7th International Natural Language Generation Conference 2012

(INLG 2012)

Utica, Illinois, USA
30 May - 1 June 2012

ISBN: 978-1-62276-498-3

Printed from e-media with permission by:

Curran Associates, Inc.
57 Morehouse Lane
Red Hook, NY 12571

Some format issues inherent in the e-media version may also appear in this print version.

Printed by Curran Associates, Inc. (2012)

For permission requests, please contact the Association for Computational Linguistics at the address below.

Association for Computational Linguistics
209 N. Eighth Street
Stroudsburg, Pennsylvania 18360

Phone: 1-570-476-8006
Fax: 1-570-476-0860

acl@aclweb.org

Additional copies of this publication are available from:

Curran Associates, Inc.
57 Morehouse Lane
Red Hook, NY 12571 USA
Phone: 845-758-0400
Fax: 845-758-2634
Email: curran@proceedings.com
Web: www.proceedings.com

Introduction

Welcome to the Seventh International Natural Language Generation Conference (INLG 2012). INLG 2012 is the biennial meeting of the ACL Special Interest Group on Natural Language Generation (SIGGEN). The INLG conference provides the premier forum for the discussion, dissemination, and archiving of research and results in the field of Natural Language Generation. Previous INLG conferences have been held in Ireland, the USA, Australia, the UK and Israel. Prior to 2000, INLG meetings were held as international workshops with a history stretching back to 1983. In 2012, INLG is being co-hosted by the University of Illinois-Chicago and the University of Wisconsin-Milwaukee; and held at Starved Rock State Park in Utica, IL, USA.

The INLG 2012 program consists of presentations of substantial, original, and previously unpublished results on all topics related to natural language generation. This year we received 27 submissions (12 full papers, 9 short papers and 6 demo proposals) from 10 different countries from around the world. As in previous years, each submission was reviewed by at least three members of an international program committee of leading researchers in the field. Based on these reviews 8 submissions were accepted as full papers, 10 as short papers, and 3 demos (1 paper was withdrawn). The accepted papers are of the highest quality and cover all of the major aspects of natural language generation.

This year, the conference program includes two keynote speakers. Kathleen McCoy, Professor of Computer and Information Sciences at the University of Delaware, will speak on *Natural Language Generation and Assistive Technologies.* James Lester, Professor of Computer Science at North Carolina State University, will speak on *Expressive NLG for Next-Generation Learning Environments: Language, Affect, and Narrative*. This year we are also delighted to host the 2012 Generation Challenges organized by Anja Belz, Albert Gatt, Alexander Koller, and Kristina Striegnitz. This is a part of INLG that has been growing in importance over the last several conferences and is a great addition to the event.

The organizing committee would like to offer their thanks to our invited speakers for agreeing to join us, to the program committee for their dedicated work, and, most of all, to the authors of all submitted papers. A conference like INLG would not happen without much help from many quarters: the organizers of the last two INLG conferences for sharing their wisdom, specifically, Mike White (OSU) for INLG 2008 and Ielka van der Sluis (Groningen) for INLG 2010; the SIGGEN board for allowing us to host the conference and for their assistance; Lin Chen (UIC), the INLG 2012 webmaster; Priscilla Rasmussen at ACL for her enormous help, always extremely prompt and offered with cheerfulness; Rich Gerber and Paolo Gai from SoftConf for setting up and supporting the START submission site for INLG 2012; Lorie Miller from AgoraNet for her assistance with registration; Margie VandeWyngaerde from Starved Rock Lodge and Conference Center for her help at every step of the way. We have also received sponsorship from CogenTex, for which we are extremely grateful. Finally, we would like to welcome you to Starved Rock and hope that you have an enjoyable and inspiring visit.

Barbara Di Eugenio and Susan McRoy
INLG 2012 Program Co-Chairs

Organizers:

Barbara Di Eugenio, University of Illinois at Chicago
Susan McRoy, University of Wisconsin–Milwaukee

Program Committee:

John Bateman, University of Bremen, Germany
Anja Belz, University of Brighton, UK
Stephan Busemann, DFKI GmbH, Germany
Giuseppe Carenini, The University of British Columbia, Canada
Nathalie Colineau, CSIRO, Australia
Robert Dale, Macquarie University, Australia
Reva Freedman, Northern Illinois University, US
Claire Gardent, CNRS/LORIA, France
Albert Gatt, University of Malta, Malta
Nancy Green, University of North Carolina at Greensboro, US
Helmut Horacek, Saarland University, Germany
Alistair Knott, University of Otago, New Zealand
Oliver Lemon, Heriot Watt University, Edinburgh, UK
Chris Mellish, The University of Aberdeen, UK
Margaret Mitchell, The University of Aberdeen, UK
Elena Not, Fondazione Bruno Kessler, Italy
Jon Oberlander, The University of Edinburgh, UK
Cecile Paris, CSIRO ICT Centre, Australia
Paul Piwek, the Open University, UK
Rashmi Prasad, University of Wisconsin—Milwaukee, US
Ehud Reiter, University of Aberdeen, UK
Graeme Ritchie, University of Aberdeen, UK
Donia Scott, University of Sussex Falmer, UK
James Shaw, Thomson Legal and Regulatory, US
Manfred Stede, Universitaet Potsdam, Germany
Amanda Stent, AT& T Labs, US
Matthew Stone, Rutgers, US
Kristina Striegnitz, Union College, US
Michael Strube, EML Research, Germany
Mariet Theune, University of Twente, The Netherlands
Takenobu Tokunaga, Tokyo Instiute of Technology, Japan
Ielka van der sluis, University of Groningen, Netherlands
Keith vanderLinden, Calvin College, US
Sebastian Varges, University of Potsdam, Germany
Leo Wanner, Universitat Pompeu Fabra, Spain
Michael White, The Ohio State University, US
Tie-jun Zhao, Harbin Institute of Technology, China

Invited Speakers:

Kathleen McCoy, University of Delaware
James Lester, North Carolina State University

Table of Contents

Natural Language Generation and Assistive Technologies
Kathleen McCoy 1

Expressive NLG for Next-Generation Learning Environments: Language, Affect, and Narrative
James Lester 2

Learning Preferences for Referring Expression Generation: Effects of Domain, Language and Algorithm
Koolen Ruud, Krahmer Emiel and Theune Mariët 3

Referring in Installments: A Corpus Study of Spoken Object References in an Interactive Virtual Environment
Kristina Striegnitz, Hendrik Buschmeier and Stefan Kopp 12

MinkApp: Generating Spatio-temporal Summaries for Nature Conservation Volunteers
Nava Tintarev, Yolanda Melero, Somayajulu Sripada, Elizabeth Tait, Rene Van Der Wal and Chris Mellish 17

Towards a Surface Realization-Oriented Corpus Annotation
Leo Wanner, Simon Mille and Bernd Bohnet 22

Generation for Grammar Engineering
Claire Gardent and German Kruszewski 31

Perceptions of Alignment and Personality in Generated Dialogue
Alastair Gill, Carsten Brockmann and Jon Oberlander 40

Optimising Incremental Generation for Spoken Dialogue Systems: Reducing the Need for Fillers
Nina Dethlefs, Helen Hastie, Verena Rieser and Oliver Lemon 49

Linguist's Assistant: A Multi-Lingual Natural Language Generator based on Linguistic Universals, Typologies, and Primitives
Tod Allman, Stephen Beale and Richard Denton 59

"Hidden semantics": what can we learn from the names in an ontology?
Allan Third 67

On generating coherent multilingual descriptions of museum objects from Semantic Web ontologies
Dana Dannélls 76

Extractive email thread summarization: Can we do better than He Said She Said?
Pablo Duboue 85

Rich Morphology Generation Using Statistical Machine Translation
Ahmed El Kholy and Nizar Habash 90

Reformulating student contributions in tutorial dialogue
Pamela Jordan, Sandra Katz, Patricia Albacete, Michael Ford and Christine Wilson 95

Working with Clinicians to Improve a Patient-Information NLG System
Saad Mahamood and Ehud Reiter 100

Sign Language Generation with Expert Systems and CCG
Alessandro Mazzei 105

Planning Accessible Explanations for Entailments in OWL Ontologies
Tu Anh T. Nguyen, Richard Power, Paul Piwek and Sandra Williams 110

Interactive Natural Language Query Construction for Report Generation
Fred Popowich, Milan Mosny and David Lindberg 115

Blogging birds: Generating narratives about reintroduced species to promote public engagement
Advaith Siddharthan, Matthew Green, Kees van Deemter, Chris Mellish and Rene van der Wal 120

Natural Language Generation for a Smart Biology Textbook
Eva Banik, Eric Kow, Nikhil Dinesh, Vinay Chaudri and Umangi Oza 125

Generating Natural Language Summaries for Multimedia
Duo Ding, Florian Metze, Shourabh Rawat, Peter Schulam and Susanne Burger 128

Midge: Generating Descriptions of Images
Margaret Mitchell, Xufeng Han and Jeff Hayes 131

Preface to Papers for GenChal
Generation Challenge 134

The Surface Realisation Task: Recent Developments and Future Plans
Anja Belz, Bernd Bohnet, Simon Mille, Leo Wanner and Michael White 136

KBGen – Text Generation from Knowledge Bases as a New Shared Task
Eva Banik, Claire Gardent, Donia Scott, Nikhil Dinesh and Fennie Liang 141

Content Selection From Semantic Web Data
Nadjet Bouayad-Agha, Gerard Casamayor, Leo Wanner and Chris Mellish 146

Shared Task Proposal: Syntactic Paraphrase Ranking
Michael White 150

Conference Program

Invited Speakers

Invited Talk I, Wednesday, May 30

1:45-2:45 *Natural Language Generation and Assistive Technologies*
Kathleen McCoy

Invited Talk II, Friday, June 1

9:00-10:00 *Expressive NLG for Next-Generation Learning Environments: Language, Affect, and Narrative*
James Lester

General Program

Lunch, Wednesday, May 30, (12:00-1:30pm)

Opening (1:30-1:45)

Invited Talk I (1:45-2:45)

Break (2:45-3:00)

Presentations, Wednesday, May 30

3:00-3:30 *Learning Preferences for Referring Expression Generation: Effects of Domain, Language and Algorithm*
Koolen Ruud, Krahmer Emiel and Theune Mariët

3:30-4:00 *Referring in Installments: A Corpus Study of Spoken Object References in an Interactive Virtual Environment*
Kristina Striegnitz, Hendrik Buschmeier and Stefan Kopp

4:00-4:30 *MinkApp: Generating Spatio-temporal Summaries for Nature Conservation Volunteers*
Nava Tintarev, Yolanda Melero, Somayajulu Sripada, Elizabeth Tait, Rene Van Der Wal and Chris Mellish

No Day Set (continued)

Dinner, Wednesday, May 30 (7:00pm)

Breakfast, Thursday, May 31 (8:30-9:30am)

Presentations, Thursday, May 31

9:30-10:00 *Towards a Surface Realization-Oriented Corpus Annotation*
Leo Wanner, Simon Mille and Bernd Bohnet

10:00-10:30 *Generation for Grammar Engineering*
Claire Gardent and German Kruszewski

Break (10:30-10:45)

Panel: Advances in Natural Language Generation (10:45-12:00)

Lunch (12:00-1:30pm)

Generation Challenge Session, Thursday, May 31 (1:30-3:00pm)

Break (3:00-3:30pm)

Presentations, Thursday, May 31

3:30-4:00 *Perceptions of Alignment and Personality in Generated Dialogue*
Alastair Gill, Carsten Brockmann and Jon Oberlander

4:00-4:30 *Optimising Incremental Generation for Spoken Dialogue Systems: Reducing the Need for Fillers*
Nina Dethlefs, Helen Hastie, Verena Rieser and Oliver Lemon

No Day Set (continued)

Poster Session, Thursday, May 31 (4:30-6:30pm)

Dinner, Thursday, May 31 (7:30pm)

Breakfast, Friday June 1(8:00-9:00am)

Invited Talk II (9:00-10:00am)

Break (10:00-10:20am)

Presentations, Friday, June 1

10:20-10:50 *Linguist's Assistant: A Multi-Lingual Natural Language Generator based on Linguistic Universals, Typologies, and Primitives*
Tod Allman, Stephen Beale and Richard Denton

10:50-11:20 *"Hidden semantics": what can we learn from the names in an ontology?*
Allan Third

11:20-11:50 *On generating coherent multilingual descriptions of museum objects from Semantic Web ontologies*
Dana Dannélls

Closing, Friday, June 1 (11:50-12:00)

Section for Poster and Demo Session

Posters, Thursday, May 31 (4:30-6:30)

Extractive email thread summarization: Can we do better than He Said She Said?
Pablo Duboue

Rich Morphology Generation Using Statistical Machine Translation
Ahmed El Kholy and Nizar Habash

Reformulating student contributions in tutorial dialogue
Pamela Jordan, Sandra Katz, Patricia Albacete, Michael Ford and Christine Wilson

No Day Set (continued)

Working with Clinicians to Improve a Patient-Information NLG System
Saad Mahamood and Ehud Reiter

Sign Language Generation with Expert Systems and CCG
Alessandro Mazzei

Planning Accessible Explanations for Entailments in OWL Ontologies
Tu Anh T. Nguyen, Richard Power, Paul Piwek and Sandra Williams

Interactive Natural Language Query Construction for Report Generation
Fred Popowich, Milan Mosny and David Lindberg

Blogging birds: Generating narratives about reintroduced species to promote public engagement
Advaith Siddharthan, Matthew Green, Kees van Deemter, Chris Mellish and Rene van der Wal

Demonstrations, Thursday, May 31 (4:30-6:30)

Natural Language Generation for a Smart Biology Textbook
Eva Banik, Eric Kow, Nikhil Dinesh, Vinay Chaudri and Umangi Oza

Generating Natural Language Summaries for Multimedia
Duo Ding, Florian Metze, Shourabh Rawat, Peter Schulam and Susanne Burger

Midge: Generating Descriptions of Images
Margaret Mitchell, Xufeng Han and Jeff Hayes

No Day Set (continued)

Section for Generation Challenge Session

GenChal Session, Thursday, May 31 (1:30-3:00)

1:30-1:40 *Preface to Papers for GenChal*
Generation Challenge

1:40-2:15 *The Surface Realisation Task: Recent Developments and Future Plans*
Anja Belz, Bernd Bohnet, Simon Mille, Leo Wanner and Michael White

2:15-2:30 *KBGen – Text Generation from Knowledge Bases as a New Shared Task*
Eva Banik, Claire Gardent, Donia Scott, Nikhil Dinesh and Fennie Liang

2:30-2:45 *Content Selection From Semantic Web Data*
Nadjet Bouayad-Agha, Gerard Casamayor, Leo Wanner and Chris Mellish

2:45-3:00 *Shared Task Proposal: Syntactic Paraphrase Ranking*
Michael White

Invited Speaker

Dr. Kathleen F. McCoy
University of Delaware

Natural Language Generation and Assistive Technologies

Abstract

Some people with disabilities find it difficult to access some forms of language. Assistive Technology is a term used to describe a class of technologies/interventions designed to enable people with disabilities to do things that their disabilitie currently make difficult. A large amount of work on Assistive Technology has focused on enabling access to language and communication; this class of interventions could greatly benefit from Natural Language Generation technologies.

This talk will briefly survey some Assistive Technology applications that have employed Natural Language Generation technologies – highlighting some of the needs in this application area along with the opportunities that it provides for investigating hard problems in Natural Language Generation. It will then highlight a project, called the SIGHT System, intended to provide access to information graphics (e.g., bar charts, line graphs) found in popular media to people who have visual impairments. This system employs Natural Language Generation technologies to generate appropriate textual summaries of the information graphics. As such, it makes contributions to several areas within the field of Natural Language Generation while also enabling access to the information in these graphics to people who cannot access it with visual means.

Biography

Dr. Kathleen F. McCoy is a professor in the Department of Computer and Information Sciences at the University of Delaware. She received her PhD from the University of Pennsylvania in 1985 with a dissertation in the area of Natural Language Generation, and has been at the University of Delaware ever since then. Shortly after joining Delaware, she began working in applying Natural Language Processing to Assistive technologies at the Center for Applied Science and Engineering in Rehabilitation at the University of Delaware and the DuPont Hospital for Children. She served as the Center's director from 2000-2009. She received a University of Delaware Excellence in Teaching Award in 1997, a University of Delaware Excellence in Advising Award in 2001, and a College of Arts and Science Outstanding Advisor Award in 2003. From 1995-2008 she served on the ACL Executive committee in various capacities including 10 years as Treasurer. She is the founding President of the ACL Special Interest Group on Speech and Language Processing for Assistive Technologies (2011). She has been an organizer of several workshops on that area associated with various ACL conferences. She was program co-chair of the User Modeling Conference in 2007, the ACM SIGACCESS Conference on Computers and Accessibility in 2009, and the General Chair of that same conference in 2011. She is a Senior Member of the ACM.

Invited Speaker

Dr. James Lester
North Carolina State University

Expressive NLG for Next-Generation Learning Environments: Language, Affect, and Narrative

Abstract

Recent years have seen the appearance of adaptive learning technologies that offer significant potential for bringing about fundamental improvements in education. A promising development in this arena is the emergence of narrative-centered learning environments, which integrate the inferential capabilities of intelligent tutoring systems with the rich gameplay supported by commercial game engines. While narrative-centered learning environments have demonstrated effectiveness in both student learning and engagement, their capabilities will increase dramatically with expressive NLG. In this talk we will introduce the principles motivating the design of narrative-centered learning environments, discuss the role of NLG in narrative-centered learning, consider the interaction of NLG, affect, and learning, and explore how next-generation learning environments will push the envelope in expressive NLG.

Biography

Dr. James Lester is a professor Department of Computer Science North Carolina State University. He received the B.A. (Highest Honors), M.S.C.S., and Ph.D. Degrees in Computer Science from the University of Texas at Austin and the B.A in History from Baylor University. A member of Phi Beta Kappa, he has served as Program Chair for the ACM conference on Intelligent User Interfaces (2001), Program Chair for the International Conference on Intelligent Tutoring Systems (2004), Conference Co-Chair for the International Conference on Intelligent Virtual Agents (2008), and on the editorial board of *Autonomous Agents and Multi-Agent Systems* (1997-2007). His research focuses on intelligent tutoring systems, computational linguistics, and intelligent user interfaces. It has been recognized by several Best Paper awards. His research interests include intelligent game-based learning environments, computational models of narrative, affective computing, creativity-enhancing technologies, and tutorial dialogue. He is Editor-In-Chief of the *International Journal of Artificial Intelligence in Education*.

Learning Preferences for Referring Expression Generation: Effects of Domain, Language and Algorithm

Ruud Koolen
Tilburg University
P.O. Box 90135
5000 LE Tilburg
The Netherlands
r.m.f.koolen@uvt.nl

Emiel Krahmer
Tilburg University
P.O. Box 90135
5000 LE Tilburg
The Netherlands
e.j.krahmer@uvt.nl

Mariët Theune
University of Twente
P.O. Box 217
7500 AE Enschede
The Netherlands
m.theune@utwente.nl

Abstract

One important subtask of Referring Expression Generation (REG) algorithms is to select the attributes in a definite description for a given object. In this paper, we study how much training data is required for algorithms to do this properly. We compare two REG algorithms in terms of their performance: the classic Incremental Algorithm and the more recent Graph algorithm. Both rely on a notion of preferred attributes that can be learned from human descriptions. In our experiments, preferences are learned from training sets that vary in size, in two domains and languages. The results show that depending on the algorithm and the complexity of the domain, training on a handful of descriptions can already lead to a performance that is not significantly different from training on a much larger data set.

1 Introduction

Most practical NLG systems include a dedicated module for Referring Expression Generation (REG) in one form or another (Mellish et al., 2006). One central problem a REG module needs to address is deciding on the contents of a description. Jordan and Walker (2005), for example, studied human-produced descriptions in a furniture scenario, and found that speakers can refer to a target in many different ways ("the yellow rug", "the $150 rug", etc.). The question, then, is how speakers decide which attributes to include in a description, and how this decision process can be modeled in a REG algorithm.

When we focus on the generation of distinguishing descriptions (which is often done in REG), it is usually assumed that some attributes are more preferred than others: when trying to identify a chair, for example, its colour is probably more helpful than its size. It is precisely this intuition of preferred attributes which is incorporated in the Incremental Algorithm (Dale and Reiter, 1995), arguably one of the most influential REG algorithms to date. The Incremental Algorithm (IA) assumes the existence of a complete, ordered list of preferred attributes. The algorithm basically iterates through this list, adding an attribute (e.g., COLOUR) to the description under construction if its value (e.g., *yellow*) helps ruling out one or more of the remaining distractors.

Even though the IA is exceptional in that it relies on a complete ordering of attributes, most current REG algorithms make use of preferences in some way (Fabbrizio et al., 2008; Gervás et al., 2008; Kelleher, 2007; Spanger et al., 2008; Viethen and Dale, 2010). The graph-based REG algorithm (Krahmer et al., 2003), for example, models preferences in terms of costs, where cheaper is more preferred. Contrary to the IA, the graph-based algorithm assumes that preferences operate at the level of attribute-value pairs (or properties) rather than at the level of attributes; in this way it becomes possible to prefer a straightforward size (*large*) over a subtle colour (*mauve, taupe*). Moreover, the graph-based algorithm looks for the cheapest overall description, and may opt for a description with a single, relatively dispreferred property ("the man with the blue eyes") when the alternative would be to combine many, relatively preferred properties ("the large, balding man with the bow tie and the striped tuxedo"). This flexibility is arguably one of the reasons why the graph-based REG approach works well: it was the best performing system in the most recent REG Challenge (Gatt et al., 2009).

But where do the preferences used in the algorithms come from? Dale and Reiter point out that preferences are domain dependent, and that determining them for a given domain is essentially an empirical question. Unfortunately, they do not specify how this particular empirical question should be answered. The general preference for colour over size is experimentally well-established (Pechmann, 1989), but for most other cases experimental data are not readily available. An alternative would be to look at human data, preferably in a "semantically transparent" corpus (van Deemter et al., 2006), that is: a corpus that contains the attributes and values of all domain objects, together with the attribute-value pairs actually included in a target reference. Such corpora are typically collected using human participants, who are asked to produce referring expressions for targets in controlled visual scenes. One example is the TUNA corpus, which is a publicly available data set containing 2280 human-produced descriptions in total, and which formed the basis of various REG Challenges. Clearly, building a corpus such as TUNA is a time consuming and labour intensive exercise, so it will not be surprising that only a handful of such corpora exists (and often only for English).

This raises an important question: how many human-produced references are needed to make a good estimate of which attributes and properties are preferred? Do we really need hundreds of instances, or is it conceivable that a few of them (collected in a semantically transparent way) will do? This is not an easy matter, since various factors might play a role: from which data set are example references sampled, what are the domains of interest, and, perhaps most importantly, which REG algorithm is considered? In this paper, we address these questions by systematically training two REG algorithms (the Incremental Algorithm and the graph-based REG algorithm) on sets of human-produced descriptions of increasing size and evaluating them on a held-out test set; we do this for two different domains (people and furniture descriptions) and two data sets in two different languages (TUNA and D-TUNA, the Dutch version of TUNA).

That size of the training set may have an impact on the performance of a REG algorithm was already suggested by Theune et al. (2011), who used the English TUNA corpus to determine preferences (costs) for the graph-based algorithm using a similar learning curve set-up as we use here. However, the current paper expands on Theune et al. (2011) in three major ways. Firstly, and most importantly, where Theune et al. reported results for only one algorithm (the graph-based one), we directly compare the performance of the graph-based algorithm and the Incremental Algorithm (something which, somewhat surprisingly, has not been done before). Secondly, we test whether these algorithms perform differently in two different languages (English and Dutch), and thirdly, we use eight training set sizes, which is more than the six set sizes that were used by Theune et al.

Below we first explain in more detail which algorithms (Section 2) and corpora (Section 3) we used for our experiments. Then we describe how we derived costs and orders from subsets of these corpora (Section 4), and report the results of our experiments focusing on effects of domain, language and size of the training set (Section 5). We end with a discussion and conclusion (Section 6), where we also compare the performance of the IA trained on small set sizes with that of the classical Full Brevity and Greedy algorithms (Dale and Reiter, 1995).

2 The Algorithms

In this section we briefly describe the two algorithms, and their settings, used in our experiment. For details about these algorithms we refer to the original publications.

The Incremental Algorithm (IA) The basic assumption underlying the Incremental Algorithm (Dale and Reiter, 1995) is that speakers "prefer" certain attributes over others when referring to objects. This intuition is formalized in the notion of a list of attributes, ranked in order of preference. When generating a description for a target, the algorithm iterates through this list, adding an attribute to the description under construction if its value helps rule out any of the distractors not previously ruled out. There is no backtracking in the IA, which means that a selected attribute is always realized in the final description, even if the inclusion of later attributes renders it redundant. In this way, the IA is capable of generating overspecified descriptions, in accordance with the human tendency to mention redundant information (Pechmann, 1989; Engelhardt et al., 2006; Arts et al., 2011). The TYPE attribute (typically realized as the head noun) has a special status in the IA. After running the algorithm it is checked whether TYPE is in the description; if not, it is added, so that TYPE is always included even if it does not rule out any distractors.

To derive preference orders from human-produced descriptions we proceeded as follows: given a set of n descriptions sampled from a larger corpus (where n is the set size, a variable we systematically control in our experiment), we counted the number of times a certain attribute occurred in the n descriptions. The most frequently occurring attribute was placed at the first position of the preferred attributes list, followed by the second most frequent attribute, etc. In the case of a tie (i.e., when two attributes occurred equally often, which typically is more likely to happen in small training sets), the attributes were ordered alphabetically. In this way, we made sure that all ties were treated in the same, comparable manner, which resulted in a complete ranking of attributes, as required by the IA.

The Graph-based Algorithm (Graph) In the graph-based algorithm (Krahmer et al., 2003), which we refer to as Graph, information about domain objects is represented as a labelled directed graph, and REG is modeled as a graph-search problem. The output of the algorithm is the cheapest distinguishing subgraph, given a particular *cost function* assigning costs to properties (i.e., attribute-value pairs). By assigning zero costs to some properties Graph is also capable of generating overspecified descriptions, including redundant properties. To ensure that the graph search does not terminate before the free properties are added, the search order must be explicitly controlled (Viethen et al., 2008). To ensure a fair comparison with the IA, we make sure that if the target's TYPE property was not originally selected by the algorithm, it is added afterwards.

In this study, both the costs and orders required by Graph are derived from corpus data. We base the property order on the frequency with which each attribute-value pair is mentioned in a training corpus, relative to the number of target objects with this property. The properties are then listed in order of decreasing frequency. Costs can be derived from the same corpus frequencies; here, following Theune et al. (2011), we adopt a systematic way of deriving costs from frequencies based on k-means clustering. Theune and colleagues achieved the best performance with $k = 2$, meaning that the properties are divided in two groups based on their frequency. The properties in the group with the highest frequency get cost 0. These 'free' properties are always included in the description if they help distinguish the target. The properties in the less frequent group get cost 1; of these properties, the algorithm only adds the minimum number necessary to achieve a distinguishing description. Ties due to properties occurring with the same frequency need not be resolved when determining the cost function, since Graph does not assume the existence of a complete ordering. Properties that did not occur in a training corpus were automatically assigned cost 1. Like we did for the IA, we listed attribute-value pairs with the same frequency in alphabetical order.

3 Corpora

Training and test data for our experiment were taken from two corpora of referring expressions, one English (TUNA) and one Dutch (D-TUNA).

TUNA The TUNA corpus (Gatt et al., 2007) is a semantically transparent corpus consisting of object descriptions in two domains (furniture and people). The corpus was collected in an on-line production experiment, in which participants were presented with visual scenes containing one target object and six distractor objects. These objects were ordered in a 5×3 grid, and the participants were asked to describe the target in such a way that it could be uniquely distinguished from its distractors. Table 1 shows the attributes and values that were annotated for the descriptions in the two domains.

There were two experimental conditions: in the +LOC condition, the participants were free to describe the target using any of its properties, including its location on the screen (represented

Furniture	
Attribute	**Possible values**
TYPE	*chair, desk, sofa, fan*
COLOUR	*green, red, blue, gray*
ORIENTATION	*front, back, left, right*
SIZE	*large, small*
X-DIMENSION	*1, 2, 3, 4, 5*
Y-DIMENSION	*1, 2, 3*

People	
Attribute	**Possible values**
TYPE	*person*
AGE	*old, young*
HAIRCOLOUR	*light, dark*
ORIENTATION	*front, left, right*
HASBEARD	*true, false*
HASGLASSES	*true, false*
HASSHIRT	*true, false*
HASSUIT	*true, false*
HASTIE	*true, false*
X-DIMENSION	*1, 2, 3, 4, 5*
Y-DIMENSION	*1, 2, 3*

Table 1: Attributes and values in the furniture and people domains. X- and Y-DIMENSION refer to an object's horizontal and vertical position in a scene grid and only occur in the English TUNA corpus.

in Table 1 as the X- and Y-DIMENSION), whereas in the -LOC condition they were discouraged (but not prevented) from mentioning object locations. However, some descriptions in the -LOC condition contained location information anyway.

D-TUNA For Dutch, we used the D-TUNA corpus (Koolen and Krahmer, 2010). This corpus uses the same visual scenes and annotation scheme as the TUNA corpus, but consists of Dutch instead of English target descriptions. Since the D-TUNA experiment was performed in laboratory conditions, its data is relatively 'cleaner' than the TUNA data, which means that it contains fewer descriptions that are not fully distinguishing and that its descriptions do not contain X- and Y-DIMENSION attributes. Although the descriptions in D-TUNA were collected in three different conditions (written, spoken, and face-to-face), we only use the written descriptions in this paper, as this condition is most similar to the data collection in TUNA.

4 Method

To find out how much training data is required to achieve an acceptable attribute selection performance for the IA and Graph, we derived orders and costs from different sized training sets. We then evaluated the algorithms, using the derived orders and costs, on a test set. Training and test sets were taken from TUNA and D-TUNA.

As Dutch training data, we used 160 furniture and 160 people items, randomly selected from the textual descriptions in the D-TUNA corpus. The remaining furniture and people descriptions (40 items each) were used for testing. As English training data, we took all -LOC data from the training set of the REG Challenge 2009 (Gatt et al., 2009): 165 furniture and 136 people descriptions. As English test data we used all -LOC data from the REG 2009 development set: 38 furniture and 38 people descriptions. We only used -LOC data to increase comparability to the Dutch data.

From the Dutch and English furniture and people training data, we selected random subsets of 1, 5, 10, 20, 30, 40 and 50 descriptions. Five different sets of each size were created, since the accidental composition of a training set could strongly influence the results. All training sets were built up in a cumulative fashion, starting with five randomly selected sets of size 1, then adding 4 items to each of them to create five sets of size 5, and so on, for each combination of language and domain. We used these different training sets to derive preference orders of attributes for the IA, and costs and property orders for Graph, as outlined above.

We evaluated the performance of the derived preference orders and cost functions on the test data for the corresponding domain and language, using the standard Dice and Accuracy metrics for evaluation. Dice measures the overlap between attribute sets, producing a value between 1 and 0, where 1 stands for a perfect match and 0 for no overlap at all. Accuracy is the percentage of perfect matches between the generated attribute sets and the human descriptions in the test set. Both metrics were used in the REG Generation Challenges.

	English furniture			
	IA		Graph	
Set size	Dice	Acc.(%)	Dice	Acc.(%)
1	0.764	36.8	0.693	24.7
5	0.829	55.3	0.756	33.7
10	0.829	55.3	0.777	39.5
20	0.829	55.3	0.788	40.5
30	0.829	55.3	0.782	40.5
40	0.829	55.3	0.793	45.3
50	0.829	55.3	0.797	45.8
All	0.829	55.3	0.810	50.0

	Dutch furniture			
	IA		Graph	
Set size	Dice	Acc.(%)	Dice	Acc.(%)
1	0.925	63.0	0.876	44.5
5	0.935	67.5	0.917	62.0
10	0.929	68.5	0.923	66.0
20	0.930	65.5	0.923	64.0
30	0.931	67.0	0.924	65.5
40	0.931	67.0	0.931	67.5
50	0.929	66.0	0.929	67.0
All	0.926	65.0	0.929	67.5

Table 2: Performance for each set size in the furniture domain. For sizes 1 to 50, means over five sets are given. The full sets are 165 English and 160 Dutch descriptions. Note that the scores of the IA for the English sets of sizes 1 to 30 were also reported in Theune et al. (2011).

	English people			
	IA		Graph	
Set size	Dice	Acc.(%)	Dice	Acc.(%)
1	0.519	7.4	0.558	12.6
5	0.605	15.8	0.617	14.5
10	0.682	21.1	0.683	20.0
20	0.710	22.1	0.716	24.7
30	0.682	15.3	0.716	26.8
40	0.716	26.3	0.723	26.3
50	0.718	27.9	0.727	26.3
All	0.724	31.6	0.730	28.9

	Dutch people			
	IA		Graph	
Set size	Dice	Acc.(%)	Dice	Acc.(%)
1	0.626	4.5	0.682	17.5
5	0.737	16.0	0.738	21.0
10	0.738	12.5	0.741	19.5
20	0.765	12.5	0.778	25.5
30	0.762	14.5	0.789	25.0
40	0.763	11.5	0.792	25.0
50	0.764	10.5	0.798	26.0
All	0.775	12.5	0.812	32.5

Table 3: Performance for each set size in the people domain. For sizes 1 to 50, means over five sets are given. The full sets are 136 English and 160 Dutch descriptions. Note that the scores of the IA for the English sets of sizes 1 to 30 were also reported in Theune et al. (2011).

5 Results

5.1 Overall analysis

To determine the effect of domain and language on the performance of REG algorithms, we applied repeated measures analyses of variance (ANOVA) to the Dice and Accuracy scores, using *set size* (1, 5, 10, 20, 30, 40, 50, all) and *domain* (furniture, people) as within variables, and *algorithm* (IA, Graph) and *language* (English, Dutch) as between variables.

The results show main effects of *domain* (Dice: $F_{(1,152)} = 56.10$, $p < .001$; Acc.: $F_{(1,152)} = 76.36$, $p < .001$) and *language* (Dice: $F_{(1,152)} = 30.30$, $p < .001$; Acc.: $F_{(1,152)} = 3.380$, $p = .07$). Regarding the two domains, these results indicate that both the IA and the Graph algorithm generally performed better in the furniture domain (Dice: M = .86, SD = .01; Acc.: M = .56, SD = .03) than in the people domain (Dice: M = .72, SD = .01; Acc.: M = .20, SD = .02). Regarding the two languages, the results show that both algorithms generally performed better on the Dutch data (Dice: M = .84, SD = .01; Acc.: M = .41, SD = .03) than on the English data (Dice: M = .74, SD = .01; Acc.: M = .34, SD = .03). There is no main effect of *algorithm*, meaning that overall, the two algorithms had an equal performance. However, this is different when we look separately at each domain and language, as we do below.

5.2 Learning curves per domain and language

Given the main effects of domain and language described above, we ran separate ANOVAs for the different domains and languages. For these four analyses, we used *set size* as a within variable, and *algorithm* as a between variable. To determine the effects of *set size*, we calculated the means of the scores of the five training sets for each set size, so that we could compare them with the scores of the entire set. The results are shown in Tables 2 and 3.

We made planned post hoc comparisons to test which is the smallest set size that does not perform significantly different from the entire training set in terms of Dice and Accuracy scores (we call this the "ceiling"). We report results both for the standard Bonferroni method, which corrects for multiple comparisons, and for the less strict LSD method from Fisher, which does not. Note that with the Bonferroni method we are inherently less likely to find statistically significant differences between the set sizes, which implies that we can expect to reach a ceiling earlier than with the LSD method. Table 4 shows the ceilings we found for the algorithms, per domain and language.

	English furniture		**Dutch furniture**	
	Dice	Accuracy	Dice	Accuracy
IA	5 (5)	5 (5)	1 (1)	1 (1)
Graph	10 (5)	40 (5)	5 (1)	5 (1)
	English people		**Dutch people**	
	Dice	Accuracy	Dice	Accuracy
IA	10 (10)	40 (1)	20 (5)	1 (1)
Graph	20 (10)	20 (1)	30 (20)	5 (1)

Table 4: Ceiling set sizes computed using LSD, with Bonferroni between brackets.

The furniture domain Table 2 shows the Dice and Accuracy scores in the furniture domain. We found significant effects of *set size* for both the English data (Dice: $F_{(7,518)} = 15.59$, $p < .001$; Acc.: $F_{(7,518)} = 17.42$, $p < .001$) and the Dutch data (Dice: $F_{(7,546)} = 5.322$, $p < .001$; Acc.: $F_{(7,546)} = 5.872$, $p < .001$), indicating that for both languages, the number of descriptions used for training influenced the performance of both algorithms in terms of both Dice and Accuracy. Although we did not find a main effect of algorithm, suggesting that the two algorithms performed equally well, we did find several interactions between *set size* and *algorithm* for both the English data (Dice: $F_{(7,518)} = 1.604$, ns; Acc.: $F_{(7,518)} = 2.282$, $p < .05$) and the Dutch data (Dice: $F_{(7,546)} = 3.970$, $p < .001$; Acc.: $F_{(7,546)} = 3.225$, $p < .01$). For the English furniture data, this interaction implies that small set sizes have a bigger impact for the IA than for Graph. For example, moving from set size 1 to 5 yielded a Dice improvement of .18 for the IA, while this was only .09 for Graph. For the Dutch furniture data, however, a reverse pattern was observed; moving from set size 1 to 5 yielded an improvement of .01 (Dice) and .05 (Acc.) for the IA, while this was .11 (Dice) and .18 (Acc.) for Graph.

Post hoc tests showed that small set sizes were generally sufficient to reach ceiling performance: the general pattern for both algorithms and both languages was that the scores increased with the size of the training set, but that the increase got smaller as the set sizes became larger. For the English furniture data, Graph reached the ceiling at set size 10 for Dice (5 with the Bonferroni test), and at set size 40 for Accuracy (again 5 with Bonferroni), while this was the case for the IA at set size 5 for both Dice and Accuracy (also 5 with Bonferroni). For the Dutch furniture data, Graph reached the ceiling at set size 5 for both Dice and Accuracy (and even at 1 with the Bonferroni test), while this was at set size 1 for the IA (again 1 with Bonferroni).

The people domain Table 3 shows the Dice and Accuracy scores in the people domain. Again, we found significant effects of *set size* for both the English data (Dice: $F_{(7,518)} = 39.46$, $p < .001$; Acc.: $F_{(7,518)} = 11.77$, $p < .001$) and the Dutch data (Dice: $F_{(7,546)} = 33.90$, $p < .001$; Acc.: $F_{(7,546)} = 3.235$, $p < .01$). Again, this implies that for both languages, the number of descriptions used for training influenced the performance of both algorithms in terms of both Dice and Accuracy. Unlike we did in the furniture domain, we found no interactions between *set size* and *algorithm*, but we did find a main effect of algorithm for the Dutch people data (Dice: $F_{(1,78)} = .751$, ns; Acc.: $F_{(1,78)} = 5.099$, $p < .05$), showing that Graph generated Dutch descriptions that were more accurate than those generated by the IA.

As in the furniture domain, post hoc tests showed that small set sizes were generally sufficient to reach ceiling performance. For the English data, Graph reached the ceiling at set size 20 for both Dice and Accuracy (with Bonferroni: 10 for Dice, 1 for Accuracy), while this was the case for the IA at set size 10 for Dice (also 10 with Bonferroni), and at set size 40 for Accuracy (and even at 1 with Bonferroni). For the Dutch data, Graph reached the ceiling at set size 30 for Dice (20 with Bonferroni), and at set size 5 for Accuracy (1 with Bonferroni). For the IA, ceiling was reached at set size 20 for Dice (Bonferroni: 5), and already at 1 for Accuracy (Bonferroni: 1).

6 Discussion and Conclusion

Our main goal was to investigate how many human-produced references are required by REG algorithms such as the Incremental Algorithm and the graph-based algorithm to determine preferences (or costs) for a new domain, and to generate "human-like" descriptions for new objects in these domains. Our results show that small data sets can be used to train these algorithms, achieving results that are not significantly different from those derived from a much larger training set. In the simple furniture domain even one training item can already be sufficient, at least for the IA. As shown in Table 4, on the whole the IA needed fewer training data than Graph (except in the English people domain, where Graph only needed a set size of 10 to hit the ceiling for Dice, while the IA needed a set size of 20).

Given that the IA ranks attributes, while the graph-based REG algorithm ranks attribute-value pairs, the difference in required training data is not surprising. In any domain, there will be more attribute-value pairs than attributes, so determining an attribute ranking is an easier task than determining a ranking of attribute-value pairs. Another advantage of ranking attributes rather than attribute-value pairs is that it is less vulnerable to the problem of "missing data". More specifically, the chance that a specific attribute does not occur in a small training set is much smaller than the chance that a specific attribute-value pair does not occur. As a consequence, the IA needs fewer data to obtain complete attribute orderings than Graph needs to obtain costs for all attribute-value pairs.

Interestingly, we only found interactions between training set size and algorithm in the furniture domain. In the people domain, there was no significant difference between the size of the training sets required by the algorithms. This could be explained by the fact that the people domain has about twice as many attributes as the furniture domain, and fewer values per attribute (see Table 1). This means that for people the difference between the number of attributes (IA) and the number of attribute-value pairs (Graph) is not as big as for furniture, so the two algorithms are on more equal grounds.

Both algorithms performed better on furniture than on people. Arguably, the people pictures in the TUNA experiment can be described in many more different ways than the furniture pictures can, so it stands to reason that ranking potential attributes and values is more difficult in the people than in the furniture domain. In a similar vein, we might expect Graph's flexible generation strategy to be more useful in the people domain, where more can be gained by the use of costs, than in the furniture domain, where there are relatively few options anyway, and a simple linear ordering may be quite sufficient.

This expectation was at least partially confirmed by the results: although in most cases the differences are not significant, Graph tends to perform numerically better than the IA in the people domain. Here we see the pay-off of Graph's more fine-grained preference ranking, which allows it to distinguish between more and less salient attribute values. In the furniture domain, most attribute values appear to be more or less equally salient (e.g., none of the colours gets notably mentioned more often), but in the people domain certain values are clearly more salient than others. In particular, the attributes HASBEARD and HASGLASSES are among the most frequent attributes in the people domain when their value is *true* (i.e., the target object can be distinguished by his beard or glasses), but they hardly get mentioned when their value is *false*. Graph quickly learns this distinction, assigning low costs and a high ranking to <HASBEARD, *true*> and <HASGLASSES, *true*> while assigning high costs and a low ranking to <HASBEARD, *false*> and <HASGLASSES, *false*>. The IA, on the other hand, does not distinguish between the values of these attributes.

Moreover, the graph-based algorithm is arguably more generic than the Incremental Algorithm, as it can straightforwardly deal with relational properties and lends itself to various extensions (Krahmer et al., 2003). In short, the larger training investment required for Graph in simple domains may be compensated by its versatility and better performance on more complex domains. To test this assumption, our experiment should be repeated using data from a more realistic and complex domain, e.g., geographic descriptions (Turner et al., 2008). Unfortunately, currently no such data sets are available.

Finally, we found that the results of both algorithms were better for the Dutch data than for the English ones. We think that this is not so much an effect of the language (as English and Dutch are highly comparable) but rather of the way the TUNA and D-TUNA corpora were constructed. The D-TUNA corpus was collected in more controlled conditions than TUNA and as a result, arguably, it contains training data of a higher quality. Also, because the D-TUNA corpus does not contain any location properties (X- and Y-DIMENSION) its furniture and people domains are slightly less complex than their TUNA counterparts, making the attribute selection task a bit easier.

One caveat of our study is that so far we have only used the standard automatic metrics on REG evaluation (albeit in accordance with many other studies in this area). However, it has been found that these do not always correspond to the results of human-based evaluations, so it would be interesting to see whether the same learning curve effects are obtained for extrinsic, task based evaluations involving human subjects. Following Belz and Gatt (2008), this could be done by measuring reading times, identification times or error rates as a function of training set size.

Comparing IA with FB and GR We have shown that small set sizes are sufficient to reach ceiling for the IA. But which preference orders (PO's) do we find with these small set sizes? And how does the IA's performance with these orders compare to the results obtained by alternative algorithms such as Dale and Reiter's (1995) classic Full Brevity (FB) and Greedy Algorithm (GR)? – a question explicitly asked by van Deemter et al. (2012). In the furniture domain, all five English training sets of size 5 yield a PO for which van Deemter et al. showed that it causes the IA to significantly outperform FB and GR (i.e., either C(olor)O(rientation)S(ize) or CSO; note that here we abstract over TYPE which van Deemter and colleagues do not consider). When we look at the English people domain and consider set size 10 (ceiling for Dice), we find that four out of five sets have a preference order where HAIRCOLOUR, HASBEARD and HASGLASSES are in the top three (again disregarding TYPE); one of these is the best performing preference order found by van Deemter and colleagues (GBH), another performs slightly less well but still significantly better than FB and GR (BGH); the other two score statistically comparable to the classical algorithms. The fifth people PO includes X- and Y-DIMENSION in the top three, which van Deemter et al. ignore. In sum: in almost all cases, small set sizes (5 and 10 respectively) yield POs with which the IA performs at least as well as the FB and GR algorithms, and in most cases significantly better.

Conclusion We have shown that with few training instances, acceptable attribute selection results can be achieved; that is, results that do not significantly differ from those obtained using a much larger training set. Given the scarcity of resources in this field, we feel that this is an important result for researchers working on REG and Natural Language Generation in general. We found that less training data is needed in simple domains with few attributes, such as the furniture domain, and more in relatively more complex domains such as the people domain. The data set being used is also of influence: better results were achieved with D-TUNA than with the TUNA corpus, which probably not so much reflects a language difference, but a difference in the way the corpora were collected.

We found some interesting differences between the IA and Graph algorithms, which can be largely explained by the fact that the former ranks attributes, and the latter attribute-value pairs. The advantage of the former (coarser) approach is that overall, fewer training items are required, while the latter (more fine-grained) approach is better equipped to deal with more complex domains. In the furniture domain both algorithms had a similar performance, while in the people domain Graph did slightly better than the IA. It has to be kept in mind that these results are based on the relatively simple furniture and people domains, and evaluated in terms of a limited (though standard) set of evaluation metrics. We hope that in the near future semantically transparent corpora for more complex domains will become available, so that these kinds of learning curve experiments can be replicated.

Acknowledgments Krahmer and Koolen received financial support from The Netherlands Organization for Scientific Research (NWO Vici grant 27770007). We thank Albert Gatt for allowing us to use his implementation of the IA, and Sander Wubben for help with k-means clustering.

References

Anja Arts, Alfons Maes, Leo Noordman, and Carel Jansen. 2011. Overspecification facilitates object identification. *Journal of Pragmatics*, 43(1):361–374.

Anja Belz and Albert Gatt. 2008. Intrinsic vs. extrinsic evaluation measures for referring expression generation. In *Proceedings of the 46th Annual Meeting of the Association for Computational Linguistics (ACL'08)*, pages 197–200.

Robert Dale and Ehud Reiter. 1995. Computational interpretation of the Gricean maxims in the generation of referring expressions. *Cognitive Science*, 19(2):233–263.

Paul E. Engelhardt, Karl G.D Bailey, and Fernanda Ferreira. 2006. Do speakers and listeners observe the Gricean Maxim of Quantity? *Journal of Memory and Language*, 54:554–573.

Giuseppe Di Fabbrizio, Amanda Stent, and Srinivas Bangalore. 2008. Trainable speaker-based referring expression generation. In *Twelfth Conference on Computational Natural Language Learning (CoNLL-2008)*, pages 151–158.

Albert Gatt, Ielka van der Sluis, and Kees van Deemter. 2007. Evaluating algorithms for the generation of referring expressions using a balanced corpus. In *Proceedings of the 11th European Workshop on Natural Language Generation (ENLG 2007)*, pages 49–56.

Albert Gatt, Anja Belz, and Eric Kow. 2009. The TUNA-REG Challenge 2009: Overview and evaluation results. In *Proceedings of the 12th European Workshop on Natural Language Generation (ENLG 2009)*, pages 174–182.

Pablo Gervás, Raquel Hervás, and Carlos Léon. 2008. NIL-UCM: Most-frequent-value-first attribute selection and best-scoring-choice realization. In *Proceedings of the 5th International Natural Language Generation Conference (INLG 2008)*, pages 215–218.

Pamela W. Jordan and Marilyn Walker. 2005. Learning content selection rules for generating object descriptions in dialogue. *Journal of Artificial Intelligence Research*, 24:157–194.

John Kelleher. 2007. DIT - frequency based incremental attribute selection for GRE. In *Proceedings of the MT Summit XI Workshop Using Corpora for Natural Language Generation: Language Generation and Machine Translation (UCNLG+MT)*, pages 90–92.

Ruud Koolen and Emiel Krahmer. 2010. The D-TUNA corpus: A Dutch dataset for the evaluation of referring expression generation algorithms. In *Proceedings of the 7th international conference on Language Resources and Evaluation (LREC 2010)*.

Emiel Krahmer, Sebastiaan van Erk, and André Verleg. 2003. Graph-based generation of referring expressions. *Computational Linguistics*, 29(1):53–72.

Chris Mellish, Donia Scott, Lynn Cahill, Daniel Paiva, Roger Evans, and Mike Reape. 2006. A reference architecture for natural language generation systems. *Natural Language Engineering*, 12:1–34.

Thomas Pechmann. 1989. Incremental speech production and referential overspecification. *Linguistics*, 27:98–110.

Ehud Reiter and Anja Belz. 2009. An investigation into the validity of some metrics for automatically evaluating NLG systems. *Computational Linguistics*, 35(4):529–558.

Philipp Spanger, Takehiro Kurosawa, and Takenobu Tokunaga. 2008. On "redundancy" in selecting attributes for generating referring expressions. In *COLING 2008: Companion volume: Posters*, pages 115–118.

Mariët Theune, Ruud Koolen, Emiel Krahmer, and Sander Wubben. 2011. Does size matter – How much data is required to train a REG algorithm? In *Proceedings of the 49th Annual Meeting of the Association for Computational Linguistics: Human Language Technologies*, pages 660–664, Portland, Oregon, USA.

Ross Turner, Somayajulu Sripada, Ehud Reiter, and Ian P. Davy. 2008. Using spatial reference frames to generate grounded textual summaries of georeferenced data. In *Proceedings of the 5th International Natural Language Generation Conference (INLG)*, pages 16–24.

Kees van Deemter, Ielka van der Sluis, and Albert Gatt. 2006. Building a semantically transparent corpus for the generation of referring expressions. In *Proceedings of the 4th International Natural Language Generation Conference (INLG 2006)*, pages 130–132.

Kees van Deemter, Albert Gatt, Ielka van der Sluis, and Richard Power. 2012. Generation of referring expressions: Assessing the Incremental Algorithm. *Cognitive Science, to appear*.

Jette Viethen and Robert Dale. 2010. Speaker-dependent variation in content selection for referring expression generation. In *Proceedings of the 8th Australasian Language Technology Workshop*, pages 81–89.

Jette Viethen, Robert Dale, Emiel Krahmer, Mariët Theune, and Pascal Touset. 2008. Controlling redundancy in referring expressions. In *Proceedings of the Sixth International Conference on Language Resources and Evaluation (LREC 2008)*, pages 239–246.

Referring in Installments: A Corpus Study of Spoken Object References in an Interactive Virtual Environment

Kristina Striegnitz*, **Hendrik Buschmeier**[†] and **Stefan Kopp**[†]
*Computer Science Department, Union College, Schenectady, NY
striegnk@union.edu
[†]Sociable Agents Group – CITEC, Bielefeld University, Germany
{hbuschme,skopp}@techfak.uni-bielefeld.de

Abstract

Commonly, the result of referring expression generation algorithms is a single noun phrase. In interactive settings with a shared workspace, however, human dialog partners often split referring expressions into installments that adapt to changes in the context and to actions of their partners. We present a corpus of human–human interactions in the GIVE-2 setting in which instructions are spoken. A first study of object descriptions in this corpus shows that references in installments are quite common in this scenario and suggests that contextual factors partly determine their use. We discuss what new challenges this creates for NLG systems.

1 Introduction

Referring expression generation is classically considered to be the problem of producing a single noun phrase that uniquely identifies a referent (Krahmer and van Deemter, 2012). This approach is well suited for non-interactive, static contexts, but recently, there has been increased interest in generation for situated dialog (Stoia, 2007; Striegnitz et al., 2011).

Most human language use takes place in dynamic situations, and psycholinguistic research on human–human dialog has proposed that the production of referring expressions should rather be seen as a process that not only depends on the context and the choices of the speaker, but also on the reactions of the addressee. Thus the result is often not a single noun phrase but a sequence of *installments* (Clark and Wilkes-Gibbs, 1986), consisting of multiple utterances which may be interleaved with feedback from the addressee. In a setting where the dialog partners have access to a common workspace, they, furthermore, carefully monitor each other's non-linugistic actions, which often replace verbal feedback (Clark and Krych, 2004; Gergle et al., 2004). The following example from our data illustrates this. *A* is instructing *B* to press a particular button.

(1) A: *the blue button*
B: [moves and then hesitates]
A: *the one you see on your right*
B: [starts moving again]
A: *press that one*

While computational models of this behavior are still scarce, some first steps have been taken. Stoia (2007) studies instruction giving in a virtual environment and finds that references to target objects are often not made when they first become visible. Instead interaction partners are navigated to a spot from where an easier description is possible. Garoufi and Koller (2010) develop a planning-based approach of this behavior. But once their system decides to generate a referring expression, it is delivered in one unit.

Thompson (2009), on the other hand, proposes a game-theoretic model to predict how noun phrases are split up into installments. While Thompson did not specify how the necessary parameters to calculate the utility of an utterance are derived from the context and did not implement the model, it provides a good theoretical basis for an implementation.

The GIVE Challenge is a recent shared task on situated generation (Striegnitz et al., 2011). In the GIVE scenario a human user goes on a treasure hunt in a virtual environment. He or she has to press a series of buttons that unlock doors and open a safe. The challenge for the NLG systems is to generate instructions in real-time to guide the user to the goal. The instructions are presented to the user as written text, which means that there is less opportunity for interleaving language and actions than with spoken instructions. While some systems generate sentence fragments in certain situations (e.g., *not this one* when the user is moving towards the wrong button), instructions are generally produced as complete sentences and replaced with a new full sentence when the context changes (a strategy which would not work for spoken instructions). Nevertheless, timing issues are a cause for errors that is cited by several teams who developed systems for the GIVE challenge, and generating appropriate feedback has been an important concern for almost all teams (see the system descriptions in (Belz et al., 2011)). Unfortunately, no systematic error analysis has been done for the interactions from the GIVE challenges. Anecdotally, however, not reacting to signs of confusion in the user's actions at all or reacting too late seem to be common causes for problems. Furthermore, we have found that the strategy of replacing instructions with complete sentences to account for a change in context can lead to confusion because it seems unclear to the user whether this new instruction is a correction or an elaboration.

In this paper we report on a study of the communicative behavior of human dyads in the GIVE environment where instead of written text instruction givers use unrestricted spoken language to direct instruction followers through the world. We find that often multiple installments are used to identify a referent and that the instruction givers are highly responsive to context changes and the instruction followers' actions. Our goal is to inform the development of a generation system that generates object descriptions in installments while taking into account the actions of its interaction partner.

2 A corpus of spoken instructions in a virtual environment

Data collection method The setup of this study was similar to the one used to collect the GIVE-2 corpus of typed instructions (Gargett et al., 2010). Instruction followers (IFs) used the standard GIVE-2 client to interact with the virtual environment. Instruction givers (IGs) could observe the followers' position and actions in the world using an interactive map, and they were also provided with the same 3D view into the scene that the IFs saw on their screen. Differently from the normal GIVE-2 scenario, the IGs did not type their instructions but gave spoken instructions, which were audio recorded as well as streamed to the IFs over the network. A log of the IFs' position, orientation and actions that was updated every 200ms was recorded in a database.

Participants were recruited in pairs on Bielefeld University's campus and received a compensation of six euros each. They were randomly assigned to the roles of IG and IF and were seated and instructed separately. To become familiar with the task, they switched roles in a first, shorter training world. These interactions were later used to devise and test the annotation schemes. They then played two different worlds in their assigned roles. After the first round, they received a questionnaire assessing the quality of the interaction; after the second round, they completed the Santa Barbara sense of direction test (Hegarty et al., 2006) and answered some questions about themselves.

Annotations The recorded instructions of the IGs were transcribed and segmented into utterances (by identifying speech pauses longer than 300ms) using Praat (Boersma and Weenink, 2011). We then created videos showing the IGs' map view as well as the IFs' scene view and aligned the audio and transcriptions with them. The data was further annotated by the first two authors using ELAN (Wittenburg et al., 2006).

Most importantly for this paper, we classified utterances into the following types:

(i) **move** (MV) – instruction to turn or to move
(ii) **manipulate** (MNP) – instruction to manipulate an object (e.g., press a button)
(iii) **reference** (REF) – utterance referring to an object
(iv) **stop** – instruction to stop moving
(v) **warning** – telling the user to not do something
(vi) **acknowledgment** (ACK) – affirmative feedback
(vii) **communication management** (CM) – indicating that the IG is planning (e.g., *uhmm, just a moment, sooo* etc.)
(viii) **negative acknowledgment** – indicating a mistake on the player's part
(ix) **other** – anything else

A few utterances which contained both move and press instructions were further split, but in general we picked the label that fit best (using the above list as a precedence order to make a decision if two labels fit equally well). The inter-annotator agreement for utterance types was $\kappa = 0.89$ (Cohen's kappa), which is considered to be very good. Since the categories were of quite different sizes (cf. Table 1), which may skew the κ statistic, we also calculated the kappa per category. It was satisfactory for all 'interesting' categories. The agreement for category REF was $\kappa = 0.77$ and the agreement for *other* was $\kappa = 0.58$. The kappa values for all other categories were 0.84 or greater. We reviewed all cases with differing annotations and reached a consensus, which is the basis for all results presented in this paper. Furthermore, we collapsed the labels *warning*, *negative acknowledgment* and *other* which only occurred rarely.

To support a later more in depth analysis, we also annotated what types of properties are used in object descriptions, the givenness status of information in instructions, and whether an utterance is giving positive or negative feedback on a user action (even if not explicitly labeled as *(negative) acknowledgment*). Finally, information about the IF's movements and actions in the world as well as the visible context was automatically calculated from the GIVE log files and integrated into the annotation.

Collected data We collected interactions between eight pairs. Due to failures of the network connection and some initial problems with the GIVE software, only four pairs were recorded completely, so that we currently have data from eight interactions with four different IGs. We are in the process of collecting additional data in order to achieve a corpus size that will allow for a more detailed statistical analysis. Furthermore, we are collecting data in English to be able to make comparisons with the existing corpus of written instructions in the GIVE world and to make the data more easily accessible to a wider audience. The corpus will be made freely available at `http://purl.org/net/sgive-corpus`.

Participants were between 20 and 30 years old and all of them are native German speakers. Two of the IGs are male and two female; three of the IFs are female. The mean length of the interactions is 5.24 minutes (SD = 1.86), and the IGs on average use 325 words (SD = 91).

Table 1 gives an overview of the kinds of utterances used by the IGs. While the general picture is similar for all speakers, there are statistically significant differences between the frequencies with which different IGs use the utterance types ($\chi^2 = 78.82, p \leq 0.001$). We did not find a significant differences (in terms of the utterance types used) between the two worlds that we used or between the two rounds that each pair played.

Table 1: Overall frequency of utterance types.

utterance type	count	%
MV	334	46.58
MNP	66	9.21
REF	65	9.07
stop	38	5.30
ACK	92	12.83
CM	97	13.53
other	25	3.49

Table 2: Transitional probabilities for utterance types.

	MV	MNP	REF	stop	ACK	CM	other	IF press
MV	.53	.08	.06	.06	.15	.08	.03	.00
MNP	.02	.03	.09	.02	.02	.02	.02	.80
REF	.00	.33	.19	.02	.14	.00	.02	.30
stop	.47	.03	.18	.03	.03	.16	.11	.00
ACK	.64	.08	.09	.03	.01	.10	.00	.05
CM	.53	.05	.10	.08	.01	.18	.05	.00
other	.44	.04	.12	.12	.08	.16	.00	.04
IF press	.21	.01	.00	.01	.36	.36	.04	.00

3 How instruction givers describe objects

We now examine how interaction partners establish what the next target button is. Overall, there are 76 utterance sequences in the data that identify a target button and lead to the IF pressing that button. We discuss a selection of seven representative examples.

(2) IG: *und dann drückst du den ganz rechten Knopf den blauen* (and then you press the rightmost button the blue one; MNP)
IF: [goes across the room and does it]

In (2) the IG generates a referring expression identifying the target and integrates it into an object manipulation instruction. In our data, 55% of the target buttons (42 out of 76) get identified in this way (which fits into the traditional view of referring expression generation). In all other cases a sequence of at least two, and in 14% of the cases more than two, utterances is used.

The transitional probabilities between utterance types shown in Table 2 suggest what some common patterns may be. For example, even though *move* instructions are so prevalent in our data, they are uncommon after *reference* or *manipulate* utterances.

Instead, two thirds of the *reference* utterances are followed by object manipulation instruction, another reference or an acknowledgement. In the remaining cases, IFs press a button in response to the reference.

(3) IG: *vor dir der blaue Knopf* (in front of you the blue button; REF)
IF: [moves across the room toward the button]
IG: *drauf drücken* (press it; MNP)

(4) IG: *und auf der rechten Seite sind zwei rote Knöpfe* (and on the right are two red buttons; REF)
IF: [turns and starts moving towards the buttons]
IG: *und den linken davon drückst du* (and you press the left one; MNP)

In (3) and (4) a first *reference* utterance is followed by a separate *object manipulation* utterance. While in (3) the first reference uniquely identifies the target, in (4) the first utterance simply directs the player's attention to a group of buttons. The second utterance then picks out the target.

(5) IG: *dreh dich nach links etwas* (turn left a little; MV)
IF: [turns left] there are two red buttons in front of him (and some other red buttons to his right)
IG: *so, da siehst du zwei rote Schalter* (so now you see two red buttons; REF)
IF: [moves towards buttons]
IG: *und den rechten davon drückst du* (and you press the right one; MNP)
IF: [moves closer, but more towards the left one]
IG: *rechts* (right; REF)

Stoia (2007) observed that IGs use *move* instructions to focus the IF's attention on a particular area. This is also common in our data. For instance in (5), the IF is asked to turn to directly face the group of buttons containing the target. (5) also shows how IGs monitor their partners' actions and respond to them. The IF is moving towards the wrong button causing the IG to repeat part of the previous description.

(6) IG: *den blauen Schalter* (the blue button; REF)
IF: [moves and then stops]
IG: *den du rechts siehst* (the one you see on your right; REF)
IF: [starts moving again]
IG: *den drücken* (press that one; MNP)

Similarly, in (6) the IG produces an elaboration when the IF stops moving towards the target, indicating her confusion.

(7) IG: *und jetzt rechts an der* (and now to the right on the; REF)
IF: [turns right, is facing the wall with the target button]
IG: *ja ... genau ... an der Wand den blauen Knopf* (yes ... right ... on the wall the blue button; ACK, REF)
IF: [moves towards button]
IG: *einmal drücken* (press once; MNP)

In (7) the IG inserts affirmative feedback when the IF reacts correctly to a portion of his utterance. As can be seen in Table 2, *reference* utterances are relatively often followed by affirmative feedback.

(8) IF: [enters room, stops, looks around, ends up looking at the target]
IG: *ja genau den grünen Knopf neben der Lampe drücken* (yes right, press the green button next to the lamp; MNP)

IGs can also take advantage of IF actions that are not in direct response to an utterance. This happens in (8). The IF enters a new room and looks around. When she looks towards the target, the IG seizes the opportunity and produces affirmative feedback.

4 Conclusions and future work

We have described a corpus of spoken instructions in the GIVE scenario which we are currently building and which we will make available once it is completed. This corpus differs from other corpora of task-oriented dialog (specifically, the MapTask corpus (Anderson et al., 1991), the TRAINS corpus (Heeman and Allen, 1995), the Monroe corpus (Stent, 2000)) in that the IG could observe the IF's actions in real-time. This led to interactions in which instructions are given in installments and linguistic and non-linguistic actions are interleaved.

This poses interesting new questions for NLG systems, which we have illustrated by discussing the patterns of utterance sequences that IGs and IFs use in our corpus to agree on the objects that need to be manipulated. In line with results from psycholinguistics, we found that the information necessary to establish a reference is often expressed in multiple installments and that IGs carefully monitor how their partners react to their instructions and quickly respond by giving feedback, repeating information or elaborating on previous utterance when necessary.

The NLG system thus needs to be able to decide when a complete identifying description can be given in one utterance and when a description in installments is more effective. Stoia (2007) as well as Garoufi and Koller (2010) have addressed this question, but their approaches only make a choice between generating an instruction to move or a uniquely identifying referring expression. They do not consider cases in which another type of utterance, for instance, one that refers to a group of objects or gives an initial ambiguous description, is used to draw the attention of the IF to a particular area and they do not generate referring expressions in installments.

The system, furthermore, needs to be able to interpret the IF's actions and decide when to insert an acknowledgment, elaboration or correction. It then has to decide how to formulate this feedback. The addressee, e.g., needs to be able to distinguish elaborations from corrections. If the feedback was inserted in the middle of a sentence, if finally has to decide whether this sentence should be completed and how the remainder may have to be adapted.

Once we have finished the corpus collection, we plan to use it to study and address the questions discussed above. We are planning on building on the work by Stoia (2007) on using machine learning techniques to develop a model that takes into account various contextual factors and on the work by Thompson (2009) on generating references in installments. The set-up under which the corpus was collected, furthermore, lends itself well to Wizard-of-Oz studies to test the effectiveness of different interactive strategies for describing objects.

Acknowledgments This research was supported by the Deutsche Forschungsgemeinschaft (DFG) in the Center of Excellence in 'Cognitive Interaction Technology' (CITEC) and by the Skidmore Union Network which was funded through an ADVANCE grant from the National Science Foundation.

References

Anne H. Anderson, Miles Bader, Ellen Gurman Bard, Elizabeth Boyle, Gwyneth Doherty, Simon Garrod, Stephen Isard, Jacqueline Kowtko, Jan McAllister, Jim Miller, Catherine Sotillo, Henry S. Thompson, and Regina Weinert. 1991. The HCRC map task corpus. *Language and Speech*, 34:351–366.

Anja Belz, Albert Gatt, Alexander Koller, and Kristina Striegnitz, editors. 2011. *Proceedings of the Generation Challenges Session at the 13th European Workshop on Natural Language Generation*, Nancy, France.

Paul Boersma and David Weenink. 2011. Praat: doing phonetics by computer. Computer program. Retrieved May 2011, from http://www.praat.org/.

Herbert H. Clark and Meredyth A. Krych. 2004. Speaking while monitoring addressees for understanding. *Journal of Memory and Language*, 50:62–81.

Herbert H Clark and Deanna Wilkes-Gibbs. 1986. Referring as a collaborative process. *Cognition*, 22:1–39.

Andrew Gargett, Konstantina Garoufi, Alexander Koller, and Kristina Striegnitz. 2010. The GIVE-2 corpus of giving instructions in virtual environments. In *Proceedings of the Seventh International Conference on Language Resources and Evaluation (LREC'10)*, pages 2401–2406, Valletta, Malta.

Konstantina Garoufi and Alexander Koller. 2010. Automated planning for situated natural language generation. In *Proceedings of the 48th Annual Meeting of the Association for Computational Linguistics*, pages 1573–1582, Uppsala, Sweden.

Darren Gergle, Robert E. Kraut, and Susan R. Fussell. 2004. Action as language in a shared visual space. In *Proceedings of the 2004 ACM Conference on Computer Supported Cooperative Work*, pages 487–496, Chicago, IL.

Peter A. Heeman and James Allen. 1995. The Trains 93 dialogues. Technical Report Trains 94-2, Computer Science Department, University of Rochester, Rochester, NY.

Mary Hegarty, Daniel R. Montello, Anthony E. Richardson, Toru Ishikawa, and Kristin Lovelace. 2006. Spatial abilities at different scales: Individual differences in aptitude-test performance and spatial-layout learning. *Intelligence*, 34:151–176.

Emiel Krahmer and Kees van Deemter. 2012. Computational generation of referring expressions: A survey. *Computational Linguistics*, 38:173–218.

Amanda Stent. 2000. The Monroe corpus. Technical Report 728/TN 99-2, Computer Science Department, University of Rochester, Rochester, NY.

Laura Stoia. 2007. *Noun Phrase Generation for Situated Dialogs*. Ph.D. thesis, Graduate School of The Ohio State University, Columbus, OH.

Kristina Striegnitz, Alexandre Denis, Andrew Gargett, Konstantina Garoufi, Alexander Koller, and Mariët Theune. 2011. Report on the second second challenge on generating instructions in virtual environments (GIVE-2.5). In *Proceedings of the Generation Challenges Session at the 13th European Workshop on Natural Language Generation*, pages 270–279, Nancy, France.

Will Thompson. 2009. *A Game-Theoretic Model of Grounding for Referential Communication Tasks*. Ph.D. thesis, Northwestern University, Evanston, IL.

Peter Wittenburg, Hennie Brugman, Albert Russel, Alex Klassmann, and Han Sloetjes. 2006. ELAN: A professional framework for multimodality research. In *Proceedings of the 5th International Conference on Language Resources and Evaluation (LREC)*, pages 1556–1559, Genoa, Italy.

MinkApp: Generating Spatio-temporal Summaries for Nature Conservation Volunteers

Nava Tintarev, Yolanda Melero, Somayajulu Sripada,
Elizabeth Tait, Rene Van Der Wal, Chris Mellish
University of Aberdeen
{n.tintarev, y.melero, yaji.sripada,
elizbeth.tait, r.vanderwal, c.mellish@abdn.ac.uk}@abdn.ac.uk

Abstract

We describe preliminary work on generating contextualized text for nature conservation volunteers. This Natural Language Generation (NLG) differs from other ways of describing spatio-temporal data, in that it deals with abstractions on data across large geographical spaces (total projected area 20,600 km^2), as well as temporal trends across longer time frames (ranging from one week up to a year). We identify challenges at all stages of the classical NLG pipeline.

1 Introduction

We describe preliminary work on summarizing spatio-temporal data, with the aim to generate contextualized feedback for wildlife management volunteers. The MinkApp project assesses the use of NLG to assist volunteers working on the Scottish Mink Initiative (SMI). This participatory initiative aims to safeguard riverine species of economic importance (e.g., salmon and trout) and species of nature conservation interest including water voles, ground nesting birds and other species that are actively preyed upon by an invasive non-native species - the American mink (Bryce et al., 2011).

2 Background

Our test ground is one of the world's largest community-based invasive species management programs, which uses volunteers to detect, and subsequently remove, American mink from an area of Scotland set to grow from 10,000 km^2 in 2010 to 20,600 km^2 by the end of 2013 (Bryce et al., 2011). Such a geographical expansion means that an increasing share of the monitoring and control work is undertaken by volunteers supported by a fixed number of staff. An important contribution of volunteers is to help collect data over a large spatial scale.

Involving members of the public in projects such as this can play a crucial role in collecting observational data (Silvertown, 2009). High profile examples of data-gathering programmes, labelled as citizen science, include Galaxy Zoo and Springwatch (Raddick et al., Published online 2010; Underwood et al., 2008). However, in such long-term and wide ranging initiatives, maintaining volunteer engagement can be challenging and volunteers must get feedback on their contributions to remain motivated to participate (Silvertown, 2009). NLG may serve the function of supplying this feedback.

3 Related work

We are particularly interested in summarizing raw geographical and temporal data whose semantics need to be computed at run time – so called spatio-temporal NLG. Such extended techniques are studied in data-to-text NLG (Molina and Stent, 2010; Portet et al., 2009; Reiter et al., 2005; Turner et al., 2008; Thomas et al., Published online 2010). Generating text from spatio-temporal data involves not just finding data abstractions, but also determining appropriate descriptors for them (Turner et al., 2008). Turner et. al (2008) present a case study in weather forecast generation where selection of spatial descriptors is partly based on domain specific (weather related) links between spatial descriptors and weather phenomena. In the current project we see an opportunity to investigate such domain specific constraints in the selection of descriptors over larger temporal and spatial scales.

4 Current Status

Over 600 volunteers currently notify volunteer managers of their ongoing mink recording efforts. Our work is informed by in-depth discussions and interviews with the volunteer managers, as well as 58 (ground level) volunteers' responses to a questionnaire about their volunteering experience. The set of volunteers involves different people, such as conservation professionals, rangers, landowners and farmers with the degree of volunteer involvement varying among them. Most volunteers check for sightings: footprints on a floating platform with a clay-based tracking plate (raft hereafter) readily used by mink, or visual sightings on land or water. Others set and check traps, and (much fewer volunteers) dispatch trapped mink.[1] In terms of feedback, volunteers currently receive regional quarterly newsletters, but tailored and contextualized feedback is limited to sporadic personal communication, mostly via email.[2]

4.1 Why NLG in this context?

Where the initiative has been successful, mink sightings are sparse. Such a lack of sightings can be demotivating for volunteers and leads to a situation in which negative records are seldom recorded (Beirne, 2011). As one volunteer stated: *"Nothing much happens on my raft so my enthusiasm wanes."* Also, 73% of the volunteers who completed the questionnaire said they checked their raft at the recommended frequency of every two weeks. Similarly, 72% said that they got in touch with their manager rarely or only every couple of months – when they needed more clay or saw footprints. NLG based feedback could motivate volunteers by informing them about the value of negative records. If they were to stop because of a lack of interest, mink are likely to reinvade the area.

In addition, volunteers who work alone can be isolated and lack natural mechanisms for information exchange with peers. We postulate that giving the volunteers contextualized feedback for an area gives them a better feeling for their contribution to the project and a better sense of how the initiative is going overall. A need for this has already been felt by volunteers: *"Knowing even more about progress in the catchment would be good - and knowing in detail about water vole returning and latest mink sightings. It would be helpful to learn about other neighboring volunteers captures sightings in 'real time'."*

5 Approach

In this section we describe the generation of text in terms of a classic NLG pipeline, (Reiter and Dale, 2000), while addressing the additional tasks of interpreting the input data (from volunteers) to meaningful messages that achieve the desired communication goals: providing information to, as well as motivating volunteers. The NLG system which will generate these texts is actively under development.

5.1 Gold standard

Our nearest comparison is a corpus of domain specific conservation newsletters containing text such as the one below. These newsletters give us an idea of the type of structure and lexical choice applied when addressing volunteers, using both temporal and spatial summaries. However, these texts are not contextualized, or adapted to a particular volunteer.

> *"With an ever expanding project area, we are progressing exceptionally well achieving and maintaining areas free of breeding mink through-out the North of Scotland. Currently, the upper Spey, upper Dee and Ythan appear to be free of breeding mink, with only a few transients passing through..."*

We would like to improve on these existing texts and aim to generate texts that are tailored and consider the context of the volunteer. The text below is developed from a template supplied from a volunteer manager in the process of corpus collection. In the following sections we describe the steps and challenges involved in the process of generating such a text.

[1] Traps are only placed once a sighting has occurred. Once placed, by law a trap must be checked daily.

[2] In this project, we are using a corpus based on newsletters from the North Scotland Mink Project and the Cairngorms Water Vole Conversation Project.

"Thank you for your helpful contribution! You may have not seen any signs this time, but in the last week two people in the Spey catchment have seen footprints on their rafts. This means there might be a female with a litter in your neighborhood – please be on the lookout in the coming weeks! Capturing her could mean removing up to 6 mink at once!"

5.2 Example input

The data we receive from volunteers includes positive and negative records from raft checks (every 14 days), visual sightings, and mink captures. Each record contains a geographical reference (x and y coordinate) and a timestamp. In addition, for trapped mink we may know the sex (male, female, or unknown) and age (juvenile, adult, or unknown).

5.3 Data analysis and interpretation

Spatial trends. The current version of the system can reason over geographical information, defining various notions of neighborhood.[3] For a given point the following attributes can be used to describe its neighborhood: geographical region (catchment and subcatchment), Euclidean distance from another point, and relative cardinal direction to another point (north, south, east, west). The system reasons about sightings and captures using facts such as:

- This point (on land or water) is in the Dee catchment.
- Three neighbors have seen footprints (within a given time window).
- One neighbor has caught a mink (within a given time window).
- The nearest mink footprint is 15 km north east of this point.

The definition of neighborhood will differ according to domain specific factors. Euclidean distance appears to be the most likely candidate for use, because sightings may belong to different geographic regions (catchments) but be very close to each other. More importantly, the definition of neighborhood is likely to depend on the geographic region (e.g. areas differ in terms of mink population density with mountainous regions less likely to be utilized than coastal regions).

Temporal trends. Aside from geographic trends, the system will also be used to portray temporal trends. These look at the change in sightings between two time intervals, identifying it as a falling, rising or steady trend in mink numbers. We are primarily observing trends between different years, but also taking into consideration the ecology of the mink including their behavior in different seasons and for quantification. For example, we need to be able to decide if an increase from 0 to 5 mink sightings in an area during breeding is worth mentioning – most likely it is, as this a common size for a litter. Another example is the definition of a 'cleared' area - Example 1 below describes a stable zero trend over a longer period of time.

...Currently, the upper Spey, upper Dee and Ythan appear to be free of breeding mink... (1)

5.4 Document planning

Content determination While useful on its own, the text that could be generated from the data analysis and interpretation described above is much more useful when domain specific rules are applied. Example 2 describes a significant year-on-year increase *for a given definition of neighborhood*, during breeding season.

IF ((month >= 6 AND month <9)
AND sightingsLastYear(area) == 0
AND sightingsThisYear >= 5)
THEN feedback +=
"It looks like the area has been reinvaded.
We should get ready to trap them to keep this
area mink free." (2)

Example rule 2 is applied in the breeding season (ca June-Aug.). It will be given a score which signifies its relative importance compared to other derived content to allow prioritization. For example,

[3] The reasoning is performed using the opensource GIS Java library Geotools, `http://geotools.org`, retrieved Jan 2012

if there are **both** female and male captures in a region, it would be more important to speak about the female capture. This is because the capture of breeding mink has a much larger positive impact on the success of the initiative.[4] This importance should be reflected in texts such as: *...Capturing her could mean removing up to 6 mink at once!...*

Document structuring Since our goal is to motivate as well as inform, the structure of the text will be affected. If we consider the example text in Section 5.1, we can roughly divide it into three summary types:

- **Personal** - "Thank you for your helpful contribution! You may have not seen any signs this time."
- **Neighbor** - "In the last week two people in the Spey catchment have seen small footprints on their rafts."
- **Biology** - "There might be a female with a litter in your neighborhood ... Capturing her could mean removing up to 6 mink at once!"

If, in contrast to the previous example, a volunteer *would* capture a mink, then the neighborhood summary can be used to emphasize the importance of rare captures.

"IF currentMonth == August AND
capture == true AND nCapturesInSummer == 0" (3)

The feedback for rule 3 might read something like: *"Well done! So far, this was the only mink captured during the breeding season in the Spey catchment!"*

5.5 Microplanning

Microplanning will need to consider the aggregation of spatio-temporal data that happens on a deeper level e.g., for a given catchment and year. This aggregation is likely to result in a surface aggregation as well deeper data aggregation, such as the catchments in Example 1. In terms of lexical choice, the system will have to use domain appropriate vocabulary. The latter example refers to "breeding mink", which informs the reader that their capture has a large impact on population control. Another example of lexical choice may be "quieter autumn" to denote a decrease in mink for an area.

The best way to communicate neighborhood to volunteers is still an open question. The texts in our corpus describe neighborhoods in terms of geographic regions (catchments and subcatchments, e.g. Spey). However, Euclidean distance may be more informative, in particular close to catchment boundaries.

6 Challenges

There are several key challenges when generating motivating text for nature conservation volunteers, using spatio-temporal NLG.

One challenge is to tailor feedback texts to individuals according to their motivations and information needs. In line with previous research in affective NLG (de Rosis and Grasso, 2000; Belz, 2003; Sluis and Mellish, 2010; Tintarev and Masthoff, 2012; Mahamood and Reiter, 2011), we continue to study the factors which are likely to have an effect on volunteer motivation. So far we have worked together with volunteer managers. We collected a corpus of texts, written by the managers, that are tailored to motivate different volunteer personas, and conducted interviews and a focus group with them. While we found that the mink managers tailored texts to different personas, interviews indicated that the biggest factor to tailor for was the definition of neighborhood. Some volunteers are interested in a local update, while others are interested in a larger overview.

A second, related challenge, regards correctly defining the reasoning over spatio-temporal facts e.g., quantifying the magnitude of significant changes (increases and decreases in sightings and captures) for different seasons, regions, and the time frames over which they occur. We believe this will lead to generating text referring to more compound abstractions such as mink free areas, or re-invasion.

A final challenge brought out by the interviews is to supply varied feedback that helps volunteers to continue to learn about mink and their habitat. This is a challenge for both content determination and microplanning.

[4] Established adult females with litters.

References

Christopher Beirne. 2011. Novel use of mark-recapture framework to study volunteer retention probabilities within an invasive non-native species management project reveals vocational and temporal trends. Master's thesis, University of Aberdeen.

Anja Belz. 2003. And now with feeling: Developments in emotional language generation. Technical Report ITRI-03-21, Information Technology Research Institute, University of Brighton.

Rosalind Bryce, Matthew K. Oliver, Llinos Davies, Helen Gray, Jamie Urquhart, and Xavier Lambin. 2011. Turning back the tide of american mink invasion at an unprecedented scale through community participation and adaptive management. *Biological Conservation*, 144:575–583.

Fiorella de Rosis and Floriana Grasso, 2000. *Affective Interactions*, volume 1814 of *Lecture Notes in Artificial Intelligence*, chapter Affective Natural Language Generation. Springer-Verlag.

Saad Mahamood and Ehud Reiter. 2011. Generating affective natural language for parents of neonatal infants. In *ENLG*.

Martin Molina and Amanda Stent. 2010. A knowledge-based method for generating summaries of spatial movement in geographic areas. *International Journal on Artificial Intelligence Tools*, 19(3):393–415.

Francois Portet, Ehud Reiter, Albert Gatt, Jim Hunter, Somayajulu Sripada, Yvonne Freer, and Cindy Sykes. 2009. Automatic generation of textual summaries from neonatal intensive care data. *Artificial Intelligence*, 173:789–816.

M. Jordan Raddick, Georgia Bracey, Pamela L. Gay, Chris J. Lintott, Phil Murray, Kevin Schawinski, Alexander S. Szalay, and Jan Vandenberg. Published online 2010. Galaxy zoo: Exploring the motivations of citizen science volunteers. *Astronomy Education Review*, 9(1), 010103, doi:10.3847/AER2009036.

Ehud Reiter and Robert Dale. 2000. *Building natural language generation systems*. Cambridge University Press.

Ehud Reiter, Somayajulu Sripada, Jim Hunter, Jin Yu, and Ian Davy. 2005. Choosing words in computer-generated weather forecasts. *Artificial Intelligence*, 167:137–169.

Jonathan Silvertown. 2009. A new dawn for citizen science. *Trends in Ecology & Evolution*, 24:467–471.

Ielka Van der Sluis and Chris Mellish, 2010. *Empirical Methods in Natural Language Generation*, volume 5980 of *Lecture Notes in Computer Science*, chapter Towards Empirical Evaluation of Affective Tactical NLG. Springer, Berlin / Heidelberg.

Kavita E. Thomas, Somayajulu Sripada, and Matthijs L. Noordzij. Published online 2010. Atlas.txt: Exploring linguistic grounding techniques for communicating spatial information to blind users. *Journal of Universal Access in the Information Society*, DOI 10.1007/s10209-010-0217-5.

Nava Tintarev and Judith Masthoff. 2012. Evaluating the effectiveness of explanations for recommender systems: Methodological issues and empirical studies on the impact of personalization. *User Modeling and User-Adapted Interaction*, (to appear).

Ross Turner, Somayajulu Sripada, Ehud Reiter, and Ian Davy. 2008. Using spatial reference frames to generate grounded textual summaries of georeferenced data. In *INLG*.

Joshua Underwood, Hilary Smith, Rosemary Luckin, and Geraldine Fitzpatrick. 2008. E-science in the classroom towards viability. *Computers & Education*, 50:535–546.

Towards a Surface Realization-Oriented Corpus Annotation

Leo Wanner
ICREA and
Universitat Pompeu Fabra
Roc Boronat 138
Barcelona, 08018, Spain
leo.wanner@upf.edu

Simon Mille
Universitat Pompeu Fabra
Roc Boronat 138
Barcelona, 08018, Spain
simon.mille@upf.edu

Bernd Bohnet
Universität Stuttgart
IMS, Pfaffenwaldring 5b
Stuttgart, 70569, Germany
bohnet@ims.uni-stuttgart.de

Abstract

Until recently, deep stochastic surface realization has been hindered by the lack of semantically annotated corpora. This is about to change. Such corpora are increasingly available, e.g., in the context of CoNLL shared tasks. However, recent experiments with CoNLL 2009 corpora show that these popular resources, which serve well for other applications, may not do so for generation. The attempts to adapt them for generation resulted so far in a better performance of the realizers, but not yet in a genuinely semantic generation-oriented annotation schema. Our goal is to initiate a debate on how a generation suitable annotation schema should be defined. We define some general principles of a semantic generation-oriented annotation and propose an annotation schema that is based on these principles. Experiments shows that making the semantic corpora comply with the suggested principles does not need to have a negative impact on the quality of the stochastic generators trained on them.

1 Introduction

With the increasing interest in data-driven surface realization, the question on the adequate annotation of corpora for generation also becomes increasingly important. While in the early days of stochastic generation, annotations produced for other applications were used (Knight and Hatzivassiloglou, 1995; Langkilde and Knight, 1998; Bangalore and Rambow, 2000; Oh and Rudnicky, 2000; Langkilde-Geary, 2002), the poor results obtained, e.g., by (Bohnet et al., 2010) with the original CoNLL 2009 corpora, show that annotations that serve well for other applications, may not do so for generation and thus need at least to be adjusted.[1] This has also been acknowledged in the run-up to the surface realization challenge 2011 (Belz et al., 2011), where a considerable amount of work has been invested into the conversion of the annotations of the CoNLL 2008 corpora (Surdeanu et al., 2008), i.e., PropBank (Palmer et al., 2005), which served as the reference treebank, into a more "generation friendly" annotation. However, all of the available annotations are to a certain extent still syntactic. Even PropBank and its generation-oriented variants contain a significant number of syntactic features (Bohnet et al., 2011b).

Some previous approaches to data-driven generation avoid the problem related to the lack of semantic resources in that they use hybrid models that imply a symbolic submodule which derives the syntactic representation that is then used by the stochastic submodule (Knight and Hatzivassiloglou, 1995; Langkilde and Knight, 1998). (Walker et al., 2002), (Stent et al., 2004), (Wong and Mooney, 2007), and (Mairesse et al., 2010) start from deeper structures: Walker et al. and Stent et al. from *deep-syntactic structures* (Mel'čuk, 1988), and Wong and Mooney and Mairesse et al. from higher order predicate logic structures. However, to the best of our knowledge,

[1]Trained on the original ConLL 2009 corpora, (Bohnet et al., 2010)'s SVM-based generator reached a BLEU score of 0.12 for Chinese, 0.18 for English, 0.11 for German and 0.14 for Spanish. Joining the unconnected parts of the sentence annotations to connected trees (as required by a stochastic realizer) improved the performance to a BLEU score of 0.69 for Chinese, 0.66 for English, 0.61 for German and 0.68 for Spanish.

none of them uses corpora annotated with the structures from which they start.

To deep stochastic generation, the use of hybrid models is not an option and training a realizer on syntactically-biased annotations is highly problematic in the case of data-to-text NLG, which starts from numeric time series or conceptual or semantic structures: the syntactic features will be simply not available in the input structures at the moment of application.[2]. Therefore, it is crucial to define a theoretically sound semantic annotation that is still good in practical terms.

Our goal is thus to discuss some general principles of a semantic generation-oriented annotation schema and offer a first evaluation of its possible impact on stochastic generation. Section2 details what kind of information is available respectively not available during data-to-text generation. Section 3 states some general principles that constrain an adequate semantic representation, while Section 4 formally defines their well-formedness. Section 5 reports then on the experiments made with the proposed annotation, and Section6 offers some conclusions.

2 What can we and what we cannot count on?

In data-to-text or ontology-to-text generation, with the standard *content selection–discourse structuring—surface generation* pipeline in place, and no hard-wired linguistic realization of the individual chunks of the data or ontology structure, the input to the surface realization module can only be an abstract structure that does not contain any syntactic (and even lexical) information. *Conceptual graphs* in the sense of Sowa (Sowa, 2000) are structures of this kind;[3] see Figure 1 for illustration ('Cmpl' = 'Completion', 'Rcpt' = 'Recipient', 'Strt' = 'Start', 'Attr' = Attribute, 'Chrc' = 'Characteristic', and 'Amt' = 'Amount'). *Content selection* accounts for the determination of the content units that are to be communicated and *Discourse Structuring* for the delimitation of *Elementary Discourse Units* (EDUs) and their organization and for the discursive relations between them (e.g., *Bcas* (*Because*) in the Figure).

In particular, such a structure cannot contain:

- non-meaningful nodes: governed prepositions (BECAUSE *of*, CONCENTRATION *of*), auxiliaries (passive *be*), determiners (*a*, *the*);
- syntactic connectors (*between* A *and* B), relative pronouns, etc.
- syntactic structure information: A modifies B, A is the subject of B, etc.

In other words, a deep stochastic generator has to be able to produce all syntactic phenomena from generic structures that guarantee a certain flexibility when it comes to their surface form (i.e., without encoding directly this type of syntactic information). For instance, *a concentration of NO2* can be realized as *a NO2 concentration*, *between 23h00 and 00h00* as *from 23h00 until 00h00*, etc. This implies that deep annotations as, for instance, have been derived so far from PennTreeBank/PropBank, in which either all syntactic nodes of the annotation are kept (as in (Bohnet et al., 2010)) or only certain syntactic nodes are removed (as THAT complementizers and TO infinitives in the shared task 2011 on surface realization (Belz et al., 2011)) still fall short of a genuine semantic annotation. Both retain a lot of syntactic information which is not accessible in genuine data-to-text generation: nodes (relative pronouns, governed prepositions and conjunctions, determiners, auxiliaries, etc.) and edges (relative clause edges, control edges, modifier vs. argumental edges, etc.).

This lets us raise the question how the annotation policies should look like to serve generation well and to what extent existing resources such as PropBank comply with them already. We believe that the answer is critical for the future research agenda in generation and will certainly play an outstanding role in the shared tasks to come.

In the next section, we assess the minimal principles which the annotation suitable for (at least) data-to-text generation must follow in order to lead to a *core semantic structure*. This core structure still ignores such important information as co-reference,

[2]Even though in this article we are particularly interested in data-to-text generation, we are convinced that clean semantic and syntactic annotations also facilitate text-to-text generation.

[3]But note that this can be any other content structure.

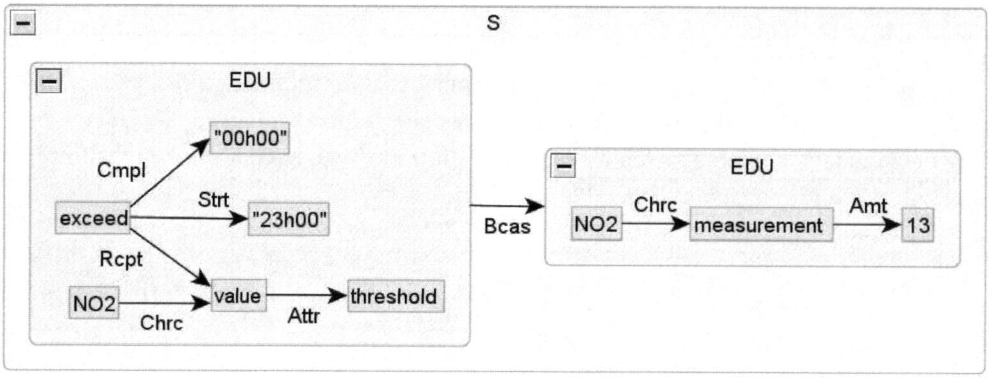

Figure 1: Sample conceptual structure as could be produced by text planning (*Because of a concentration of NO2 of 13*$\mu g/m^3$*, the NO2 threshold value was exceeded between 23h00 and 00h00*)

scope, presupposition, etc.: this information is obviously necessary, but it is not absolutely vital for a sufficient restriction of the possible choices faced during surface generation. Further efforts will be required to address its annotation in appropriate depth.

3 The principles of generation-suitable semantic annotation

Before talking about generation-suitable annotation, we must make some general assumptions concerning NLG as such. These assumptions are necessary (but might not always be sufficient) to cover deep generation in all its subtleties: (i) data-to-text generation starts from an abstract conceptual or semantic representation of the content that is to be rendered into a well-formed sentence; (ii) data-to-text generation is a series of equivalence mappings from more abstract to more concrete structures, with a chain of inflected words as the final structure; (iii) the equivalence between the source structure S_s and the target structure S_t is explicit and self-contained, i.e., for the mapping from S_s to S_t, only features contained in S_s and S_t are used. The first assumption is in the very nature of the generation task in general; the second and the third are owed to requirements of statistical generation (although a number of rule-based generators show these characteristics as well).

The three basic assumptions give rise to the following four principles.

1. Semanticity: The semantic annotation must capture the meaning and only the meaning of a given sentence. Functional nodes (auxiliaries, determiners, governed conjunctions and prepositions), node duplicates and syntactically-motivated arcs should not appear in the semantic structure: they reflect grammatical and lexical features, and thus already anticipate how the meaning will be worded. For example, *meet*-AGENT→*the* (*directors*), *meet*-LOCATION→*in* (*Spain*), *meet*-TIME→*in* (*2002*) cited in (Buch-Kromann et al., 2011) as semantic annotation of the phrase *meeting between the directors in Spain in 2002* in the Copenhagen Dependency Treebank does not meet this criterion: *the*, and both *ins* are functional nodes. Node duplicates such as the relative pronoun *that* in the PropBank annotation (*But Panama illustrates that their their substitute is a system*) *that*←R-A0-*produces* (*an absurd gridlock*) equally reflect syntactic features, as do syntactically-motivated arc labels of the kind 'R(elative)-A0'.

The PropBank annotation of the sentence cited above also intermingles predicate-argument relations ('Ai') with syntactico-functional relations ('AM-MNR'): *gridlock*−AM-MNR→*absurd*. The predicate-argument analysis of modifiers suggests namely that they are predicative semantemes that take as argument the node that governs them in the syntactic structure; in the above structure: $absurd$−A1→$gridlock$. This applies also to locatives, temporals and other "circumstantials", which are most conveniently represented as two-place semantemes: $house$←A1−$location$−A2→$Barcelona$, $party$←A1−$time$−A2→$yesterday$, and so on. Although not realized at the surface, $location$, $time$, etc. are crucial.

2. Informativity: A propositional semantic annotation must be enriched by *information structure* features that predetermine the overall syntactic structure (paratactic, hypotactic, parenthetical, ...), the internal syntactic structure (subject/object, clefted or not, any element fronted or not, etc.), determiner distribution, etc. in the sentence. Otherwise, it will be always underspecified with respect to its syntactic equivalence in that, as a rule, a single semantic structure will correspond to a number of syntactic structures. This is not to say that with the information structure in place we will always achieve a 1:1 correspondence between the semantic and syntactic annotations; further criteria may be needed—including prosody, style, presupposedness, etc. However, information structure is crucial.

The most relevant information structure features are those of Thematicity, Foregroundedness and Givenness.[4]

Thematicity specifies what the utterance states (marked as *rheme*) and about what it states it (marked as *theme*).[5] Theme/rheme determines, in the majority of cases, the subject-object structure and the topology of the sentence. For instance,[6] $[John]_{theme}$←A1$-[see$–A2→$Maria]_{rheme}$ may be said to correspond to $John$←subject$-see-$dir.obj→$Maria$ and $[John$←A1$-see]_{rheme}$–A2 →$[Maria]_{theme}$ to $John$ ←obj$-see_{pass}-$subject →$Maria$. For the generation of relative sentence structures such as *John bought a car which was old and ugly*, we need to accommodate for a recursive definition of thematicity: $[John]_{theme}$←A1$-[buy-$A2→$[c1 : car]_{theme}$←A1$-[old]_{rheme}$; $c1$←A1 $-[ugly]_{rheme}]_{rheme}$.[7] With no recursive (or *secondary* in Mel'čuk's terms) thematicity, we would get *John bought an old and ugly car*.[8]

It is quite easy to find some counter-examples to the default theme/rheme–syntactic feature correlation, in particular in the case of questions and answers. For instance, the neutral answer to the question *What will John bake tomorrow?*, *John will bake a cake*, would be split as follows: $[John$←A1$-bake]_{theme}$ –A2→$[cake]_{rheme}$. In this case, the main verb at the surface, *bake*, is included in the theme and not in the rheme. Consider also the sentence *In a cross-border transaction, the buyer is in a different region of the globe from the target*, where the main theme is *in a cross-border transaction*, i.e., not the subject of the sentence (with the subject *the buyer* being the embedded theme of the main rheme). In these cases, the correlation is more complex, but it undoubtedly exists and needs to be distilled during the training phase.

Foregroundedness captures the "prominence" of the individual elements of the utterance for the speaker or hearer. An element is 'foregrounded' if it is prominent and 'backgrounded' if it is of lesser prominence; elements that are neither foregrounded nor backgrounded are 'neutral'. A number of correlations can be identified: (i) a 'foregrounded' A1 argument of a verb will trigger a clefting construction; e.g., $[John]_{foregr;theme}$←A1$-[see$–A2→$Maria]_{rheme}$ will lead to *It was John who saw Maria*; similarly, $[John$←A1$-bake]_{foregr;theme}$ –A2→$[cake]_{rheme}$ will lead to *What John will bake is a cake*; (ii) a 'foregrounded' A2 argument of a verb will correspond to a clefting construction or a dislocation: *It was Maria, whom John saw*; (iii) a 'foregrounded' A1 or A2 argument of a noun will result in an *argument promotion*, as, e.g., *John's arrival* (instead of *arrival of John*); (iv) a 'foregrounded' circumstantial will be fronted: *Under this tree he used to rest*; (v) marking a part of the semantic structure as 'backgrounded' will lead to a parenthetical construction: *John (well known among the students and professors alike) was invited as guest speaker*. If no elements

[4]We use mainly the terminology and definitions (although in some places significantly simplified) of (Mel'čuk, 2001), who, to the best of our knowledge, establishes the most detailed correlation between information structure and syntactic features.

[5]Similar notions are *topic/focus* (Sgall et al., 1986) and *topic/comment* (Gundel, 1988).

[6]As in PropBank, we use 'Ai' as argument labels of predicative lexemes, but for us, 'A1' stands for the first argument, 'A2' for the second argument, etc. That is, in contrast to PropBank, we do not support the use of 'A0' to refer to a lexeme's external argument since the distinction between external and internal arguments is syntactic.

[7]$c1$ is a "handle" in the sense of *Minimal Recursion Semantics* (Copestake et al., 1997).

[8]We believe that operator scopes (e.g., negations and quantifiers) can, to a large extent, be encoded within the thematic structure; see (Cook and Payne, 2006) for work in the LFG-framework on German, which provides some evidence for this. However, it must be stated that very little work has been done on the subject until now.

are marked as foregrounded/backgrounded, the default syntactic structure and the default word order are realized.

Givenness captures to what extent an information element is present to the hearer. The elementary givenness markers 'given' and 'new' correlate in syntax with determiner distribution. Thus, the 'new' marker of an object node will often correspond to an indefinite or zero determiner of the corresponding noun: *A masked man was seen to enter the bank* (*man* is newly introduced into the discourse). The 'given' marker will often correlate with a definite determiner: *The masked man* (whom a passer-by noticed before) *was seen to enter the bank.* To distinguish between demonstratives and definite determiners, a gradation of givenness markers as suggested by Gundel et al. (Gundel et al., 1989) is necessary: '$\text{given}_{1/2/3}$'.

As already for Thematicity, numerous examples can be found where the giveness-syntactic feature correlation deviates from the default correlation. For instance, in *I have heard a cat, the cat of my neighbour*, there would be only one single (given) node *cat* in the semantic structure, which does not prevent the first appearance of *cat* in the sentence to be indefinite. In *A warrant permits a holder that he acquire one share of common stock for $17.50 a share*, *warrant* is given, even if it is marked by an indefinite determiner. Again, this only shows the complexity of the annotation of the information structure, but it does not call into question the relevance of the information structure to NLG.

As one of the few treebanks, the Prague Dependency Treebank (PDT) (Hajič et al., 2006) accounts for aspects of the information structure in that it annotates *Topic-Focus Articulation* in terms of various degrees of *contextual boundness*, which are correlated with word order and intonation (Mikulová et al., 2006, p.152).

3. Connectivity: The semantic annotation must ensure that the annotation of an utterance forms a connected structure: without a connected structure, generation algorithms that imply a traversal of the input structure will fail to generate a grammatical sentence. For instance, the PropBank annotation of the sentence *But Panama illustrates that their substitute is a system that produces an absurd gridlock* (here shown partially) does not comply with this principle since it consists of four unconnected meaning-bearing substructures (the single node 'but' and the subtrees governed by 'illustrate', 'produce' and 'substitute'): *but* | *Panama*←A0–*illustrate*–A1→*that* | *system*←A0–*produce*–A1→*gridlock*–AM-MNR→*absurd* | *substitute*–A0→*their*.

4 Outline of a Generation-Oriented Annotation

The definitions below specify the syntactic well-formedness of the semantic annotation. They do not intend to and cannot substitute a detailed annotation manual, which is indispensable to achieve a semantically accurate annotation.

Definition 1: [Semantic Annotation of a sentence S, SA]
SA of S in the text T in language $\mathcal{L}$ is a pair $\langle S_{sem}, S_{inf}\rangle$, where S_{sem} is the semantic structure of S (ensuring Semanticity and Connectivity), and S_{inf} is the information structure of S (ensuring Informativity).

Let us define each of the two structures of the semantic annotation in turn.

Definition 2: [Semantic Structure of a sentence S, S_{sem}]
S_{sem} of S is a labeled acyclic directed connected graph (V, E, γ, λ) defined over the vertex label alphabet $L := L_S \cup M_C \cup M_T \cup M_t \cup M_a$ (such that $L_S \cap (M_C \cup M_T \cup M_t \cup M_a) = \emptyset$) and the edge label alphabet $R_{sem} \subseteq$ {A1, A2, A3, A4, A5, A6}, with
– V as the set of vertices;
– E as the set of directed edges;
– γ as the function that assigns each $v \in V$ an element $l \in L$;
– λ as the function that assigns each $e \in E$ an element $a \in R_{sem}$;
– L_S as the meaning bearing lexical units (LUs) of S;
– $M_C \subseteq$ {LOC, TMP, EXT, MNR, CAU, DIR, SPEC, ELAB, ADDR} as the "circumstantial meta semantemes" (with the labels standing for 'locative', 'temporal', 'temporal/spatial extension', 'manner', 'cause', 'direction', 'specification', 'elaboration', and 'addressee');
– $M_T \subseteq$ {TIME, TCST} as the "temporal meta semantemes" (with the labels standing for 'time' and

'time constituency');
– $M_t \subseteq \{\texttt{past*}, \texttt{present*}, \texttt{future*}\}$ as the "time value semantemes";
– $M_a \subseteq \{\texttt{imperfective*}, \texttt{durative*}, \texttt{semelfactive*}, \texttt{iterative*}, \texttt{telic*}, \texttt{atelic*}, \texttt{nil*}\}$ as the "aspectual value semantemes"[9]

such that the following conditions hold:

(a) the edges in S_{sem} are in accordance with the valency structure of the lexical units (LUs) in S: If l_p–Ai→$l_r \in S_{sem}$ ($l_p, l_r \in L_S$, $i \in \{1, 2, 3, \ldots\}$), then the semantic valency of l_p possesses at least i slots and l_r fulfils the semantic restrictions of the i-th slot
(b) the edges in S_{sem} are exhaustive: If $\gamma(n_r) = l_r \in L$ instantiates in S the i-th semantic argument of $\gamma(n_p) = l_p$, then l_p–Ai→$l_r \in S_{sem}$
(c) S_{sem} does not contain any duplicated argument edges: If $\gamma(n_p)$–Ai→$\gamma(n_r)$, $\gamma(n_p)$ –Aj→ $\gamma(n_q) \in S_{sem}$ (with $n_p, n_r, n_q \in N$) then Ai ≠ Aj and $n_r \neq n_q$
(d) circumstantial LUs in S are represented in S_{sem} by two-place meta-semantemes: If $l_r \in L_{sem}$ is a locative/temporal/ manner/cause/direction/specification/elaboration/addressee LU and in the syntactic dependency structure of S, l_r modifies l_p, then l_r←A2-α-A1→$l_p \in S_{sem}$ (with $\alpha \in$ LOC, TMP, MNR, CAU, DIR, SPEC, ELAB, ADDR)
(e) verbal tense is captured by the two-place predicate TIME: If $l_p \in L_{sem}$ is a verbal LU then l_r←A2-TIME-A1→$l_p \in S_{sem}$, with $l_r \in M_t$
(f) verbal aspect is captured by the two-place predicate TCST: If $l_p \in L_{sem}$ is a verbal LU then l_r←A2-TCST-A1→$l_p \in S_{sem}$, with $l_r \in M_a$.

(a) implies that no functional node is target of an argument arc: this would contradict the semantic valency conditions of any lexeme in S. (b) ensures that no edge in S_{sem} is missing: if a given LU is an argument of another LU in the sentence, then there is an edge from the governor LU to the argument LU. (c) means that no predicate in S_{sem} possesses in S two different instances of the same argument slot. The circumstantial meta-semantemes in (d) either capture the semantic role of a circumstantial that would otherwise get lost or introduce a predicate type for a name. Most of the circumstantial meta-semantemes reflect PropBank's modifier relations 'AM-X' (but in semantic, not in syntactico-functional terms), such that their names are taken from PropBank or are inspired by PropBank. LOC takes as A1 a name of a location of its A2: *Barcelona* ←A1-LOC-A2→*live*-A1→*John*; TMP a temporal expression: *yesterday* ←A1-TMP-A2→*arrive*-A1→*John*; MNR a manner attribute: *player*←A1-MNR-A2→*solo*; CAU the cause: *accept*←A1-CAU-A2→*reason* in *This is the reason why they accepted it*; DIR a spatial direction: *run around*←A2-DIR-A1→*circles* in *I'm running around in circles*; SPEC a "context specifier": *should*←A2-SPEC-A1→thought in *You should leave now, just a thought*; ELAB an appositive attribute *company*←A1-ELAB-A2 →*bank* in *This company, a bank, closed*; and ADDR direct address: *come*←A1-ADDR-A2→*John* in *John, come here!*

Definition 3: [Information Structure of a sentence S, S_{inf}]
Let S_{sem} of S be defined as above. S_{inf} of S is an undirected labeled hypergraph (V, I) with V as the set of vertices of S and I the set of hyperedges, with $I := \{$theme$_i$ (i = 1, 2, ...), rheme$_i$ (i = 1, 2, ...), given$_j$ (j = 1,...,3), new, foregrounded, backgrounded$\}$. The following conditions apply:
(a) thematicity is recursive, i.e., a thematic hyperedge contains under specific conditions embedded theme/rheme hyperedges: If $\exists n_k \in$ theme$_i$ such that $\gamma(n_k) = l_p$ is a verbal lexeme and l_p -A1→$l_r \in S_{sem}$, then ∃ theme$_{i+1}$, rheme$_{i+1}$ ∈ theme$_i$
(b) theme and rheme hyperedges of the same recursion level, given and new hyperedges, and foregrounded and backgrounded hyperedges are disjoint: theme$_i$ ∩ rheme$_i$ = ∅ (i = 1, 2, ...), given$_j$ ∩ new = ∅ (j = 1,...,3), foregr. ∩ backgr. = ∅
(c) any node in S_{sem} forms part of either theme or rheme: $\forall n_p \in S_{sem} : n_p \in$ theme$_1$ ∪ rheme$_1$.

Consider in Figure 2 an example of SA with its two structures.[10] All syntactic nodes have been removed, and all the remaining nodes are connected in terms of a predicate–argument structure, with no use of any syntactically motivated edge, so as to ensure that the structure complies with the Semanticity and Connectivity principles. Figure 2 illustrates the three main aspects of Informativity: (i) thematic-

[9]The aspectual feature names are mainly from (Comrie, 1976).

[10]The meta-semanteme TCST is not shown in the figure.

ity, with the two theme/rheme oppositions; (ii) foregroundedness, with the backgrounded part of the primary rheme; and (iii) givenness, with the attribute *givenness* and the value *2* on the node *program*. The information structure constrains the superficial realization of the sentence in that the primary theme will be the subject of the sentence, and the main node of the primary rheme pointing to it will be the main verb of the same sentence. The secondary theme and rheme will be realized as an embedded sentence in which *you* will be the subject, that is, forcing the realization of a relative clause. However, it does not constrain the appearance of a relative pronoun. For instance: *we obtained technologies you do not see anywhere else* and *we obtained technologies that you do not see anywhere else* are possible realizations of this structure. Leaving the relative pronoun in the semantic structure would force one realization to occur when it does not have to (both outputs are equally correct and meaning-equivalent to the other). Similarly, marking *the Soviet space program* as backgrounded leaves some doors open when it comes to surface realization: *Cosmos, the Soviet space program* vs. *Cosmos (the Soviet space program)* vs. *the Soviet space program Cosmos* (if *Cosmos* is backgrounded too) are possible realizations of this substructure.

ELABORATION is an example of a meta-node needed to connect the semantic structure: *Cosmos* and *program* have a semantic relation, but neither is actually in the semantic frame of the other—which is why the introduction of an extra node cannot be avoided. In this case, we could have a node *NAME*, but *ELABORATION* is much more generic and can actually be automatically introduced without any additional information.

5 Experiments

Obviously, the removal of syntactic features from a given standard annotation, with the goal to obtain an increasingly more semantic annotation, can only be accepted if the quality of (deep) stochastic generation does not unacceptably decrease. To assess this aspect, we converted automatically the PropBank annotation of the WSJ journal as used in the CoNLL shared task 2009 into an annotation that complies with all of the principles sketched above for deep statistical generation and trained (Bohnet et al., 2010)'s generator on this new annotation.[11] For our experiments, we used the usual training, development and test data split of the WSJ corpus (Langkilde-Geary, 2002; Ringger et al., 2004; Bohnet et al., 2010); Table 1 provides an overview of the used data.

set	section	# sentences
training	2 - 21	39218
development	24	1334
test	23	2400

Table 1: Data split of the used data in the WSJ Corpus

The resulting BLEU score of our experiment was 0.64, which is comparable with the accuracy reported in (Bohnet et al., 2010) (namely, 0.659), who used an annotation that still contained all functional nodes (such that their generation task was considerably more syntactic and thus more straightforward).

To assess furthermore whether the automatically converted PropBank already offers some advantages to other applications than generation, we used it in a semantic role labeling (SRL) experiment with (Bjö rkelund et al., 2010)'s parser. The achieved overall accuracy is 0.818, with all analysis stages (including the predicate identification stage) being automatic, which is a rather competitive figure. In the original CoNLL SRL setting with Oracle reading, an accuracy of 0.856 is achieved.

Another telling comparison can be made between the outcomes of the First Surface Realization Shared Task (Belz et al., 2011), in which two different input representations were given to the competing teams: a shallow representation and a deep representation. The shallow structures were unordered syntactic dependency trees, with all the tokens of the sentence, and the deep structures were predicate-argument graphs with some nodes removed (see Section 2). Although the performance of shallow generators was higher than the performance of the deep generators (the StuMaBa shallow generator (Bohnet et al., 2011a) obtained a BLEU score of 0.89, as opposed to 0.79 of the StuMaBa deep gen-

[11]Obviously, our conversion can be viewed only preliminary. It does not take into account all the subtleties that need to be taken account—for instance, with respect to the information structure; see also Section 6.

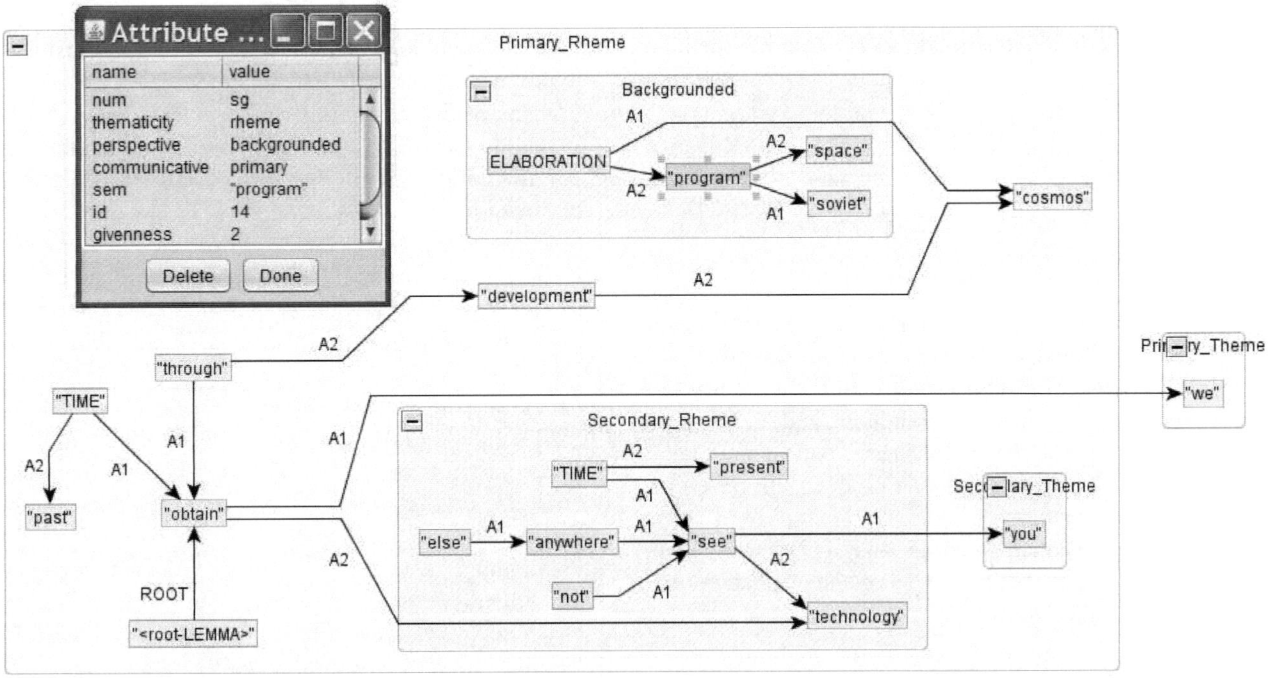

Figure 2: Illustration of the semantic annotation of the sentence *Through the development of Cosmos, the Soviet space program, we obtained technologies you do not see anywhere else.*

erator), the difference is not as striking as one would expect.[12]

6 Conclusions

Our experiments and the Surface Realization Shared Task 2011 suggest that making the deep annotation more semantic does not necessarily imply an unsurmountable problem for stochastic generation. We can thus conclude that deriving automatically a deep semantic annotation from PropBank allowed us to obtain very promising results, both for NLG and SRL. By sticking to universal predicate-argument structures, as PropBank does, we maintain the potential of the corpus to be mapped to other, more idiosyncratic, annotations. Still, automatic conversion will always remain deficient. Thus, a flawless identification of semantic predication cannot be guaranteed. For instance, when an actancial arc points to a preposition, it is not clear how to deduce whether this preposition is semantic or lexical. Also, the treatment of phraseological nodes is problematic, as is the annotation of a comprehensive information structure: the criteria for the automatic derivation of the information structure from the syntactic structure and the topology of a sentence can only be superficial and likely to be even less efficient in longer and complex sentences. The annotation of intersentential coreferences and the identification of gapped elements are further major hurdles for an automatic derivation of a truly semantic resource. As a consequence, we believe that new annotation policies are needed to obtain a high quality semantic resource. The best strategy is to start with a conversion of an existing semantically annotated treebank such as PropBank, revising and extending the result of this conversion in a manual concerted action—always following truly semantic annotation policies.

[12]Note that our results mentioned above cannot be directly compared with the StuMaBa results during the Generation Challenges 2011 because the realizers are different.

Acknowledgments

We would like to thank the reviewers for their valuable comments and suggestions and the Penn Treebank/PropBank/NomBank team, without whom our experiments would not be possible. Many thanks also to Mike White for the useful discussions on some of the topics discussed in the paper. Although we might still not agree on all of the details, he made us see the task of generation-oriented annotation from another angle and revise some of our initial assumptions.

References

S. Bangalore and O. Rambow. 2000. Exploiting a Probabilistic Hierarchical Model for Generation. In *Proc. of COLING '00*.

A. Belz, M. White, D. Espinosa, D. Hogan, and A. Stent. 2011. The First Surface Realization Shared Task: Overview and Evaluation Results. In *ENLG11*.

A. Björkelund, B. Bohnet, L. Hafdell, and P. Nugues. 2010. A high-performance syntactic and semantic dependency parser. In *Proc. of COLING '10: Demonstration Volume*.

B. Bohnet, L. Wanner, S. Mille, and A. Burga. 2010. Broad coverage multilingual deep sentence generation with a stochastic multi-level realizer. In *Proc. of COLING '10*.

B. Bohnet, S. Mille, B. Favre, and L. Wanner. 2011a. <STUMABA>: From Deep Representation to Surface. In *ENLG11*.

B. Bohnet, S. Mille, and L. Wanner. 2011b. Statistical language generation from semantic structures. In *Proc. of International Conference on Dependency Linguistics*.

M. Buch-Kromann, M. Gylling-Jørgensen, L. Jelbech-Knudsen, I. Korzen, and H. Müller. 2011. The inventory of linguistic relations used in the Copenhagen Dependency Treebanks. www.cbs.dk/ content/download/149771/1973272/file.

B. Comrie. 1976. *Aspect*. Cambridge University Press, Cambridge.

P. Cook and J. Payne. 2006. Information Structure and Scope in German. In *LFG06*.

A. Copestake, D. Flickinger, and I. Sag. 1997. Minimal recursion semantics. Technical report, CSLI, Stanford University, Stanford.

J. Gundel, N. Hedberg, and R. Zacharski. 1989. Giveness, Implicature and Demonstrative Expressions in English Discourse. In *CLS-25, Part II (Parasession on Language in Context)*, pages 89–103. Chicago Linguistics Society.

J.K. Gundel. 1988. "Universals of Topic-Comment Structure". In M. Hammond, E. Moravčik, and J. Wirth, editors, *Studies in Syntactic Typology*. John Benjamins, Amsterdam & Philadelphia.

J. Hajič, J. Panevová, E. Hajičová, P. Sgall, P. Pajas, J. Štěpánek, J. Havelka, M. Mikulová, and Z. Žabokrtský. 2006. Prague Dependency Treebank 2.0.

K. Knight and V. Hatzivassiloglou. 1995. Two-level, many paths generation. In *Proc. of ACL '95*.

I. Langkilde and K. Knight. 1998. Generation that exploits corpus-based statistical knowledge. In *Proc. of COLING/ACL '98*.

I. Langkilde-Geary. 2002. An empirical verification of coverage and correctness for a general-purpose sentence generator. In *Proc. of 2nd INLG Conference*.

F. Mairesse, M Gašić, F. Juričíč, S Keizer, B. Thomson, K. Yu, and S. Young. 2010. Phrase-based statistical language generation using graphical models and active learning. In *Proc. of ACL '10*.

I.A. Mel'čuk. 1988. *Dependency Syntax: Theory and Practice*. SUNY Press, Albany.

I.A. Mel'čuk. 2001. *Communicative Organization in Natural Language (The Semantic-Communicative Structure of Sentences)*. Benjamins Academic Publishers, Amsterdam.

M. Mikulová et al. 2006. Annotation on the tectogrammatical level in the Prague Dependency Treebank: Reference book. www.cbs.dk/content/download/149771/ 1973272/file.

A.H. Oh and A.I. Rudnicky. 2000. Stochastic language generation for spoken dialogue systems. In *Proc. of ANL/NAACL Workshop on Conversational Systems*.

M. Palmer, D. Gildea, and P. Kingsbury. 2005. The proposition bank: An annotated corpus of semantic roles. *Computational Linguistics*, 31(1):71–105.

E. Ringger, M. Gamon, R.C. Moore, D. Rojas, M. Smets, and S. Corston-Oliver. 2004. Linguistically informed statistical models of constituent structure for ordering in sentence realization. In *Proceedings of COLING*, pages 673–679.

P. Sgall, E. Hajičová, and J. Panevová. 1986. *The Meaning of the Sentence in its Semantic and Pragmatic Aspects*. Reidel Publishing Company, Dordrecht.

J. F. Sowa. 2000. *Knowledge Representation: Logical, Philosophical, and Computational Foundations*. Brooks Cole Publishing Co., Pacific Grove, CA, USA.

A. Stent, R. Prasad, and M. Walker. 2004. Trainable sentence planning for complex information presentation in spoken dialog systems. In *Proc. of ACL '04*.

Mihai Surdeanu, Richard Johansson, Adam Meyers, Lluís Màrquez, and Joakim Nivre. 2008. The CoNLL-2008 shared task on joint parsing of syntactic and semantic dependencies. In *Proceedings of the 12th CoNLL-2008*.

M.A. Walker, O.C. Rambow, and M. Rogati. 2002. Training a sentence planner for spoken dialogue using boosting. *Computer Speech and Language*, 16:409–433.

Y.W. Wong and R.J. Mooney. 2007. Generation by inverting a semantic parser that uses statistical machine translation. In *Proc. of the HLT Conference*.

Generation for Grammar Engineering

Claire Gardent
CNRS, LORIA, UMR 7503
Vandoeuvre-lès-Nancy, F-54000, France
claire.gardent@loria.fr

German Kruszewski
Inria, LORIA, UMR 7503
Villers-lès-Nancy, F-54600, France
german.kruszewski@inria.fr

Abstract

While in Computer Science, grammar engineering has led to the development of various tools for checking grammar coherence, completion, under- and over-generation, in Natural Langage Processing, most approaches developed to improve a grammar have focused on detecting under-generation and to a much lesser extent, over-generation. We argue that generation can be exploited to address other issues that are relevant to grammar engineering such as in particular, detecting grammar incompleteness, identifying sources of overgeneration and analysing the linguistic coverage of the grammar. We present an algorithm that implements these functionalities and we report on experiments using this algorithm to analyse a Feature-Based Lexicalised Tree Adjoining Grammar consisting of roughly 1500 elementary trees.

1 Introduction

Grammar engineering, the task of developing large scale computational grammars, is known to be error prone. As the grammar grows, the interactions between the rules and the lexicon become increasingly complex and the generative power of the grammar becomes increasingly difficult for the grammar writer to predict.

While in Computer Science, grammar engineering has led to the development of various tools for checking grammar coherence, completion, under- and over-generation (Klint et al., 2005), in Natural Langage Processing, most approaches developed to improve a grammar have focused on detecting under-generation (that is cases where the grammar and/or the lexicon fails to provide an analysis for a given, grammatical, input) and to a lesser degree over-generation.

In this paper, we argue that generation can be exploited to address other issues that are relevant to grammar engineering. In particular, we claim that it can be used to:

- Check grammar completeness: for each grammar rule, is it possible to derive a syntactically complete tree ? That is, can each grammar rule be used to derive a constituent.
- Analyse generation and over-generation: given some time/recursion upper bounds, what does the grammar generate? How much of the output is over-generation? Which linguistic constructions present in a language are covered by the grammar?

We present a generation algorithm called GRADE (GRAmmar DEbugger) that permits addressing these issues. In essence, this algorithm implements a top-down grammar traversal guided with semantic constraints and controlled by various parameterisable constraints designed to ensure termination and linguistic control.

The GRADE algorithm can be applied to any generative grammar i.e., any grammar which uses a start symbol and a set of production rules to generate the sentences of the language described by that grammar. We present both an abstract description of this algorithm and a concrete implementation which takes advantage of Definite Clause Grammars to implement grammar traversal. We then present the results of several experiments where we use the GRADE algorithm to examine the output of SEMTAG, a Feature-Based Lexicalised Tree Adjoining Grammar (FB-LTAG) for French.

The paper is structured as follows. Section 2 summarises related work. Section 3 presents the GRADE algorithm. Section 4 introduces the grammar used for testing and describes an implementation of GRADE for FB-LTAG. Section 5 presents the results obtained by applying the GRADE algorithm to SEMTAG. We show that it helps (i) to detect sources of grammar incompleteness (i.e., rules that do not lead to a complete derivation) and (ii) to identify overgeneration and analyse linguistic coverage. Section 6 concludes.

2 Related Work

Two main approaches have so far been used to improve grammars: treebank-based evaluation and error mining techniques. We briefly review this work focusing first, on approaches that are based on parsing and second, on those that exploit generation.

Debugging Grammars using Parsing Over the last two decades, *Treebank-Based evaluation* has become the standard way of evaluating parsers and grammars. In this framework (Black et al., 1991), the output of a parser is evaluated on a set of sentences that have been manually annotated with their syntactic parses. Whenever the parse tree produced by the parser differs from the manual annotation, the difference can be traced back to the parser (timeout, disambiguation component), the grammar and/or to the lexicon. Conversely, if the parser fails to return an output, undergeneration can be traced back to missing or erroneous information in the grammar or/and in the lexicon.

While it has supported the development of robust, large coverage parsers, treebank based evaluation is limited to the set of syntactic constructions and lexical items present in the treebank. It also fails to directly identify the most likely source of parsing failures. To bypass these limitations, *error mining techniques* have been proposed which permit detecting grammar and lexicon errors by parsing large quantities of data (van Noord, 2004; Sagot and de la Clergerie, 2006; de Kok et al., 2009). The output of this parsing process is then divided into two sets of parsed and unparsed sentences which are used to compute the "suspicion rate" of n-grams of word forms, lemmas or part of speech tags whereby the suspicion rate of an item indicates how likely a given item is to cause parsing to fail. Error mining was shown to successfully help detect errors in the lexicon and to a lesser degree in the grammar.

Debugging Grammars using Generation Most of the work on treebank-based evaluation and error mining target undergeneration using parsing. Recently however, some work has been done which exploits generation and more specifically, surface realisation to detect both under- and over-generation.

Both (Callaway, 2003) and the Surface Realisation (SR) task organised by the Generation Challenge (Belz et al., 2011) evaluate the output of surface realisers on a set of inputs derived from the Penn Treebank. As with parsing, these approaches permit detecting under-generation in that an input for which the surface realiser fails to produce a sentence points to shortcomings either in the surface realisation algorithm or in the grammar/lexicon. The approach also permits detecting overgeneration in that a low BLEU score points to these inputs for which the realiser produced a sentence that is markedly different from the expected answer.

Error mining approaches have also been developed using generation. (Gardent and Kow, 2007) is similar in spirit to the error mining approaches developed for parsing. Starting from a set of manually defined semantic representations, the approach consists in running a surface realiser on these representations; manually sorting the generated sentences as correct or incorrect; and using the resulting two datasets to detect grammatical structures that systematically occur in the incorrect dataset. The approach however is only partially automatised since both the input and the output need to be manually produced/annotated. More recently, (Gardent and Narayan, 2012) has shown how the fully automatic error mining techniques used for parsing could be adapted to mine for errors in the output of a surface realiser tested on the SR input data. In essence, they present an algorithm which enumerate the subtrees in the input data that frequently occur in surface realisation failure (the surface realiser fails to generate a sentence) and rarely occur in surface realisation success. In this way, they can identify subtrees in the input that are predominantly associated with generation failure.

In sum, tree-bank based evaluation permits detecting over- and under-generation while error mining techniques permits identifying sources of errors; Treebank-based evaluation requires a reference corpus while error mining techniques require a way to sort good from bad ouput; and in all cases, generation-based grammar debugging requires input to be provided (while for parsing, textual input is freely available).

Discussion The main difference between the GRADE approach and both error mining and treebank based evaluation is that GRADE is grammar based. No other input is required for the GRADE algorithm to work than the grammar[1]. Whereas existing approaches identify errors by processing large amounts of data, GRADE identifies errors by traversing the grammar. In other words, while other approaches assess the coverage of a parser or a generator on a given set of input data, GRADE permits systematically assessing the linguistic coverage and the precision of the constructs described by the grammar independently of any input data.

Currently, the output of GRADE needs to be manually examined and the sources of error manually identified. Providing an automatic means of sorting GRADE 's output into good and bad sentences is developed however, it could be combined with error mining techniques so as to facilitate interpretation.

3 The GraDE Algorithm

How can we explore the quirks and corners of a grammar to detect inconsistencies and incorrect output?

In essence, the GRADE algorithm performs a top-down grammar traversal and outputs the sentences generated by this traversal. It is grammar neutral in that it can be applied to any generative grammar i.e., any grammar which includes a start symbol and a set of production rules. Starting from the string consisting of the start symbol, the GRADE algorithm recursively applies grammar rules replacing one occurrence of its left-hand side in the string by its right-hand side until a string that contains neither the start symbol nor designated nonterminal symbols is produced.

Since NL grammars describe infinite sets of sentences however, some means must be provided to control the search and output sets of sentences that are linguistically interesting. Therefore, the GRADE algorithm is controlled by several user-defined parameters designed to address termination (Given that NL grammars usually describe an infinite set of sentences, how can we limit sentence generation to avoid non termination?), linguistic control (How can we control sentence generation so that the sentences produced cover linguistic variations that the linguist is interested in ?) and readibility (How can we constrain sentence generation in such a way that the output sentences are meaningful sentences rather than just grammatical ones?).

3.1 Ensuring termination

To ensure termination, GRADE supports three user-defined control parameters which can be used simultaneously or in isolation namely: a time out parameter; a restriction on the number and type of recursive rules allowed in any derivation; and a restriction on the depth of the derivation tree.

Each of these restrictions is implemented as a restriction on the grammar traversal process as follows.

Time out. The process halts when the time bound is reached.

Recursive Rules. For each type of recursive rule, a counter is created which is initialised to the values set by the user and decremented each time a recursive rule of the corresponding type is used. When all counters are null, recursive rules can no longer be used. The type of a recursive rule is simply the main category expanded by that rule namely, N, NP, V, VP and S. In addition, whenever a rule is applied, the GRADE algorithm arbitrarily divides up the recursion quotas of a symbol among the symbol's children. If it happens to divide them a way that cannot be fulfilled, then it fails, backtracks, and divides them some other way.

[1]Although some semantic input is possible.

Derivation Depth. A counter is used to keep track of the depth of the derivation tree and either halts (if no other rule applies) or backtracks whenever the set depth is reached.

3.2 Linguistic Coverage and Output Readibility

GRADE provides several ways of controlling the linguistic coverage and the readibility of the output sentences.

Modifiers. As we shall show in Section 5, the recursivity constraints mentioned in the previous section can be used to constrain the type and the number of modifiers present in the output.

Root Rule. Second, the "root rule" i.e., the rule that is used to expand the start symbol can be constrained in several ways. The user can specify which rule should be used; which features should label the lhs of that rule; which subcategorisation type it should model; and whether or not it is a recursive rule. For instance, given the FB-LTAG we are using, by specifying the root rule to be used, we can constrain the generated sentences to be sentences containing an intransitive verb in the active voice combining with a canonical nominal subject. If we only specify the subcategorisation type of the root rule e.g., transitive, we can ensure that the main verb of the generated sentences is a transitive verb; And if we only constrain the features of the root rule to indicative mode and active voice, then we allow for the generation of any sentence whose main verb is in the indicative mode and active voice.

Input Semantics. Third, in those cases where the grammar is a reversible grammar associating sentences with both a syntactic structure and a semantic representation, the content of the generated sentences can be controlled by providing GRADE with an input semantics. Whenever a core semantics is specified, only rules whose semantics includes one or more literal(s) in the core semantics can be used. Determiner rules however are selected independent of their semantics. In this way, it is possible to constrain the output sentences to verbalise a given meaning without having to specify their full semantics (the semantic representations used in reversible grammars are often intricate representations which are difficult to specify manually) and while allowing for morphological variations (tense, number, mode and aspect can be left unspecified and will be informed by the calls to the lexicon embedded in the DCG rules) as well as variations on determiners[2]. For instance, the core semantics {`run(E M)`, `man(M)`} is contained in, and therefore will generate, the flat semantics for the sentences *The man runs, The man ran, A man runs, A man ran, This man runs, My man runs, etc.*.

4 Implementation

In the previous section, we provided an abstract description of the GRADE algorithm. We now describe an implementation of that algorithm tailored for FB-LTAGs equipped with a unification-based compositional semantics. We start by describing the grammar used (SEMTAG), we then summarise the implementation of GRADE for FB-LTAG.

4.1 SemTAG

For our experiments, we use the FB-LTAG described in (Crabbé, 2005; Gardent, 2008). This grammar, called SEMTAG, integrates a unification-based semantics and can be used both for parsing and for generation. It covers the core constructs for non verbal constituents and most of the verbal constructions for French. The semantic representations built are MRSs (Minimal Recursion Semantic representations, (Copestake et al., 2001)).

More specifically, a tree adjoining grammar (TAG) is a tuple $\langle \Sigma, N, I, A, S \rangle$ with Σ a set of terminals, N a set of non-terminals, I a finite set of initial trees, A a finite set of auxiliary trees, and S a distinguished non-terminal ($S \in N$). Initial trees are trees whose leaves are labeled with substitution nodes (marked with a downarrow) or terminal categories[3]. Auxiliary trees are distinguished by a foot node (marked with a star) whose category must be the same as that of the root node.

[2]The rules whose semantics is not checked during derivation are specified as a parameter of the system and can be modified at will e.g., to include adverbs or auxiliaries. Here we choosed to restrict underspecification to determiners.

[3]Due to space limitation we here give a very sketchy definition of FB-LTAG. For a more detailed presentation, see (Vijay-Shanker and Joshi, 1988).

Two tree-composition operations are used to combine trees: substitution and adjunction. Substitution inserts a tree onto a substitution node of some other tree while adjunction inserts an auxiliary tree into a tree. In a Feature-Based Lexicalised TAG (FB-LTAG), tree nodes are furthermore decorated with two feature structures (called **top** and **bottom**) which are unified during derivation; and each tree is anchored with a lexical item. Figure 1 shows an example toy FB-LTAG with unification semantics.

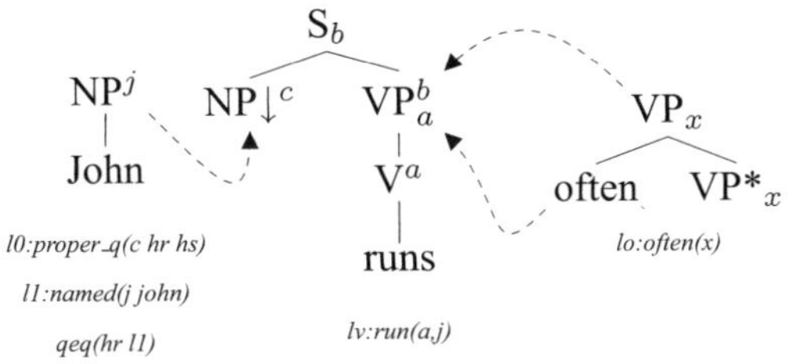

⇒ *l0:proper_q(c hr hs) l1:named(j john), qeq(hr, l1), lv:run(a,j), lv:often(a)*

Figure 1: MRS for "John often runs"

4.2 GraDe for FB-LTAG

The basic FB-LTAG implementation of GRADE is described in detail in (Gardent et al., 2011; Gardent et al., 2010). In brief, this implementation takes advantage of the top-down, left-to-right, grammar traversal implemented in Definite Clause Grammars by translating the FB-LTAG to a DCG. In the DCG formalism, a grammar is represented as a set of Prolog clauses and Prolog's query mechanism provides a built-in top-down, depth-first, traversal of the grammar. In addition, the DCG formalism allows arbitrary Prolog goals to be inserted into a rule. To implement a controlled, top-down grammar traversal of SEMTAG, we simply convert SEMTAGto a Definite Clause Grammar (DCG) wherein arbitrary Prolog calls are used both to ground derivations with lexical items and to control Prolog's grammar traversal so as to respect the user defined constraints on recursion and on linguistic coverage. In addition, we extended the approach to handle semantic constraints (i.e., to allow for an input semantic to constrain the traversal) as discussed in Section 3. That is, for a subset of the grammar rules, a rule will only be applied if its semantics subsumes a literal in the input semantics.

For more details, on the FB-LTAG implementation of the GRADE algorithm and of the conversion from FB-LTAG to DCG, we refer the reader to (Gardent et al., 2011; Gardent et al., 2010).

5 Grammar Analysis

Depending on which control parameters are used, the GRADE algorithm can be used to explore the grammar from different viewpoints. In what follows, we show that it can be used to check grammar completeness (Can all rules in the grammar be used so as to derive a constituent?); to inspect the various possible realisations of syntactic functors and of their arguments (e.g., Are all possible syntactic realisations of the verb and of its arguments generated and correct?); to explore the interactions between basic clauses and modifiers; and to zoom in on the morphological and syntactic variants of a given core semantics (e.g., Does the grammar correctly account for all such variants ?).

5.1 Checking for Grammar Completeness

We first use GRADE to check, for each grammar rule, whether it can be used to derive a complete constituent i.e., whether a derivation can be found such that all leaves of the derivation tree are terminals (words). Can all trees anchored by a verb for instance, be completed to build a syntactically complete clause? Trees that cannot yield a complete constituent points to gaps or inconsistencies in the grammar.

To perform this check, we run the GRADE algorithm on verb rules, allowing for up to 1 adjunction on either a noun, a verb or a verb phrase and halting when either a derivation has been found or all possible rule combinations have been tried. Table 1 shows the results per verb family[4]. As can be seen, there are strong differences between the families with e.g., 80% of the trees failing to yield a derivation in the n0Vs1int (Verbs with interrogative sentential complement) family against 0% in the ilV

[4]The notational convention for verb types is from XTAG and reads as follows. Subscripts indicate the thematic role of the verb argument. n indicates a nominal, Pn a PP and s a sentential argument. pl is a verbal particle. Upper case letters describe the syntactic functor type: V is a verb, A an adjective and BE the copula. For instance, n0Vn1 indicates a verb taking two nominal arguments (e.g., *like*) .

Tree Family	Trees	Fails	Fails/Trees
CopulaBe	60	1	1%
ilV	2	0	0%
n0V	10	0	0%
n0ClV	9	0	0%
n0ClVn1	45	2	4%
n0ClVden1	36	3	8%
n0ClVpn1	29	3	10%
n0Vn1	84	3	3%
n0Vn1Adj2	24	6	25%
n0Van1	87	3	3%
n0Vden1	38	3	7%
n0Vpn1	30	3	10%
ilVcs1	2	0	0%
n0Vcs1	30	23	74%
n0Vas1	15	10	66%
n0Vn1Adj2	24	0	0%
s0Vn1	72	9	12%
n0Vs1int	15	12	80%
n0Vn1n2	24	0	0%
n0Vn1an2	681	54	7%

Table 1: Checking for Gaps in the Grammar

(impersonal with expletive subject, "it rains") and the n0V (intransitive, "Tammy sings"). In total, approximatively 10% (135/1317) of the grammar rules cannot yield a derivation.

5.2 Functor/Argument Dependencies

To check grammar completeness, we need only find one derivation for any given tree. To assess the degree to which the grammar correctly generates all possible realisations associated with a given syntactic functor however, all realisations generated by the grammar need to be produced. To restrict the output to sentences illustrating functor/argument dependencies (no modifiers), we constrain adjunction to the minimum required by each functor. In most cases, this boils down to setting the adjunction counters to null for all categories. One exception are verbs taking a sentential argument which require one S adjunction. We also allow for one N-adjunction and one V-adjunction to allow for determiners and the inverted subject clitic (t'il). In addition, the lexicon is restricted to avoid lexical or morphological variants.

We show below some of the well-formed sentences output by GRADE for the n0V (intransitive verbs) family.

> Elle chante (*She sings*), La tatou chante-t'elle? (*Does the armadillo sing?*), La tatou chante (*The armadillo sings*), La tatou qui chante (*The armadillo which sings*), Chacun chante -t'il (*Does everyone sing?*), Chacun chante (*Everyone sings*), Quand chante chacun? (*When does everyone sing?*), Quand chante la tatou? (*When does the armadillo sing?*) Quand chante quel tatou? (*When does which armadillo sing?*), Quand chante Tammy? (*When does Tammy sing?*), Chante-t'elle? (*Does she sing?*) Chante -t'il? (*Does he sing?*), Chante! (*Sing!*), Quel tatou chante ? (*Which armadillo sing?*), Quel tatou qui chante ..? (*Which armadillo who sings ..?*) Tammy chante-t'elle? (*Does Tammy sing?*), Tammy chante (*Tammy sings*), une tatou qui chante chante (*An armadillo which sings sings*), C'est une tatou qui chante (*It is an armadillo which sings*), ...

The call on this family returned 55 distinct MRSs and 65 distinct sentences of which only 28 were correct. Some of the incorrect cases are shown below. They illustrate the four main sources of overgeneration. The agreement between the inverted subject clitic and the subject fails to be enforced (a); the inverted nominal subject fails to require a verb in the indicative mode (b); the inverted subject clitic fails to be disallowed in embedded clauses (c); the interrogative determiner *quel* fails to constrain its nominal head to be a noun (d,e).

> (a) Chacun chante-t'elle? (*Everyone sings?*) (b) Chantée chacun? (*Sung everyone?*) (c) La tatou qui chante-t'elle? (*The armadillo which does she sing?*) (d) Quel chacun chante ? (*Which everyone sings?*) (e) quel tammy chante ? (*Which Tammy sings?*)

5.3 Interactions with Modifiers

Once basic functor/argument dependencies have been verified, adjunction constraints can be used to explore the interactions between e.g., basic clauses and modification[5]. Allowing for N-adjunctions for instance, will produce sentences including determiners and adjectives. Similarly, allowing for V adjunction will permit for auxiliaries and adverbs to be used; and allowing for VP or S adjunctions will licence the use of raising verbs and verbs subcategorising for sentential argument.

We queried GRADE for derivations rooted in n0V (intransitive verbs) and with alternatively, 1N, 2N, 1V and 1VP adjunction. Again a restricted lexicon was used to avoid structurally equivalent but lexically distinct variants. The following table shows the number of sentences output for each query.

0	1S	1VP	1V	1N	2N
36	170	111	65	132	638

As the examples below show, the generated sentences unveil two further shortcomings in the grammar: the inverted subject clitic fails to be constrained to occur directly after the verb (1) and the order and compatibility of determiners are unrestricted (2).

(1) a. Semble-t'il chanter? / * Semble chanter t'il? (*Does he seems to sing?*)

b. Chante-t'il dans Paris? / * Chante dans Paris-t'il? (*Does he sing in Paris?*)

c. Chante-t'il beaucoup? / * Chante beaucoup-t'il? (*Does he sing a lot?*)

d. Veut-t'il que Tammy chante? / * Veut que Tammy chante-t'il? (*Does he want that Tammy sings?*

(2) * Un quel tatou, *Quel cette tatou, Ma quelle tatou (*Un which armadillo, Which this armadillo, My which armadillo*)

5.4 Inspecting Coverage and Correctness

In the previous sections, GRADE was used to generate MRSs and sentences *ex nihilo*. As mentioned above however, a core semantics can be used to restrict the set of output sentences to sentences whose MRS include this core semantics. This is useful for instance, to systematically inspect all variations output by the grammar on a given input. These variations include all morphological variations supported by the lexicon (number, tense, mode variations) and the syntactic variations supported by the grammar for the same MRSs (e.g., active/passive). It also includes the variations supported by GRADE in that some rules are not checked for semantic compatibility thereby allowing for additional materials to be added. In effect, GRADE allows for the inclusion of arbitrary determiners and auxiliaries.

Tree Family	MRS	Sent.	S/MRS
ilV	7	52	7.4
n0V	65	161	2.4
n0ClV	30	62	2.0
n0ClVn1	20	25	1.25
n0ClVden1	10	15	1.5
n0ClVpn1	40	63	1.57
n0Vn1	20	110	5.5
n0Van1	30	100	3.33
n0Vden1	5	15	3.00
n0Vpn1	25	76	3.04
ilVcs1	1	1	1.00
n0Vcs1	200	660	3.3
n0Vas1	35	120	3.42
n0Vn1Adj2	10	15	1.5
s0Vn1	4	24	6.00
n0Vn1n2	10	48	4.80
n0Vn1an2	5	45	9.00

Table 2: Producing Variants

Table 2 shows the number of MRSs and sentences output for each verb family given a matching core semantics and a morphological lexicon including verbs in all simple tenses (3rd person only) and nouns in singular and plural[6]. The ratio S/M of sentences on MRSs produced by one GRADE call shows how the underspecified core semantics permits exploring a larger number of sentences generated by the grammar than could be done by generating from fully specified MRSs. For the n0Vn1an2 class, for instance, the GRADE call permits generating 9 times more sentences in average than generating from a single MRS.

[5]Recall that in FB-LTAG, adjunction is the operation which permits applying recursive rules (i.e., auxiliary trees). Hence allowing for adjunctions amounts to allowing for modification with the exception already noted above of certain verbs subcategorising for sentential arguments.

[6]The lexicon used in this experiment includes more morphological variants than in the experiment of Section 5.2 where the focus was on syntactic rather than morphological variants. Hence the different number of generated sentences.

6 Conclusion

When using a grammar for generation, it is essential, not only that it has coverage (that it does not undergenerate) but also that it be precise (that it does not overgenerate). Nonetheless, relatively little work has been done on how to detect overgeneration. In this paper, we presented an algorithm and a methodology to explore the sentences generated by a grammar; we described an implementation of this algorithm based on DCGs (GRADE); and we illustrated its impact by applying it to an existing grammar. We showed that GRADE could be used to explore a grammar from different viewpoints: to find gaps or inconsistencies in the rule system; to systematically analyse the grammar account of functor/argument dependencies; to explore the interaction between base constructions and modifiers; and to verify the completeness and correctness of syntactic and morphological variants.

There are many directions in which to pursue this research. One issue is efficiency. Unsurprisingly, the computational complexity of GRADE is formidable. For the experiments reported here, runtimes are fair (a few seconds to a few minutes depending on how much output is required and on the size of the grammar and of the lexicon). As the complexity of the generated sentences and the size of the lexicons grow, however, it is clear that runtimes will become unpractical. We are currently using YAP Prolog tabling mechanism for storing intermediate results. It would be interesting however to compare this with the standard tabulating algorithms used for parsing and surface realisation.

Another interesting issue is that of the interaction between GRADE and error mining. As mentioned in Section 2, GRADE could be usefully complemented by error mining techniques as a means to automatically identify the most probable causes of errors highlighted by GRADE and thereby of improving the grammar. To support such an integration however, some means must be provided of sorting GRADE 's output into "good" and "bad" output i.e., into sentences that are grammatical and sentences that are over-generated by the grammar. We plan to investigate whether language models could be used to identify those sentences that are most probably incorrect. In a first step, simple and highly constrained input would be used to generate from the grammar and the lexicon a set of correct sentences using GRADE . Next these sentences would be used to train a language model which could be used to detect incorrect sentences produced by GRADE on more complex, less constrained input.

Other issues we are currently pursueing are the use of GRADE (i) for automating the creation of grammar exercises for learners of french and (ii) for creating a bank of MRSs to be used for the evaluation and comparison of data-to-text generators. The various degrees of under-specification supported by GRADE permit producing either many sentences out of few input (e.g., generate all basic clauses whose verb is of a given subcategorisation type as illustrated in Section 5.2); or fewer sentences out a more constrained input (e.g., producing all syntactic and morphological variants verbalising a given input semantics). We are currently exploring how semantically constrained GRADE calls permit producing variants of a given meaning; and how these variants can be used to automatically construct grammar exercises which illustrate the distinct syntactic and morphological configurations to be acquired by second language learners. In contrast, more underspecified GRADE calls can be used to automatically build a bank of semantic representations and their associated sentences which could form the basis for an evaluation of data-to-text surface realisers. The semantics input to GRADE are simplified representations of MRSs. During grammar traversal, GRADE reconstructs not only a sentence and its associated syntactic tree but also its full MRS. As a result, it is possible to produce a generation bank which, like the Redwook Bank, groups together MRSs and the sentences verbalising these MRSs. This bank however would reflect the linguistic coverage of the grammar rather than the linguistic constructions present in the corpus parsed to produce the MRS. It would thus provide an alternative way to test the linguistic coverage of existing surface realisers.

Acknowledgments

The research presented in this paper was partially supported by the European Fund for Regional Development within the framework of the INTERREG IVA Allegro Project.

References

Anja Belz, Michael White, Dominic Espinosa, Eric Kow, Deirdre Hogan, and Amanda Stent. 2011. The first surface realisation shared task: Overview and evaluation results. In *Proc. of the 13th European Workshop on Natural Language Generation*.

E. Black, S. Abney, D. Flickinger, C. Gdaniec, R. Grishman, P. Harrison, D. Hindle, Ingria R., F. Jelinek, J. Klavans, M. Liberman, M. Marcus, S. Roukos, B. Santorini, and T. Strzalkowski. 1991. A procedure for quantitatively comparing the syntactic coverage of english grammars. In *Proceedings of the DARPA Speech and Natural Language Workshop*, page 306311.

Charles B. Callaway. 2003. Evaluating coverage for large symbolic NLG grammars. In *18th IJCAI*, pages 811–817, Aug.

Ann Copestake, Alex Lascarides, and Dan Flickinger. 2001. An algebra for semantic construction in constraint-based grammars. In *Proceedings of the 39th Annual Meeting of the Association for Computational Linguistics*, Toulouse, France.

Benoit Crabbé. 2005. *Reprsentation informatique de grammaires d'arbres fortement lexicalisées : le cas de la grammaire d'arbres adjoints.* Ph.D. thesis, Nancy University.

Daniël de Kok, Jianqiang Ma, and Gertjan van Noord. 2009. A generalized method for iterative error mining in parsing results. In *ACL2009 Workshop Grammar Engineering Across Frameworks (GEAF)*, Singapore.

Claire Gardent and Eric Kow. 2007. Spotting overgeneration suspect. In *11th European Workshop on Natural Language Generation (ENLG)*.

Claire Gardent and Shashi Narayan. 2012. Error mining on dependency trees. In *Proceedings of ACL*.

Claire Gardent, Benjamin Gottesman, and Laura Perez-Beltrachini. 2010. Benchmarking surface realisers. In *COLING 2010 (Poster Session)*, Beijing, China.

Claire Gardent, Benjamin Gottesman, and Laura Perez-Beltrachini. 2011. Using regular tree grammar to enhance surface realisation. *Natural Language Engineerin*, 17:185–201. Special Issue on Finite State Methods and Models in Natural Language Processing.

Claire Gardent. 2008. Integrating a unification-based semantics in a large scale lexicalised tree adjoining grammar for french. In *COLING'08*, Manchester, UK.

Paul Klint, Ralf Lämmel, and Chris Verhoef. 2005. Toward an engineering discipline for grammarware. *ACM Transactions on Software Engineering Methodology*, 14(3):331–380.

Benoit Sagot and Eric de la Clergerie. 2006. Error mining in parsing results. In ACL, editor, *Proceedings of the ACL 2006*, pages 329–336, Morristown, NJ, USA.

Gertjan van Noord. 2004. Error mining for wide-coverage grammar engineering. In ACL, editor, *Proceedings of the ACL 2004*, pages 446–454, Morristown, NJ, USA.

K. Vijay-Shanker and Aravind Joshi. 1988. Feature Structures Based Tree Adjoining Grammars. *Proceedings of the 12th conference on Computational linguistics*, 55:v2.

Perceptions of Alignment and Personality in Generated Dialogue

Alastair J. Gill
University of Surrey
Guildford GU2 7XH, UK
A.Gill@surrey.ac.uk

Carsten Brockmann and **Jon Oberlander**
University of Edinburgh
Edinburgh EH8 9AB, UK
Carsten.Brockmann@gmx.net
J.Oberlander@ed.ac.uk

Abstract

Variation in language style can lead to different perceptions of the interaction, and different behaviour outcomes. Using the CRAG 2 language generation system we examine how accurately judges can perceive character personality from short, automatically generated dialogues, and how alignment (similarity between speakers) alters judge perceptions of the characters' relationship. Whilst personality perception of our dialogues is consistent with perceptions of human behaviour, we find that the introduction of alignment leads to negative perceptions of the dialogues and the interlocutors' relationship. A follow up evaluation study of the perceptions of different forms of alignment in the dialogues reveals that while similarity at polarity, topic and construction levels is viewed positively, similarity at the word level is regarded negatively. We discuss our findings in relation to the literature and in the context of dialogue systems.

1 Introduction

Personality describes characteristics which are central to human behaviour, and has implications for social interactions: It can affect performance on collaborative processes, and can increase engagement when incorporated within virtual agents (Hernault et al., 2008). In addition, personality has also been shown to influence linguistic style, both in written and spoken language (Pennebaker and King, 1999; Gill and Oberlander, 2002). Whilst individuals often possess individual styles of self-expression, such as those influenced by personality, in a conversation they may align or match the linguistic style of their partner: For example, by entraining, or converging, on a mutual vocabulary. Such alignment is associated with increased familiarity, trust, and task success (Shepard et al., 2001). People also adjust their linguistic styles when interacting with computers, and this affects their perceptions of the interaction (Porzel et al., 2006). However, when humans – or machines – are faced with a choice of matching the language of their conversational partner, this often raises a conflict: matching the language of an interlocutor may mean subduing one's own linguistic style. Better understanding these processes relating to language choice and interpersonal perception can inform our knowledge of human behaviour, but also have important implications for the design of dialogue systems and user interfaces.

In this paper, we present and evaluate novel automated natural language generation techniques, via the Critical Agent Dialogue system version 2 (CRAG 2), which enable us to generate dynamic, short-term alignment effects along with stable, long-term personality effects. We use it to investigate the following questions: Can personality be accurately judged from short, automatically generated dialogues? What are the effects of alignment between characters? How is the quality of the characters' relationship perceived? Additionally, in our evaluation study we examine perceptions of the different forms of alignment present in the dialogues, for example at the word, phrase or polarity levels. In the following we review relevant literature, before describing the CRAG 2 system and experimental method, and then presenting our results and discussion.

2 Background

Researchers from several traditions have studied aspects of similarity in dialogue, naming it: entrainment, alignment, priming, accommodation, coordination or convergence. For current purposes, we gloss over some important differences, and borrow the term 'alignment', because we will go on to adopt Pickering and Garrod's theoretical mechanisms in our system. Alignment usually means that if something has happened once in a dialogue (for instance, referring to an object as a vase), it is likely to happen again—and hence, alternatives become less likely (for instance, referring to the same object as a jug) (Pickering and Garrod, 2004). From this view, interlocutors align the representations they use in production and comprehension and the process is an automatic, labour-saving device, but there are of course limits to periods over which alignment processes operate; in corpus studies long-term adaptation predicts communicative success (Reitter, 2008). Alternative approaches view similarity as a process of negotiation leading to the establishment of common ground (Brennan and Clark, 1996), or a relatively conscious process resulting from attraction (Shepard et al., 2001). Although increased similarity (*convergence*) is generally regarded positively, it can sometimes arise during disagreement (Niederhoffer and Pennebaker, 2002), with cultural differences influencing both convergence and perceptions of others (Bortfeld and Brennan, 1997). Wizard-of-Oz studies have also shown convergence with a natural language interface (Brennan, 1996; Porzel et al., 2006).

Embodied conversational agents (Cassell et al., 2000) are implemented computer characters that exhibit multimodal behaviour; the technology can be exploited to give life to automatically generated scripted dialogues and to make them more engaging (van Deemter et al., 2008; Hernault et al., 2008). Aspects of the agents' personalities and their interests can be pre-configured and affect their dialogue strategies; the generation is template-based. A common way to describe personality is using the *Big Five* traits: Extraversion (preference for, and behavior in, social situations); Neuroticism (tendency to experience negative thoughts and feelings); Openness (reflects openness to new ideas); Agreeableness (how we tend to interact with others); and Conscientiousness (how organised and persistent we are in pursuing our goals). Relationships between personality dimensions and language use appear to be robust: For instance, in monological writing (essays and e-mails) high Extraverts use more social words, positive emotion words, and express more certainty; high Agreeableness scorers use more first person singular and positive emotion words, and fewer articles and negative emotion words (Pennebaker and King, 1999; Gill and Oberlander, 2002).

Personality can not only be projected through, but also perceived from, asynchronous textual communication. The extraversion dimension is generally perceived most accurately in a variety of contexts, while it was more difficult for raters to recognise neuroticism (Gill et al., 2006; Li and Chignell, 2010) Taking into account the difference between the language actually used by people with certain personality, and the language which others *expect* them to use, natural language generation (NLG) systems can exploit either to project personality. Perhaps the closest previous work to what we present here is the Personality Generator (PERSONAGE) (Mairesse and Walker, 2010) which mapped psychological findings relating to the personality to the components of the NLG system (e.g., content planning, sentence planning and realisation). Evaluation by human raters showed similar accuracy in perception of extraversion in the generated language compared with human-authored texts. There is evidence that computer users attribute personality to interfaces, and rate more highly those interfaces that exploit language associated with the user's own personality, and become more similar to the user over time (Isbister and Nass, 2000).

We now turn to describing our automated natural language generation techniques, implemented in CRAG 2, followed by a description of our experimental method and evaluation.

3 Generation Method

Dialogues are composed by CRAG 2, a Java program that provides a framework for generating dialogues between two computer characters discussing a movie. For more details of this system, see Brockmann (2009). Within CRAG 2, linguistic personality and alignment are modelled using the OPENNLP

CCG Library (OPENCCG) natural language realiser (White, 2006b). The realiser consults a grammar adapted to the movie review domain to allow the generation of utterances about the following topics: Action scenes, characters, dialogue, film, music, plot or special effects. The realiser also has access to a set of n-gram language models, used to compute probability scores of word sequences. The general conversational language model (LM) is based on data from the SWITCHBOARD corpus and a small corpus of movie reviews. The general LM is used for fallback probabilities, and is integrated with the personality and alignment language models (described below) using linear interpolation.

3.1 Personality Models

Language models were trained on a corpus of weblogs from authors of known personality (Nowson et al., 2005). For each personality dimension, the language data were divided up into high, medium and low bands so that the probability of a word sequence given a personality type could be derived; see Nowson et al. (2005) for further discussion of the positively skewed distribution of the openness dimension in bloggers. Each individual weblog was used 5 times, once for each dimension. The five models corresponding to the character's assigned personality are uniformly interpolated to give the final personality model, which is then combined with the general model (respective weights, 0.7 and 0.3).

3.2 Alignment via Cache Language Models

Meanwhile, alignment is modelled via cache language models (CLMs). For each utterance to be generated, a language model is computed based on the utterance that was generated immediately before it. This CLM is then combined with the personality LM. A character's propensity to align corresponds to the weight given to the CLM during this combination, and can be set to a value between 0 and 1.

3.3 Character Specification and Dialogue Generation

The characters are parameterised for their personality by specifying values (on a scale from 0 to 100) for the five dimensions: extraversion (E), neuroticism (N), agreeableness (A), conscientiousness (C) and openness (O). This parameterisation determines the extent to which utterances are weighted for their overlap with the personality generation model for each trait. Also, each character receives an agenda of topics they wish to discuss, along with polarities (POSITIVE/NEGATIVE) that indicate their opinion on each topic.

The character with the higher E score begins the dialogue, and their first topic is selected. Once an utterance has been generated, the other character is selected, and the system selects which topic should come next. This process continues until there are no topics left on the agenda of the current speaker. The system creates a simple XML representation of the character's utterance, using the specified topic and polarity. Following the method described in Foster and White (2004), the basic utterance specification is transformed, using stylesheets written in the Extensible Stylesheet Language Transformations (XSLT) language, into an OPENCCG logical form. We make use of the facility for defining optional and alternative inputs (White, 2006a) and underspecified semantics to mildly overgenerate candidate utterances.

Optional interjections (*I mean*, *you know*, *sort of*) and conversational markers (*right*, *but*, *and*, *well*) are added where appropriate given the discourse history. Using synonyms (e.g., *plot* = *story*, *comedy* = *humour*) and combining sentence types and optional expressions, up to 3000 possibilities are created per utterance, and the best candidate is chosen by the specific combination of n-gram models appropriate for dialogue history, personality and alignment.

4 Experimental Method

4.1 Participants

Data were collected from 80 participants with a variety of educational and occupational backgrounds using an online study (via the Language Experiments Portal; www.language-experiments.org). To ensure integrity of responses, submissions taking less than five minutes (five cases), or more than 45 minutes (one case) were examined in relation to the other responses before being included in the analysis. The demographics were as follows: 43 participants (54%) were native, and 37 (46%) non-native, speakers of English; 34 (42%) male, 46 (58%) fe-

Dialogue Type	Character	Personality Parameter Setting					Propensity to
		E	N	A	C	O	Align
1) High E	I	75	50	25	25	50	0
vs. Low E	II	25	50	75	75	50	0 or 0.7
2) Low E	I	25	50	25	25	50	0
vs. High E	II	75	50	75	75	50	0 or 0.7
3) High N	I	50	75	25	25	50	0
vs. Low N	II	50	25	75	75	50	0 or 0.7
4) Low N	I	50	25	25	25	50	0
vs. High N	II	50	75	75	75	50	0 or 0.7

Table 1: Dialogue type parameter settings.

male. Median age range was 25–29 (mode = 20–24). Other demographic information (right/left-handedness, area of upbringing, occupation) were collected, but are not considered here.

4.2 Materials

To be able to compare human judges' perceptions of characters demonstrating different personalities, and dialogues without and with alignment, dialogues were generated in four different dialogue types, as shown in Table 1. Each dialogue type sets the two computer characters to opposing extremes on either the E or the N dimension, while keeping the respective other dimension at a middle, or neutral, level (for example, in Dialogue Type 1, Character I is High E, Character II is Low E, and both characters are Mid N). Furthermore, Character I is always Low A and C, and Character II is always High A and C. All characters are set to Mid O.

Two dialogues were generated per type, giving a total of 8 dialogues, with aligning versions of each of these dialogues subsequently generated (giving 16 dialogues in total). The movie under discussion and the characters' respective agendas and their opinions about the topics were randomly assigned. Each dialogue was eight utterances long, with characters taking turns, each of them producing four utterances altogether. In each alignment dialogue, the High A/High C Character II aligned. The weight for the cache language model was set to 0.7. In both aligning and non-aligning versions of the dialogues, utterances for the non-aligning speaker were the same. The generation of utterances for the aligning speaker was seeded with the respective previous utterance functioning as the dialogue history. From the list of generated possible utterances, the top-ranked utterance was chosen.

4.2.1 Example Dialogue

To give an impression of the generated dialogues, Table 2 shows an example of Dialogue Type 1 (High E versus Low E) where the characters discuss the movie *Mystic River* (the first row of Table 1 gives the full parameter settings). The other generation parameters are (valence of opinions follows each topic): Character I, agenda (PLOT/−, CHARACTERS/−, MUSIC/−, FILM/−); further opinions (SPECIAL EFFECTS/−, ACTION SCENES/+, DIALOGUE/−); Character II, agenda (ACTION SCENES/+, SPECIAL EFFECTS/+, PLOT/−, DIALOGUE/−); further opinions (CHARACTERS/−, FILM/−, MUSIC/−).

Alignment is switched on for Character II, with examples of their utterances from the non-aligning dialogues included beneath. As can be seen, the aligned utterances closely match the surface form of their primes. The personality language models' influence on language choice can be seen when the High E Character I uses the phrase *I mean I didn't think*, while the (non-aligning) Low E Character II prefers *I (kind of) thought* throughout. Finally, the Low A/Low C Character I has a strategy of switching topics in order to follow his own agenda.

4.3 Procedure

An introductory web page explained the task and described the four personality dimensions of interest (E, N, A and C; adjectives relating to each personality type were included for reference after each dialogue). The first page also contained an example dialogue similar to those that would be displayed during the experiment. The participants were then presented with eight dialogues (two per type; one with, one without alignment). The dialogues were presented in random order and randomly chosen from the pool of available dialogues. One complete dialogue was shown at a time, and the participants were asked to judge which of the two characters scored higher on the E, N, A and C dimensions (using the previous personality descriptions and adjectives). They also answered questions probing their

	PLOT:
I	"I mean I didn't think that the story was great."
II	"I mean the story wasn't great."
	Without alignment:
	"Yes I mean I thought that it wasn't nicely tied up."
	CHARACTERS:
I	"And I mean I thought there was no characterization at all."
II	"I mean I thought there was no characterization at all."
	Without alignment:
	"Yeah there was no characterization at all I mean."
	MUSIC:
I	"I mean I didn't think that the music was great."
II	"I mean the music wasn't great."
	Without alignment:
	"Yeah I kind of thought that the music was also very bad you know."
	FILM:
I	"I mean I didn't think the film was good."
II	"I mean the film wasn't good."
	Without alignment:
	"I mean I kind of thought that it was a bit dull."

Table 2: Example Dialogue.

perceptions of the characters' relationship. They assessed on a seven-point Likert scale how well the characters 'got on' with each other (*very badly–very well*), interpreted as indicating positivity or rapport between characters, and how smoothly the conversation went (*not at all smoothly–very smoothly*), indicating how natural and coherent the interactions were. The participants were asked to rate each dialogue independently from the others.The experiment was open to both native and non-native speakers of English; upon supplying an email address, participants were entered into a draw for an Amazon gift token. All data were analysed anonymously. Note that this is a further evaluation of data previously presented in Brockmann (2009).

5 Experimental Results

5.1 Personality perception

To study the perception of personality in our dialogues, a nominal logistic regression was run on the perception ratings obtained from the judges. Here agreement between generated personality and rater judgements was coded as a binary value (agreement=1; disagreement=0), and entered into the regression model as the dependent variable (DV). The following independent variables (IVs) were entered into the model: Dialogue Alignment as a binary variable (alignment=1; no alignment=0); Personality Trait judged as a categorical variable ("Extraversion", "Neuroticism'", "Agreeableness", "Conscientiousness"). We also included an interaction variable, Generated Alignment × Personality Trait Rated. We ran this model in order to understand how each of the independent variables, such as Personality Trait judged, or combinations of variables (in the case of the interactions) best explain the accuracy of the personality perception judgements relative to our generated personality language (the DV). Throughout this section we report the parameter estimates and corresponding one degree of freedom for the more conservative Likelihood Ratio Chi Square effect tests for N=1920 (with the exception of the four-level variable, Personality Trait DF=3, and Participant ID DF=79).

The whole model is significant ($\chi^2 = 128.22$, $p < .0041$, R Square (U)= .05; although note that R Square (U) is not comparable to regular R Square, and therefore cannot be interpreted as a percentage of variance explained; model DF= 89). To investigate effects of native/non-native speaker effects on personality judgement accuracy, this variable was included in earlier models as a binary variable (Native Speaker: native=1; non-native=0), but no significant effect was found ($\chi^2 = 0.98, p = .3228$). Therefore data from all participants are included in the analyses here, and the native/non-native variable is not included in the model. For the interactions, there is a significant relationship between Dialogue Alignment and accuracy in judgement of Personality Trait ($\chi^2 = 13.67, p = .0034$). Further examination of this relationship shows that in the case of Agreeableness, accuracy decreases when alignment is present in the dialogue ($\chi^2 = 10.90, p = .0010$), whereas in the case of Conscientiousness, perception accuracy significantly increases with alignment ($\chi^2 = 4.38, p = .0364$). This is shown in Figure 1.

There is a significant main effect for Personality Trait judged ($\chi^2 = 17.04, p = .0007$): parameter estimates show that accuracy of judgement is significantly more accurate for Extraversion ($\chi^2 = 7.21, p = .0073$), but less accurate for Agreeableness ($\chi^2 = 5.54, p = .0186$) and Conscientiousness ($\chi^2 = 8.09, p = .0044$). No main effect was found for Dialogue Alignment relative to accuracy of personality judgement ($\chi^2 = 2.16, p = .1420$).

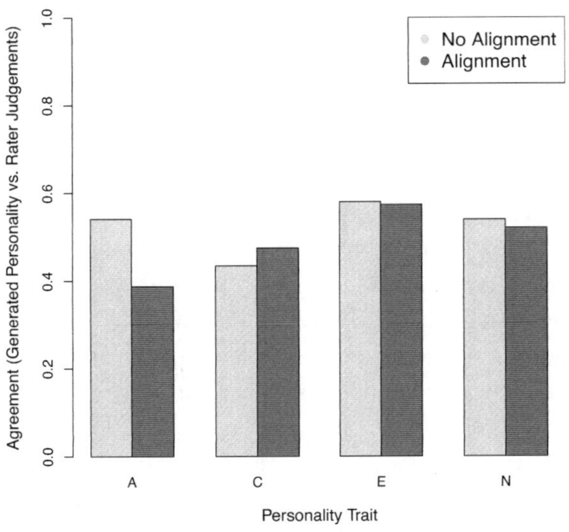

Figure 1: Accuracy of personality judgements.

5.2 Ratings of 'Getting on' and 'Smoothness'

In the following we are interested in examining what dialogue characteristics lead to the rater judgements of 'getting on'. Using an ordinal logistic regression (DV: how well the characters were judged to 'get on', seven point scale from 'very badly' to 'very well') the following independent variables, coded as described in the previous section, were entered into the model: Dialogue Alignment and Native Speaker (Personality Trait was also entered into the model, but did not reach significance). Participant ID was included in the model to account for the repeated measures design. Again, we use likelihood ratio effect tests and note parameter estimates for one degree of freedom (N=2560). The whole model is significant ($\chi^2 = 1396.75$, $p < .0001$, R Square (U)= .15; model DF=89): A main effect for Dialogue Alignment ($\chi^2 = 244.94$, $p < .0001$), shows alignment decreased perceptions of 'getting on'.

Similarly, ordinal logistic regressions were used to probe influencing factors in decisions of rating dialogue smoothness (DV: smoothness rated on a seven point scale from 'not at all smoothly' to 'very smoothly'). The following independent variables, coded as described in the previous section, were entered into the model: Dialogue Alignment and Native Speaker (again Personality Trait did not reach significance for inclusion). Again, Participant ID was included in the model to account for the repeated measures design (parameter estimates and likelihood ratio effect tests are for one degree of freedom, N=2560, Condition, DF=3; Participant ID, DF=78). The whole model is significant ($\chi^2 = 1291.28$, $p < .0001$), with an R Square (U) of 0.13 (model DF=89). There are strong main effects for Dialogue Alignment ($\chi^2 = 188.27$, $p < .0001$), and Native Speaker ($\chi^2 = 110.00$, $p < .0001$). Examination of the parameter estimates reveals negative relationships between ratings of smoothness and Native Speaker, and Dialogue Alignment, implying that native speakers significantly rated the dialogues as being less smooth than the non-native speakers, and also that dialogues with alignment were rated significantly less smooth than those without alignment.

6 Evaluation Method

To better understand the linguistic alignment processes which drive the participants' judgements in the previous experiment, we performed further analysis. In particular, we coded the forms of alignment present in each utterance of each dialogue, relative to the previous utterance. The forms of alignment were coded as follows: Polarity (matching a positive or negative opinion), Topic (whether the topic is the same or shifts), Word (instances of alignment of individual words of the previous utterance), Phrase (alignment of phrases), Construction (alignment at a grammatical construction level). Each instance of alignment for a given utterance was counted, with an overall score generated for the whole dialogue. This coding procedure was performed by one researcher and subsequently evaluated by a second, with disputes resolved by mutual agreement. In the following analysis we do not distinguish between dialogues intentionally generated with alignment and those without, but instead include all dialogues in the analysis to examine which objectively measured forms of alignment relate to the judges' perceptions for personality, 'getting on' and 'smoothness'.

7 Evaluation Results

7.1 Alignment Forms and Personality

Accuracy of judgements of personality ratings and dialogue alignment was analysed for each of the four personality traits (A, C, E, N) independently using nominal logistic regression (DV: rater vs. generated personality agreement coded 0 or 1; IVs: occurrence scores for Polarity, Topic, Word, Phrase, and Construction). For Agreeableness the whole model is significant ($\chi^2 = 85.74$, $p < .0001$, R Square (U)= .10; model DF=5, N=640), with Topic alignment ($\chi^2 = 16.68$, $p < .0001$), followed by Polarity ($\chi^2 = 10.13$, $p = .0015$) and Construction ($\chi^2 = 6.19$, $p = .0128$) alignment all positively related to perceptions of Agreeableness. For Conscientiousness (whole model $\chi^2 = 11.26$, $p = .0465$, R Square (U)= .01; DF=5, N=640), Polarity alignment is inversely related to perceptions of Conscientiousness ($\chi^2 = 5.12$, $p = .0236$). In the case of Neuroticism and Extraversion, the models are not significant ($\chi^2 = 5.37$, $p = .3719$, and $\chi^2 = 1.49$, $p = .2226$, respectively; both DF=5, N=320).

7.2 Alignment Forms and 'Getting On' and 'Smoothness'

The relationship between the different forms of alignment present in the dialogues and the judges' ratings of 'getting on' and 'smoothness' were evaluated in two separate ordinal logistic models, in which they were entered as the dependent variable. The five alignment types (Polarity, Topic, Word, Phrase, and Construction) were entered as independent variables. Participant ID was also entered into the model as an independent variable, since multiple responses were collected from each participant.

Ratings of 'getting on' (whole model $\chi^2 = 1595.10$, $p < .0001$, R Square (U)= .17; DF=84, N=2560) show that Polarity ($\chi^2 = 385.45$, $p < .0001$), Construction ($\chi^2 = 72.30$, $p < .0001$) and Topic ($\chi^2 = 16.68$, $p = .0014$) alignment all relate to greater scores of perceived getting on. Conversely, Word alignment leads to reduced scores of perceived getting on ($\chi^2 = 14.13$, $p = .0002$). For ratings of dialogue 'smoothness' ($\chi^2 = 1519.31$, $p = .0014$, R Square (U)= .16; DF=84, N=2560), again Polarity ($\chi^2 = 209.55$, $p < .0001$), Topic ($\chi^2 = 39.39$, $p < .0001$) and Construction ($\chi^2 = 28.01$, $p < .0001$) alignment all lead to increased ratings of 'smoothness'. Similarly, Word alignment has a negative impact upon perceptions of dialogue 'smoothness' ($\chi^2 = 29.24$, $p < .0001$).

8 Discussion

We now discuss the perception and evaluation results of the CRAG 2 system in greater detail. In terms of personality perception, extraversion is accurately perceived, with agreeableness and conscientiousness less so, which matches findings from personality perception studies in other contexts, including text based computer-mediated communication (Li and Chignell, 2010; Gill et al., 2006). It is interesting to note, however, that alignment helps perception of conscientiousness, but hurts ratings of agreeableness. Reduced accuracy in perception of agreeableness, which is important to relationships, may have a negative impact on the use of dialogues in collaborative settings (Rammstedt and Schupp, 2008). Further work could usefully examine ways in which these characteristics can be generated in more readily perceptible ways. Interestingly, personality perception is unaffected by whether the judges are native English speakers or not. This is a notable finding, and apparently implies that the social information relating to personality is available in the text only environment, or through the generation process, it is equally accessible to native and non-native English speakers. Native speaking judges were more critical in rating dialogue smoothness and characters getting on, perhaps indicating a finer-grained awareness of linguistic cues in interpersonal interaction, or else just greater confidence in making negative judgements of their native language.

Our finding that our generated alignment actually decreases the perceived positivity of the relationship is contrary to what is generally predicted by the literature (Brennan and Clark, 1996; Shepard et al., 2001; Pickering and Garrod, 2004); but cf. Niederhoffer and Pennebaker (2002). Likewise, we would also have expected the dialogues with alignment to have been perceived to have gone more smoothly. However, in our evaluation of the different types of alignment, we note that alignment per se is not necessarily a bad thing: Generally alignment of Polarity, Topic, and Construction are seen positively leading to higher ratings of 'getting on', 'smoothness', and increased accurate perception of Agreeableness; repetition of individual words is however viewed negatively, and leads to lower ratings of 'getting on' and 'smoothness'.

There are a number of possible explanations for these negative responses to our generated dialogue alignment. They hinge on understanding what is involved in generating alignment, or similar behaviour, in dialogue participants. First, it could be that our dialogues encode the 'wrong' type of similarity. For example, the alignment and entrainment approaches to similarity usually study task-based dialogues, which often focus on establishing a shared vocabulary for referencing objects (i.e., at the word level). In such cases, the similarity arises either through priming mechanisms, or the establishment of common ground. Given that we used an alignment model to generate similarity in our dialogues, this kind of repetition or similarity may seem incongruent or out of place in dialogues that are not task-based (cf. negative impact of word-level alignment).

A second explanation might be that similarity relates to positive outcomes when it occurs over a longer, rather than shorter, period of time (Reitter, 2008). In the current study the dialogues consisted of eight turns, thus similarity was not generated over a long period. Indeed, linguistic similarity over a longer period of time may be more consistent with perceptions of social similarity, such as in-group, rather than outgroup, membership (Shepard et al., 2001). Indeed, in such contexts word choice *is* an important feature in dialogue and would be useful to incorporate into a dialogue model to simulate ingroup membership.

Third, in communication accommodation theory it is 'convergence' – the process of *increasing* similarity between interlocutors – which is important, rather than similarity alone. In the current study, convergence was not examined since the dialogues were generated with static levels of alignment.

So how do these findings relate back to the area of dialogue generation for applied contexts? Similarly to findings for the PERSONAGE system (Mairesse and Walker, 2010), personality in our generated dialogues is perceived with similar accuracy to the way humans perceive personality of other humans. This suggests that our CRAG 2 system can create believable characters to whom the user can potentially relate while auditing the dialogues, or using a dialogue-based interface. That alignment can have negative effects on dialogue perception we propose is due to the form of alignment depicted in these generated dialogues (i.e., task-based nature emphasising similarity at the word level), rather than alignment in general. We do not take this result to necessarily indicate that alignment in generated dialogues should be avoided. Rather, its implementation should be carefully considered, especially to ensure that the form of similarity achieved makes sense in the communicative context. Indeed, as we show in the evaluation of the generated dialogues, alignment at the Polarity, Topic, and Construction levels is generally viewed positively, however in contrast alignment at the Word level tends to be viewed more negatively. One of the key suggestions arising from this study is that the different forms of dialogue similarity cannot simply be used interchangeably, with alignment found in task-based dialogues which may include many instances of word-level repetition and alignment not necessarily appropriate in non-task dialogues, and thus not automatically resulting in perceptions of positivity. We note that non-native speakers were more forgiving in their ratings of the dialogues containing alignment. Given that they were equally able to perceive the personality of the characters, this may be due to non-native speakers having fewer expectations of alignment behaviour in dialogue. Indeed in some contexts, greater alignment, and thus repetition, may be beneficial for non-native speakers auditing dialogues.

To conclude, personality in our generated dialogues was perceived with comparable accuracy to human texts, but alignment or similarity between speakers – especially at the word level – regarded negatively. We would like to see future work examine further the responses to different forms of alignment, including convergence, in generated dialogue.

9 Acknowledgements

We acknowledge Edinburgh-Stanford Link funding, and the partial support of the Future and Emerging Technologies programme FP7-COSI-ICT of the European Commission (project QLectives, grant no.: 231200). We thank Amy Isard, Scott Nowson and Michael White for their assistance in this work. A version of the paper was presented at the Twentieth Society for Text and Discourse conference; thanks to Herb Clark, Max Louwerse and Michael Schober for their insights regarding linguistic similarity.

References

[Bortfeld and Brennan1997] H. Bortfeld and S. E. Brennan. 1997. Use and acquisition of idiomatic expressions in referring by native and non-native speakers. *Discourse Processes*, 23:119–147.

[Brennan and Clark1996] Susan E. Brennan and Herbert H. Clark. 1996. Conceptual pacts and lexical choice in conversation. *Journal of Experimental Psychology: Learning, Memory, and Cognition*, 22(6):1482–1493, November.

[Brennan1996] Susan E. Brennan. 1996. Lexical entrainment in spontaneous dialog. In *International Symposium on Spoken Dialog*, pages 41–44.

[Brockmann2009] Carsten Brockmann. 2009. *Personality and Alignment Processes in Dialogue: Towards a Lexically-Based Unified Model.* Ph.D. thesis, University of Edinburgh, UK.

[Cassell et al.2000] Justine Cassell, Joseph Sullivan, Scott Prevost, and Elizabeth Churchill, editors. 2000. *Embodied Conversational Agents.* MIT Press, Cambridge, MA, USA.

[Foster and White2004] Mary Ellen Foster and Michael White. 2004. Techniques for text planning with XSLT. In *Proceedings of the 4th Workshop on NLP and XML (NLPXML-04) at the 42nd Annual Meeting of the Association for Computational Linguistics (ACL-04)*, pages 1–8, Barcelona, Spain.

[Gill and Oberlander2002] Alastair J. Gill and Jon Oberlander. 2002. Taking care of the linguistic features of extraversion. In *Proceedings of the 24th Annual Conference of the Cognitive Science Society (CogSci2002)*, pages 363–368, Fairfax, VA, USA.

[Gill et al.2006] Alastair J. Gill, Jon Oberlander, and Elizabeth Austin. 2006. Rating e-mail personality at zero acquaintance. *Personality and Individual Differences*, 40(3):497–507.

[Hernault et al.2008] Hugo Hernault, Paul Piwek, Helmut Prendinger, and Mitsuru Ishizuka. 2008. Generating dialogues for virtual agents using nested textual coherence relations. In *Proceedings of Intelligent Virtual Agents*, pages 139–145.

[Isbister and Nass2000] Katherine Isbister and Clifford Nass. 2000. Consistency of personality in interactive characters: verbal cues, non-verbal cues, and user characteristics. *International Journal of Human–Computer Studies*, 53(2):251–267.

[Li and Chignell2010] J. Li and M. Chignell. 2010. Birds of a feather: How personality influences blog writing and reading. *Int. J. Human-Computer Studies*, 68:589–602.

[Mairesse and Walker2010] François Mairesse and Marilyn Walker. 2010. Towards personality-based user adaptation: Psychologically informed stylistic language generation. *User Modeling and User-Adapted Interaction*, 20(3):227–278.

[Niederhoffer and Pennebaker2002] Kate G. Niederhoffer and James W. Pennebaker. 2002. Linguistic style matching in social interaction. *Journal of Language and Social Psychology*, 21(4):337–360.

[Nowson et al.2005] S. Nowson, J. Oberlander, and A.J. Gill. 2005. Weblogs, genres and individual differences. In *Proceedings of the 27th Annual Conference of the Cognitive Science Society*, pages 1666–1671.

[Pennebaker and King1999] James W. Pennebaker and Laura A. King. 1999. Linguistic styles: Language use as an individual difference. *Journal of Personality and Social Psychology*, 77(6):1296–1312.

[Pickering and Garrod2004] Martin J. Pickering and Simon Garrod. 2004. Toward a mechanistic psychology of dialogue. *Behavioral and Brain Sciences*, 27(2):169–225.

[Porzel et al.2006] Robert Porzel, Annika Scheffler, and Rainer Malaka. 2006. How entrainment increases dialogical efficiency. In *Proceedings of Workshop on on Effective Multimodal Dialogue Interfaces.*

[Rammstedt and Schupp2008] Beatrice Rammstedt and Jürgen Schupp. 2008. Only the congruent survive – personality similarities in couples. *Personality and Individual Differences*, 45(6):533–535.

[Reitter2008] David Reitter. 2008. *Context Effects in Language Production: Models of Syntactic Priming in Dialogue Corpora.* Ph.D. thesis, University of Edinburgh, UK.

[Shepard et al.2001] Carolyn A. Shepard, Howard Giles, and Beth A. Le Poire. 2001. Communication accommodation theory. In W. Peter Robinson and Howard Giles, editors, *The New Handbook of Language and Social Psychology*, chapter 1.2, pages 33–56. John Wiley & Sons, Chichester, UK.

[van Deemter et al.2008] Kees van Deemter, Brigitte Krenn, Paul Piwek, Martin Klesen, Marc Schröder, and Stefan Baumann. 2008. Fully generated scripted dialogue for embodied agents. *Artificial Intelligence*, 172(10):1219–1244.

[White2006a] Michael White. 2006a. CCG chart realization from disjunctive inputs. In *Proceedings of the 4th International Natural Language Generation Conference (INLG-06)*, pages 9–16, Sydney, Australia.

[White2006b] Michael White. 2006b. Efficient realization of coordinate structures in Combinatory Categorial Grammar. *Research on Language and Computation*, 4(1):39–75.

Optimising Incremental Generation for Spoken Dialogue Systems: Reducing the Need for Fillers

Nina Dethlefs, Helen Hastie, Verena Rieser and Oliver Lemon
Heriot Watt University
EH14 4AS, Edinburgh
n.s.dethlefs | h.hastie | v.t.rieser | o.lemon@hw.ac.uk

Abstract

Recent studies have shown that incremental systems are perceived as more reactive, natural, and easier to use than non-incremental systems. However, previous work on incremental NLG has not employed recent advances in statistical optimisation using machine learning. This paper combines the two approaches, showing how the *update*, *revoke* and *purge* operations typically used in incremental approaches can be implemented as state transitions in a Markov Decision Process. We design a model of incremental NLG that generates output based on micro-turn interpretations of the user's utterances and is able to optimise its decisions using statistical machine learning. We present a proof-of-concept study in the domain of Information Presentation (IP), where a learning agent faces the trade-off of whether to present information as soon as it is available (for high reactiveness) or else to wait until input ASR hypotheses are more reliable. Results show that the agent learns to avoid long waiting times, fillers and self-corrections, by re-ordering content based on its confidence.

1 Introduction

Traditionally, the smallest unit of speech processing for interactive systems has been a full utterance with strict, rigid turn-taking. Components of these interactive systems, including NLG systems, have so far treated the utterance as the smallest processing unit that triggers a module into action. More recently, work on incremental systems has shown that processing smaller 'chunks' of user input can improve the user experience (Skantze and Schlangen, 2009; Buss et al., 2010; Skantze and Hjalmarsson, 2010; Baumann et al., 2011). Incrementality in NLG systems enables the system designer to model several dialogue phenomena that play a vital role in human discourse (Levelt, 1989) but have so far been absent from NLG systems. These include more natural turn-taking through rapid system responses, grounding through the generation of backchannels and feedback, and barge-ins (from both user and system). In addition, corrections and self-corrections through constant monitoring of user and system utterances play an important role, enabling the system to recover smoothly from a recognition error or a change in the user's preferences. Some examples of the phenomena we are targeting are given in Fig. 1.

Skantze and Hjalmarsson (2010) present a model of incremental speech generation in which input processing and output planning are parallel processes and the system can self-monitor its own generation process. In an evaluation with human users they showed that their incremental system started to speak significantly faster than a non-incremental system (roughly 600 ms) and was perceived as significantly more polite and efficient. Users also indicated that they knew better when to start speaking themselves. Alternative approaches to incremental NLG include Kilger and Finkler (1995) who present an early approach based on Tree-Adjoining Grammar, and Purver and Otsuka (2003) who define an incremental generator based on Dynamic Syntax. Both of these generators can monitor their own output and initiate corrections if necessary.

Over recent years, adaptive and data-driven ap-

Self-correction (the system made a mistake)

USR	I want Italian food in the centre of town ...
SYS	OK. I found 35 Indian restaurants ...
USR	No, I want Italian.
SYS	oh sorry ...
SYS	I have 24 Italian restaurants in the city centre ...

Correction (the user changed their mind)

USR	I want Indian food in the centre of town ...
SYS	There are 35 Indian ...
USR	Oh sorry, I meant Italian.
SYS	OK, Italian ...
SYS	I have 24 Italian restaurants ...

Re-ordering (from high to low confidence)

USR	I want Italian food ...
SYS	[waits]
USR	in the city centre.
SYS	I have 120 places in the city centre ...
USR	I love Italian ...
SYS	24 of them Italian ...

Holding the floor

USR	I want cheap Italian food ...
SYS	ok let me see
SYS	I have 3 cheap Italian places ...

Figure 1: Example phenomena generated with the trained policy. The agent has learnt to produce backchannels when the user pauses, monitor and (self-)correct its output, and present information according to its confidence.

proaches to NLG have also been developed and shown to outperform the previous (handcrafted, rule-based) methods for specific problems (Rieser et al., 2010; Janarthanam and Lemon, 2010; Dethlefs and Cuayáhuitl, 2011). This work has established that NLG can fruitfully be treated as a data-driven statistical planning process, where the objective is to maximise expected utility of the generated utterances (van Deemter, 2009), by adapting them to the context and user. Statistical approaches to sentence planning and surface realisation have also been explored (Stent et al., 2004; Belz, 2008; Mairesse et al., 2010; Angeli et al., 2010). The advantages of data-driven methods are that NLG is more robust in the face of noise, can adapt to various contexts and, trained on real data, can produce more natural and desirable variation in system utterances.

This paper describes an initial investigation into a novel NLG architecture that combines incremental processing with statistical optimisation. In order to move away from conventional strict-turn taking, we have to be able to model the complex interactions observed in human-human conversation. Doing this in a deterministic fashion through hand-written rules would be time consuming and potentially inaccurate, with no guarantee of optimality. In this paper, we demonstrate that it is possible to learn incremental generation behaviour in a reward-driven fashion.

2 Previous Work: Incremental Processing Architectures

The smallest unit of processing in incremental systems is called *incremental unit* (IU). Its instantiation depends on the particular processing module. In speech recognition, IUs can correspond to phoneme sequences that are mapped onto words (Baumann and Schlangen, 2011). In dialogue management, IUs can correspond to dialogue acts (Buss et al., 2010). In speech synthesis, IUs can correspond to speech unit sequences which are mapped to segments and speech plans (Skantze and Hjalmarsson, 2010). IUs are typically linked to other IUs by two types of relations: *same-level* links connect IUs sequentially and express relationships at the same level; *grounded-in* links express hierarchical relations between IUs.

2.1 Buffer-Based Incremental Processing

A general abstract model of incremental processing based on buffers and a processor was developed by Schlangen and Skantze (2009) and is illustrated in Figure 2. It assumes that the *left buffer* of a module, such as the NLG module, receives IUs from one or more other processing modules, such as the dialogue manager. These input IUs are then passed on to the *processor*, where they are mapped to corresponding (higher-level) IUs. For an NLG module, this could be a mapping from the dialogue act *present(cuisine=Indian)* to the realisation *'they serve Indian food'*. The resulting IUs are passed on to the *right buffer* which co-incides with the left buffer of another module (for example the speech synthesis module in our example). Same-level links are indicated as dashed arrows in Figure 2 and grounded-in links as stacked boxes of IUs.

The figure also shows that the mapping between IUs can be a one-to-many mapping (IU1 and IU2 are mapped to IU3) or a one-to-one mapping (IU3 is

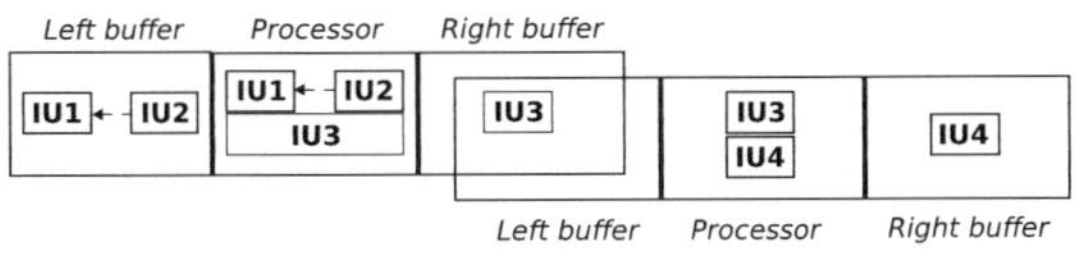

Figure 2: The buffer-based model showing two connected modules (from Skantze and Hjalmarsson (2010).

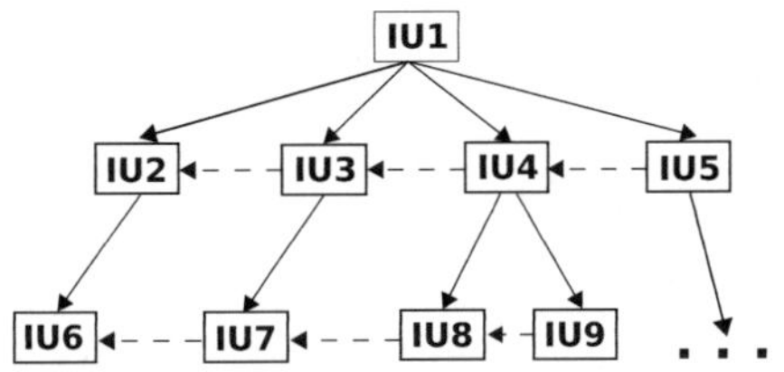

Figure 3: The ISU-model for incremental processing (adapted from Buss and Schlangen (2011)).

mapped to IU4). The model distinguishes four operations that handle information processing: *update, revise, purge* and *commit.* Whenever new IUs enter the module's left buffer, the module's knowledge base is *updated* to reflect the new information. Such information typically corresponds to the current best hypothesis of a preceding processing module. As a property of incremental systems, however, such hypotheses can be *revised* by the respective preceding module and, as a result, the knowledge bases of all subsequent modules need to be *purged* and *updated* to the newest hypothesis. Once a hypothesis is certain to not be revised anymore, it is *committed.* For concrete implementations of this model, see Skantze and Schlangen (2009), Skantze and Hjalmarsson (2010), Baumann and Schlangen (2011).

An implementation of an incremental dialogue manager is based on the Information State Update (ISU) model (Buss et al., 2010; Buss and Schlangen, 2011). The model is related in spirit to the buffer-based architecture, but all of its input processing and output planning is realised by ISU rules. This is true for the incremental 'house-keeping' actions update, revise, etc. and all types of dialogue acts. The incremental ISU model is shown in Figure 3. Note that this hierarchical architecture transfers well to the "classical" division of NLG levels into utterance (IU1), content selection (IU2 - IU5) and surface realisations (IU6 - IU9, etc.).

2.2 Beat-Driven Incremental Processing

In contrast to the buffer-based architectures, alternative incremental systems do not reuse previous partial hypotheses of the user's input (or the system's best output) but recompute them at each processing step. We follow Baumann et al. (2011) in calling them *'beat-driven'* systems. Raux and Eskenazi (2009) use a cost matrix and decision theoretic principles to optimise turn-taking in a dialogue system under the constraint that users prefer no gaps and no overlap at turn boundaries. DeVault et al. (2009) use maximum entropy classification to support responsive overlap in an incremental system by predicting the completions of user utterances.

2.3 Decision-making in Incremental Systems

Some of the main advantages of the buffer- and ISU-based approaches include their inherently incremental mechanisms for updating and revising system hypotheses. They are able to process input of varying size and type and, at the same time, produce arbitrarily complex output which is monitored and can be modified at any time. On the other hand, current models are based on deterministic decision making and thus share some of the same drawbacks that non-incremental systems have faced: (1) they rely on hand-written rules which are time-consuming and expensive to produce, (2) they do not provide a mechanism to deal with uncertainty introduced by varying user behaviour, and (3) they are unable to generalise and adapt flexibly to unseen situations.

For NLG in particular, we have seen that incrementality can enhance the responsiveness of systems and facilitate turn-taking. However, this advantage was mainly gained by the system producing semantically empty fillers such as *um, let me see, well*, etc. (Skantze and Hjalmarsson, 2010). It is an open research question whether such markers of planning or turn-holding can help NLG systems, but for now it seems that they could be reduced to a minimum by optimising the *timing and order of Information Presentation.* In the following, we develop a model for incremental NLG that is based on reinforcement learning (RL). It learns the best moment to present information to the user, when faced with the options of presenting information as soon as it becomes available or else waiting until the in-

Type	Example
Comparison	The restaurant *Roma* is in the medium price range, but does not have great food. The *Firenze* and *Verona* both have great food but are more expensive. The *Verona* has good service, too.
Recommendation	Restaurant *Verona* has the best overall match with your query. It is a bit more expensive, but has great food and service.
Summary	I have 43 Italian restaurants in the city centre that match your query. 10 of them are in the medium price range, 5 are cheap and 8 are expensive.

Table 1: Examples of IP as a *comparison, recommendation* and *summary* for a user looking for Italian restaurants in the city centre that have a good price for value.

put hypotheses of the system are more stable. This also addresses the general trade-off that exists in incremental systems between the processing speed of a system and the output quality.

3 Information Presentation Strategies

Our domain of application will be the Information Presentation phase in an interactive system for restaurant recommendations, extending previous work by Rieser et al. (2010), (see also Walker et al. (2004) for an alternative approach). Rieser et al. incrementally construct IP strategies according to the predicted user reaction, whereas our approach focuses on timing and re-ordering of information according to dynamically changing input hypotheses. We therefore implement a simplified version of Rieser et al.'s model. Their system distinguished two steps: the selection of an IP strategy and the selection of attributes to present to the user. We assume here that the choice of attributes is determined by matching the types specified in the user input, so that our system only needs to choose a strategy for presenting its results (in the future, though, we will include attribute selection into the decision process). Attributes include *cuisine, food quality, location, price range* and *service quality* of a restaurant. The system then performs a database lookup and chooses among three main IP strategies *summary, comparison, recommendation* and several ordered combinations of these. Please see Rieser et al. (2010) for details. Table 1 shows examples of the main types of presentation strategies we address.

4 Optimising Incremental NLG

To optimise the NLG process within an incremental model of dialogue processing, we define an RL agent with incremental states and actions for the IP task. An RL agent is formalised as a Markov Decision Process, or MDP, which is characterised as a four-tuple $< S, A, T, R >$, where S is a set of states representing the status of the NLG system and all information available to it, A is a set of NLG actions that combine strategies for IP with handling incremental updates in the system, T is a probabilistic transition function that determines the next state s' from the current state s and the action a according to a conditional probability distribution $P(s'|s, a)$, and R is a reward function that specifies the reward (a numeric value) that an agent receives for taking action a in state s. Using such an MDP, the NLG process can be seen as a finite sequence of states, actions and rewards $\{s_0, a_0, r_1, s_1, a_1, ..., r_{t-1}, s_t\}$, where t is the time step. Note that a learning episode falls naturally into a number of time steps at each of which the agent observes the current state of the environment s_t, takes an action a_t and makes a transition to state s_{t+1}. This organisation into discrete time steps, and the notion of a state space that is accessible to the learning agent at any time allows us to implement the state *update*, *revoke* and *purge* operations typically assumed by incremental approaches as state updates and transitions in an MDP. Any change in the environment, such as a new best hypothesis of the recogniser, can thus be represented as a transition from one state to another. At each time step, the agent then takes the currently best action according to the new state. The best action in an incremental framework can include *correcting* a previous output, *holding the floor* as a marker of planning, or to *wait* until presenting information.[1]

[1] We treat these actions as part of NLG content selection here, but are aware that in alternative approaches, they could

States
incrementalStatus {0=none,1=holdFloor,2=correct,3=selfCorrect}
presStrategy {0=unfilled,1=filled}
statusCuisine {0=unfilled,1=low,2=medium,3=high,4=realised}
statusFood {0=unfilled,1=low,2=medium,3=high,4=realised}
statusLocation {0=unfilled,1=low,2=medium,3=high,4=realised}
statusPrice {0=unfilled,1=low,2=medium,3=high,4=realised}
statusService {0=unfilled,1=low,2=medium,3=high,4=realised}
userReaction {0=none,1=select,2=askMore,3=other}
userSilence={0=false,1=true}
Actions
IP: compare, recommend, summarise, summariseCompare, summariseRecommend, summariseCompareRecommend,
Slot-ordering: presentCuisine, presentFood, presentLocation, presentPrice, presentService,
Incremental: backchannel, correct, selfCorrect, holdFloor, waitMore
Goal State $0, 1, 0 \vee 4, 0 \vee 4, 0 \vee 4, 0 \vee 4, 0 \vee 4, 1, 0 \vee 1$

Figure 4: The state and action space of the learning agent. The goal state is reached when all items (that the user may be interested in) have been presented.

Once information has been presented to the user, it is *committed* or *realised*. We again represent realised IUs in the agent's state representation, so that it can monitor its own output. The goal of an MDP is to find an optimal policy π^* according to which the agent receives the maximal possible reward for each visited state. We use the Q-Learning algorithm (Watkins, 1989) to learn an optimal policy according to $\pi^*(s) = \arg\max_{a \in A} Q^*(s, a)$, where Q^* specifies the expected reward for executing action a in state s and then following policy π^*.

5 Experimental Setting

5.1 The State and Action Space

The agent's state space needs to contain all information relevant for choosing an optimal IP strategy and an optimal sequence of incremental actions. Figure 4 shows the state and action space of our learning agent. The states contain information on the incremental and presentation status of the system. The variable 'incrementalStatus' characterises situations in which a particular (incremental) action is triggered. For example, a `holdFloor` is generated when the user has finished speaking, but the system has not yet finished its database lookup. A `correction` is needed when the system has to modify already presented information (because the user changed their preferences) and a `selfCorrection` is needed when previously presented information is modified because the system made a mistake (in recognition or interpretation). The variable 'presStrategy' indicates whether a strategy for IP has been chosen. It is 'filled' when this is the case, and 'unfilled' otherwise. The variables representing the status of the cuisine, food, location, price and service indicate whether the slot is of interest to the user (0 means that the user does not care about it), and what input confidence score is currently associated with its value. Once slots have been presented, they are *realised* and can only be changed through a correction or self-correction.

The variable 'userReaction' shows the user's reaction to an IP episode. The user can select a restaurant, provide more information to further constrain the search or do something else. The 'userSilence' variable indicates whether the user is speaking or not. This can be relevant for holding the floor or generating backchannels. The action set comprises IP actions, actions which enable us to learn the ordering of slots, and actions which allow us to capture incremental phenomena. The complete state-action space size of this agent is roughly 3.2 million. The agent reaches its goal state (defined w.r.t. the state variables in Figure 4) when an IP strategy has been chosen and all relevant attributes have been presented.

5.2 The Simulated Environment

Since a learning agent typically needs several thousand interactions to learn a reasonable policy, we train it in a simulated environment with two components. The first one deals with different IP strategies generally (not just for the incremental case), and the second one focuses on incrementally updated user input hypothesis during the interaction.

To learn a good IP strategy, we use a user simulation by Rieser et al. (2010),[2] which was estimated from human data and uses bi-grams of the form $P(a_{u,t}|IP_{s,t})$, where $a_{u,t}$ is the predicted user reaction at time t to the system's IP strategy $IP_{s,t}$ in state s at time t. We distinguish the user reactions of

also be the responsibility of a dialogue manager.

[2]The simulation data are available from `http://www.classic-project.org/`.

select a restaurant, *addMoreInfo* to the current query to constrain the search, and *other*. The last category is considered an undesired user reaction that the system should learn to avoid. The simulation uses linear smoothing to account for unseen situations. In this way, we can then predict the most likely user reaction to each system action.

While the IP strategies can be used for incremental and non-incremental NLG, the second part of the simulation deals explicitly with the dynamic environment updates during an interaction. We assume that for each restaurant recommendation, the user has the option of filling any or all of the attributes *cuisine, food quality, location, price range* and *service quality*. The possible values of each attribute and possible confidence scores are shown in Table 2 and denote the same as described in Section 5.1.

At the beginning of a learning episode, we assign each attribute a possible value and confidence score with equal probability. For food and service quality, we assume that the user is never interested in bad food or service. Subsequently, confidence scores can change at each time step. (In future work these transition probabilities will be estimated from a data collection, though the following assumptions are realistic, based on our experience.) We assume that a confidence score of 0 changes to any other value with a likelihood of 0.05. A confidence score of 1 changes with a probability of 0.3, a confidence score of 2 with a probability of 0.1 and a confidence score of 3 with a probability of 0.03. Once slots have been realised, their value is set to 4. They cannot be changed then without an explicit correction. We also assume that realised slots change with a probability of 0.1. If they change, we assume that half of the time, the user is the origin of the change (because they changed their mind) and half of the time the system is the origin of the change (because of an ASR or interpretation error). Each time a confidence score is changed, it has a probability of 0.5 to also change its value. The resulting input to the NLG system are data structures of the form *present(cuisine=Indian), confidence=low*.

5.3 The Reward Function

The main trade-off to optimise for IP in an incremental setting is the *timing and order of presentation*. The agent has to decide whether to present

Attribute	Values	Confidence
Cuisine	Chinese, French, German, Indian, Italian, Japanese, Mexican, Scottish, Spanish, Thai	0, 1, 2, 3, 4
Food	bad, adequate, good, very good	0, 1, 2, 3, 4
Location	7 distinct areas of the city	0, 1, 2, 3, 4
Price	cheap, expensive, good-price-for-value, very expensive	0, 1, 2, 3, 4
Service	bad, adequate, good, very good	0, 1, 2, 3, 4

Table 2: User goal slots for restaurant queries with possible values and confidence scores.

information as soon as it becomes available or else wait until confidence for input hypotheses is more stable. Alternatively, it can reorder information to account for different confidence scores. We assign the following rewards[3]: $+100$ if the user selects an item, 0 if the user adds more search constraints, -100 if the user does something else or the system needs to self-correct, -0.5 for holding the floor, and -1 otherwise. In addition, the agent receives an increasing negative reward for the waiting time, $waiting\_time^2$ (to the power of two), in terms of the number of time steps passed since the last item was presented. This reward is theoretically $-\infty$. The agent is thus penalised stronger the longer it delays IP. The rewards for user reactions are assigned at the end of each episode, all other rewards are assigned after each time step. One episode stretches from the moment that a user specifies their initial preferences to the moment in which they choose a restaurant. The agent was trained for 10 thousand episodes.

6 Experimental Results

After training, the RL agent has learnt the following incremental IP strategy. It will present information slots as soon as they become available if they have a medium or high confidence score. The agent will then order attributes so that those slots with the highest confidence scores are presented first and slots with lower confidence are presented later (by which time they may have achieved higher confidence). If no information is known with medium or high con-

[3]Handcrafted rewards are sufficient for this proof-of-concept study, and can be learned from data for future models (Rieser and Lemon, 2011).

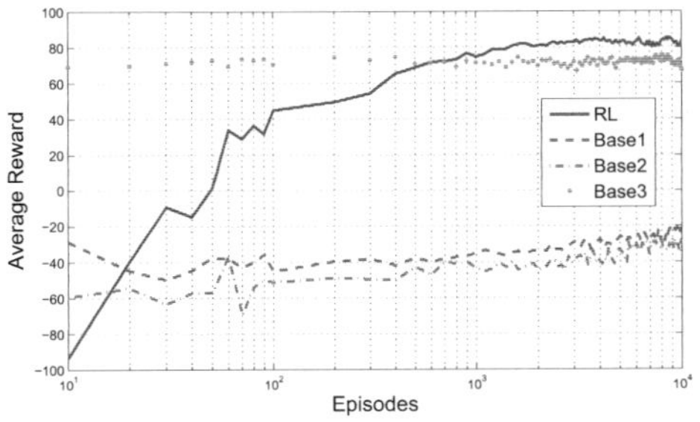

Figure 5: Performance in terms of rewards (averaged over 10 runs) for the RL agent and its baselines.

fidence, the agent will hold the floor or wait. In this way, it can prevent self-corrections and minimise waiting time—both of which yield negative rewards. It can thus start speaking very early (avoiding long pauses or semantically empty utterances) and still has a low likelihood of having to self-correct.

For a comparison of the learnt policy with possible hand-crafted policies (because current incremental NLG systems are rule-based), we designed three baselines. **Baseline 1** always presents information as soon as it is available, i.e. never waits. **Baseline 2** always waits until all information is known with high confidence (i.e. until all confidence scores are 3). **Baseline 3** was chosen to be more ambitious. It always presents information as soon as possible, using a decreasing order of confidence to minimise self-corrections (i.e. very similar to the learnt policy). It chooses randomly among slots with equal confidence. All baseline policies have an optimised IP strategy (recommend/summary etc.) and differ only in their incremental processing strategies. Baseline 1 is most similar to the current approach used in spoken dialogue systems, where the Dialogue Manager triggers an NLG component as soon as a task-relevant user utterance is processed.

Here we do not compare the different strategies for IP generally because this has been done by Rieser et al. (2010), even if not for incremental NLG. Figure 5 shows the performance of all behaviours in terms of average rewards. Baseline 1 obtains on average roughly 100 reward points less than the RL agent. This corresponds to the (negative) reward of one self-correction (-100). Since information is always presented as soon as it is available, this baseline needs to produce on average one

Baseline 1 (present information as soon as it becomes available)

USR Please show me Italian places
$(cuisine = Indian; conf\_score = 0.2)$
SYS I have found 35 Indian ...
USR No, ITALIAN
$(cuisine = Italian; conf\_score = 0.8)$
SYS Oh, you meant Italian. I have 104 Italian places in Edinburgh. 24 in the city centre, 21 in the New Town, 14 in ...
USR Show me some in the city centre
$(location = centre; conf\_score = 0.6)$
SYS OK. I found 24 Italian restaurants in the city centre ...

Baseline 2 (always wait until confidence is high)

USR Do you have Italian restaurants in the centre of town?
$cuisine = Italian; conf\_score = 0.4$
$location = centre; conf\_score = 0.2$
SYS *waits*
USR Italian in the centre.
$cuisine = Italian, conf\_score = 0.7$
$location = centre, conf\_score = 0.5$
SYS I have 104 Italian restaurants.
USR *waits*
SYS *waits*
USR city centre please
$location = centre, conf\_score = 0.7$
SYS I have 24 Italian restaurants in the city centre ...

Baseline 3 (present information in decreasing order of confidence)

USR I want Italian food ...
$cuisine = Indian, conf\_score = 0.2$
$location = centre, conf\_score = 0.3$
SYS hmm (holding turn) ...
USR in the centre of town
$location = centre, conf\_score = 0.9$
SYS In the centre, let me see, Indian ...
USR Italian, please.
$cuisine = Italian, conf\_score = 0.7$
SYS Oh I see. I have 24 Italian places in the centre ...

Figure 6: Example dialogues generated with the baseline policies for a user who wants Italian food in the city centre. Confidence scores for cuisine and location variables for the restaurants are shown as updated.

self-correction per episode. Baseline 2 needs to wait until all information is known with high confidence and obtains on average 125 to 130 rewards less than the RL agent. This corresponds to approximately 11 time steps of waiting (for input to reach higher confidence) before presentation since 11 is (approximately) the square root of 130. Baseline 3 is roughly a reward of -10 worse than the RL agent's behaviour, which is due to a combination of more self-corrections, even if they just occur occasionally, and a higher number of turn holding markers. The latter is due to the baseline starting to present as soon as possible, so that whenever all confidence scores are too low to start presenting, a turn holding marker is generated. The learning agent learns to outperform all baselines significantly, by presenting information slots in decreasing order of confidence, combined with waiting and holding the floor at appropriate moments. Anticipating the rewards for waiting vs. holding the floor at particular moments is the main reason that the learnt policy outperforms Baseline 3. Subtle moments of timing as in this case are difficult to hand-craft and more appropriately balanced using optimisation. An absolute comparison of the last 1000 episodes of each behaviour shows that the improvement of the RL agent corresponds to 126.8% over Baseline 1, to 137.7% over Baseline 2 and to 16.76% over Baseline 3. All differences are significant at $p < 0.001$ according to a paired t-test and have a high effect size $r > 0.9$. The high percentage improvement of the learnt policy over Baselines 1 and 2 is mainly due to the high numeric values chosen for the rewards as can be observed from their qualitative behaviour. Thus, if the negative numeric values of, e.g., a self-correction were reduced, the percentage reward would reduce, but the policy would not change qualitatively. Figure 1 shows some examples of the learnt policy including several incremental phenomena. In contrast, Figure 6 shows examples generated with the baselines.

7 Conclusion and Future Directions

We have presented a novel framework combining incremental and statistical approaches to NLG for interactive systems. In a proof-of-concept study in the domain of Information Presentation, we optimised the *timing and order* of IP. The learning agent optimises the trade-off of whether to present information as soon as it becomes available (for high responsiveness) or else to wait until input hypotheses were more stable (to avoid self-corrections). Results in a simulated environment showed that the agent learns to avoid self-corrections and long waiting times, often by presenting information in order of decreasing confidence. It outperforms three hand-crafted baselines due to its enhanced adaptivity. In previous work, incremental responsiveness has mainly been implemented by producing semantically empty fillers such as *um, let me see, well*, etc. (Skantze and Hjalmarsson, 2010). Our work avoids the need for these fillers by content reordering.

Since this paper has focused on a proof-of-concept study, our goal has not been to demonstrate the superiority of automatic optimisation over hand-crafted behaviour. Previous studies have shown the advantages of optimisation (Janarthanam and Lemon, 2010; Rieser et al., 2010; Dethlefs et al., 2011). Rather, our main goal has been to demonstrate that incremental NLG can be phrased as an optimisation problem and that reasonable action policies can be learnt so that an application within an incremental framework is feasible. This observation allows us to take incremental systems, which so far have been restricted to deterministic decision making, one step further in terms of their adaptability and flexibility. To demonstrate the effectiveness of a synergy between RL and incremental NLG on a large scale, we would like to train a fully incremental NLG system from human data using a data-driven reward function. Further, an evaluation with human users will be required to verify the advantages of different policies for Information Presentation.

Regarding the scalability of our optimisation framework, RL systems are known to suffer from the *curse of dimensionality*, the problem that their state space grows exponentially according to the number of variables taken into account. While the application of flat RL is therefore limited to small-scale problems, we can use RL with a divide-and-conquer approach, *hierarchical RL*, which has been shown to scale to large-scale NLG applications (Dethlefs and Cuayáhuitl, 2011), to address complex NLG tasks.

Future work can take several directions. Currently, we learn the agent's behaviour offline, before the interaction, and then execute it statistically. More adaptivity towards individual users and situations could be achieved if the agent was able to learn from ongoing interactions using *online learning*. In addition, current NLG systems tend to assume that the user's goals and situational circumstances are known with certainty. This is often an unrealistic assumption that future work could address using POMDPs (Williams and Young, 2007).

Acknowledgements

The research leading to this work has received funding from EC's FP7 programmes: (FP7/2011-14) under grant agreement no. 287615 (PARLANCE); (FP7/2007-13) under grant agreement no. 216594 (CLASSiC); (FP7/2011-14) under grant agreement no. 270019 (SPACEBOOK); (FP7/2011-16) under grant agreement no. 269427 (STAC).

References

Gabor Angeli, Percy Liang, and Dan Klein. 2010. A simple domain-independent probabilistic approach to generation. In *Proc. of EMNLP*, pages 502–512.

Timo Baumann and David Schlangen. 2011. Predicting the Micro-Timing of User Input for an Incremental Spoken Dialogue System that Completes a User's Ongoing Turn. In *Proc. of 12th Annual SIGdial Meeting on Discourse and Dialogue*, Portland, OR.

Timo Baumann, Okko Buss, and David Schlangen. 2011. Evaluation and Optimisation of Incremental Processors. *Dialogue and Discourse*, 2(1).

Anja Belz. 2008. Automatic Generation of Weather Forecast Texts Using Comprehensive Probabilistic Generation-Space Models. *Natural Language Engineering*, 14(4):431–455.

Okko Buss and David Schlangen. 2011. DIUM—An Incremental Dialogue Manager That Can Produce Self-Corrections. In *Proc. of the Workshop on the Semantics and Pragmatics of Dialogue (SemDIAL / Los Angelogue)*, Los Angeles, CA.

Okko Buss, Timo Baumann, and David Schlangen. 2010. Collaborating on Utterances with a Spoken Dialogue Systen Using an ISU-based Approach to Incremental Dialogue Management. In *Proc. of 11th Annual SIGdial Meeting on Discourse and Dialogue.*

Nina Dethlefs and Heriberto Cuayáhuitl. 2011. Combining Hierarchical Reinforcement Learning and Bayesian Networks for Natural Language Generation in Situated Dialogue. In *Proc. of the 13th European Workshop on Natural Language Generation (ENLG)*, Nancy, France.

Nina Dethlefs, Heriberto Cuayáhuitl, and Jette Viethen. 2011. Optimising Natural Language Generation Decision Making for Situated Dialogue. In *Proceedings of the 12th Annual Meeting on Discourse and Dialogue (SIGdial)*, Portland, Oregon, USA.

David DeVault, Kenji Sagae, and David Traum. 2009. Can I finish? Learning when to respond to incremental interpretation result in interactive dialogue. In *Proc. of the 10th Annual SigDial Meeting on Discourse and Dialogue*, Queen Mary University, UK.

Srini Janarthanam and Oliver Lemon. 2010. Learning to Adapt to Unknown Users: Referring Expression Generation in Spoken Dialogue Systems. In *Proc. of the 48th Annual Meeting of the Association for Computational Linguistics (ACL)*, pages 69–78, July.

Anne Kilger and Wolfgang Finkler. 1995. Incremental generation for real-time applications. Technical report, DFKI Saarbruecken, Germany.

Willem Levelt. 1989. *Speaking: From Intenion to Articulation.* MIT Press.

François Mairesse, Milica Gašić, Filip Jurčíček, Simon Keizer, Blaise Thomson, Kai Yu, and Steve Young. 2010. Phrase-based statistical language generation using graphical models and active learning. In *Proc. of the Annual Meeting of the Association for Computational Linguistics (ACL)*, pages 1552–1561.

Matthew Purver and Masayuki Otsuka. 2003. Incremental Generation by Incremental Parsing. In *Proceedings of the 6th UK Special-Interesting Group for Computational Linguistics (CLUK) Colloquium.*

Antoine Raux and Maxine Eskenazi. 2009. A Finite-State Turn-Taking Model for Spoken Dialog Systems. In *Proc. of the 10th Conference of the North American Chapter of the Association for Computational Linguistics—Human Language Technologies (NAACL-HLT)*, Boulder, Colorado.

Verena Rieser and Oliver Lemon. 2011. *Reinforcement Learning for Adaptive Dialogue Systems: A Data-driven Methodology for Dialogue Management and Natural Language Generation.* Book Series: Theory and Applications of Natural Language Processing, Springer, Berlin/Heidelberg.

Verena Rieser, Oliver Lemon, and Xingkun Liu. 2010. Optimising Information Presentation for Spoken Dialogue Systems. In *Proc. of the 48th Annual Meeting of the Association for Computational Linguistics (ACL)*, Uppsala, Sweden.

David Schlangen and Gabriel Skantze. 2009. A General, Abstract Model of Incremental Dialogue Processing. In *Proc. of the 12th Conference of the European Chapter of the Association for Computational Linguistics*, Athens, Greece.

Gabriel Skantze and Anna Hjalmarsson. 2010. Towards Incremental Speech Generation in Dialogue Systems. In *Proc. of the 11th Annual SigDial Meeting on Discourse and Dialogue*, Tokyo, Japan.

Gabriel Skantze and David Schlangen. 2009. Incremental Dialogue Processing in a Micro-Domain. In *Proc. of the 12th Conference of the European Chapter of the Association for Computational Linguistics*, Athens, Greece.

Amanda Stent, Rashmi Prasad, and Marilyn Walker. 2004. Trainable sentence planning for complex information presentation in spoken dialogue systems. In

Proc. of the Annual Meeting of the Association for Computational Linguistics.

Kees van Deemter. 2009. What game theory can do for NLG: the case of vague language. In *12th European Workshop on Natural Language Generation (ENLG)*.

Marilyn Walker, Steve Whittaker, Amanda Stent, Pretaam Maloor, Johanna Moore, and G Vasireddy. 2004. Generation and Evaluation of User Tailored Responses in Multimodal Dialogue. *Cognitive Science*, 28(5):811–840.

Chris Watkins. 1989. *Learning from Delayed Rewards*. PhD Thesis, King's College, Cambridge, UK.

Jason Williams and Steve Young. 2007. Partially Observable Markov Decision Processes for Spoken Dialog Systems. *Computer Speech and Language*, 21(2):393–422.

Linguist's Assistant: A Multi-Lingual Natural Language Generator based on Linguistic Universals, Typologies, and Primitives

Tod Allman
Graduate Institute of Applied Linguistics
7500 W. Camp Wisdom Rd.
Dallas, TX 75236
tod_allman@gial.edu

Stephen Beale
University of Maryland, Baltimore County
1000 Hilltop Circle
Baltimore, MD 21250
sbeale@csee.umbc.edu

Richard Denton
Dartmouth College
6127 Wilder Lab
Hanover, NH 03755
richard.e.denton@dartmouth.edu

Abstract

Linguist's Assistant (LA) is a large scale semantic analyzer and multi-lingual natural language generator designed and developed entirely from a linguist's perspective. The system incorporates extensive typological, semantic, syntactic, and discourse research into its semantic representational system and its transfer and synthesizing grammars. LA has been tested with English, Korean, Kewa (Papua New Guinea), Jula (Cote d'Ivoure), and North Tanna (Vanuatu), and proof-of-concept lexicons and grammars have been developed for Spanish, Urdu, Tagalog, Chinantec (Mexico), and Angas (Nigeria). This paper will summarize the major components of the NLG system, and then present the results of experiments that were performed to determine the quality of the generated texts. The experiments indicate that when experienced mother-tongue translators use the drafts generated by LA, their productivity is typically quadrupled without any loss of quality.

1 Introduction

The fundamental goal underlying LA was to develop a system capable of generating high quality texts in a wide variety of languages, particularly minority and endangered languages. Drafts produced by LA are always easily understandable, grammatically correct, semantically equivalent to the source documents, and at approximately a sixth grade reading level. Because the system is based on linguistic research, LA is expected to work well for typologically diverse languages; it works equally well for languages that are coranking or clause chaining, highly isolating or highly polysynthetic, fusional or agglutinative, etc. A natural language generator of this type is practical only when translating large quantities of texts into many different languages. Therefore semantic representations for a large variety of texts are being developed for LA. This system is a tool which enables linguists to document a language and simultaneously generate numerous texts for the speakers of that language. A model of LA is shown in Figure 1.

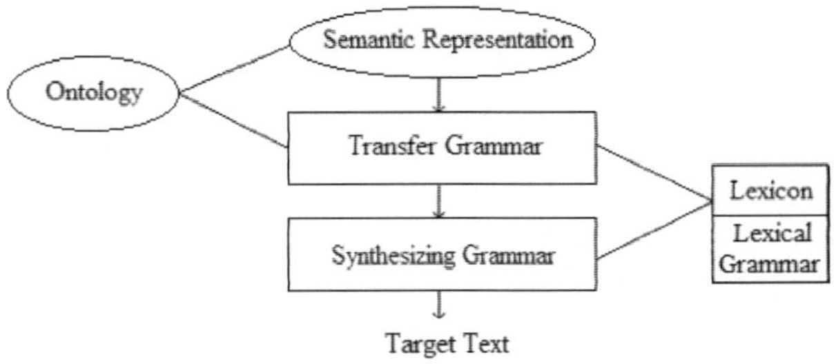

Figure 1. Model of Linguist's Assistant

As seen in the figure, there are five primary components: 1) the ontology, 2) the semantic representations, 3) the lexicon, 4) the transfer grammar, and 5) the synthesizing grammar. The two components in ovals are static knowledge which is supplied with LA, and the three items in rectangles are user-supplied target language knowledge. The final product of LA is target text.

2 The Ontology

One of the foundational principles of Natural Semantic Metalanguage theory (Goddard & Wierzbicka, 1994; Wierzbicka, 1996) proposes that there is a small set of innate concepts which are present in every language. These innate concepts can be used to explicate every word in every language. If semantic representations were developed using only these innate primitives, the problem of lexical mismatch between languages would be eliminated. However, building semantic representations using only the innate concepts is unwieldy, so semantically simple molecules were identified in a principled manner. For our semantic molecules, we elected to use the defining vocabulary in Longman's Contemporary English Dictionary (2003). By using these semantically simple concepts, the problem of lexical mismatch between source and target languages is significantly reduced. There are certainly still instances of lexical mismatch, and we have an approach for dealing with them which will be described below. LA also permits the automatic insertion of semantically complex concepts into the semantic representations, but only if the linguist indicates that the target language has a lexical equivalent.

3 LA's Semantic Representational System

The development of an adequate method of meaning representation for LA's source texts proved to be a challenge. Formal semantics (Cann, 1993; Rosner, 1992), conceptual semantics (Jackendoff, 1990) and generative semantics (Lakoff, 1987) were each considered but found unsuitable because they didn't include sufficient information for minority languages. Therefore a new format was developed specifically for LA's semantic representational system. LA's semantic representations are comprised of a controlled, English influenced metalanguage augmented by a feature system which was designed to accommodate a wide variety of languages. Fundamentally these semantic representations consist of concepts, structures, and features. The concepts that are permitted in the semantic representations are all semantically simple as was described earlier. The structures permitted in the semantic representations are a small restricted set of English-like sentence structures. The feature system developed for LA includes semantic, syntactic, and discourse information. The feature values have been gleaned from a wide variety of diverse languages. Table 1 shows a few examples of these features and their values.

Object Number	Singular, Dual, Trial, Quadrial, Plural, Paucal
Object Participant Tracking	First Mention, Routine, Interrogative, Frame Inferable, Exiting, Restaging, Generic
Object Proximity	Near Speaker and Listener, Near Speaker, Near Listener, Remote within Sight, Remote out of Sight, Temporally Near, Temporally Remote, Contextually Near with Focus
Event Time	Discourse, Present, Immediate Past, Earlier Today, Yesterday, 2 to 3 days ago, 4 to 6 days ago, 1 to 4 weeks ago, 1 to 5 months ago, 6 to 12 months ago, …, Immediate Future, Later Today, Tomorrow, 2 to 3 days from now, …
Proposition Illocutionary Force	Declarative, Imperative, Content Interrogative, Yes-No Interrogative
Proposition Salience Band (Longacre, 1996)	Pivotal Storyline, Script Predictable Actions, Backgrounded Actions, Flashback, Setting, Irrealis, Evaluation, Cohesive Material
Object Phrase Semantic Role	Agent, Patient, State, Source, Destination, Instrument, Beneficiary, Addressee

Table 1. Several Features and their Values

The semantic representation for "Paulus started walking from the market to a village named Terpen" is shown in Figure 2.

Figure 2. LA's Semantic Representational System

As seen in Figure 2, every concept, phrase, and proposition has numerous features associated with it; the letters and numbers below the concepts and beside the phrase and proposition boundaries represent specific feature values. For example, the phrase containing *Paulus* has its Semantic Role set to Agent, the phrase containing *market* has its Semantic Role set to Source, the phrase containing *village* has its Semantic Role set to Destination, the event *walk* has its Time set to Discourse and its Aspect set to Inceptive, the proposition's Illocutionary Force is set to Declarative and its Salience Band is set to Pivotal Storyline, etc.

4 LA's Lexicon

The target lexicon serves as a repository for all of the target language's words and their associated features and forms. Within the lexicon a linguist defines the features that are pertinent to each syntactic category for his particular target language. For example, each noun can be assigned a gender value, an honorific value, a class value, etc. Similarly the required forms are defined in the target lexicon (e.g., English verbs have a stem plus a past tense form, a perfect participle form, a gerund form, and a third singular present form). Then lexical spellout rules are used to generate the various forms of each target word. All instances of suppletion are entered into the target lexicon manually.

5 LA's Transfer Grammar

The purpose of LA's transfer grammar[1] is to restructure the English influenced semantic representations in order to produce a new underlying representation that is appropriate for the target language. This new underlying representation consists of the target language's words, structures, and features. For example, many languages have rules that are based on grammatical relations, but the object phrases in the semantic representations are marked with semantic roles rather than grammatical relations. Therefore a rule in the transfer grammar must generate grammatical relations from the semantic roles. For another example, many languages in the world are clause chaining rather than coranking, so a rule in the transfer grammar must build appropriate clause chains from the coranking propositions in the semantic representations. A model of LA's transfer grammar is shown in Figure 3. The transfer grammar consists of nine different types of rules, several of which will be briefly described below.

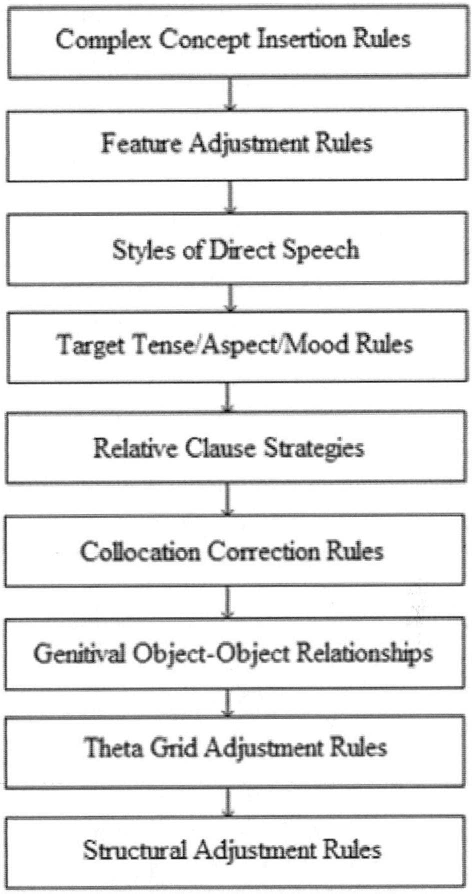

Figure 3. Model of LA's Transfer Grammar

Complex Concept Insertion Rules: These rules are prebuilt for specific complex concepts and may be activated by the user if his target language has a lexical equivalent for a particular complex concept. For example, the concept *blind* is semantically complex and is not permitted in the semantic representations. Whenever the adjective "blind" is used attributively in a source document, it is replaced in the semantic representations with the relative clause *who is not able to see*. But if the target language has a lexical equivalent for *blind*, the user can activate the complex concept insertion rule which will replace all occurrences of *who is not able to see* in the semantic representations with *blind*.

Styles of Direct Speech: Many languages employ techniques for indicating relative status when two people talk to one another. Therefore in the semantic representations all propositions that are di-

[1] The translation process is often divided into three fundamental steps: 1) analysis: analyze the source document to determine its meaning, 2) transfer: reconstruct that meaning using the target language's lexemes, structures, and world view, and 3) synthesis: synthesize the final surface forms. The term "Transfer Grammar" here refers to the grammar in LA that performs the second step of the translation process.

rect speech are marked with five features indicating: 1) the general category of the speaker (e.g., father, mother, child, political leader, religious leader, employer, employee, etc.), 2) the general category of the listener, 3) the speaker's attitude, 4) the speaker's approximate age, and 5) the age of the speaker relative to the listener. Linguists are able to define the styles of direct speech that are pertinent to the target language, and then use these features and rules to set the style appropriately. Subsequent rules then insert the appropriate pronouns or honorific morphology to indicate the relative status of the speaker to the listener.

Relative Clause Strategies: Extensive typological research has been done regarding relative clauses (Comrie 1989:138, Givón 1990:645), and linguists have found that languages apply a limited number of strategies to a limited number of grammatical relations in what is commonly called the NP Accessibility Hierarchy (Keenan & Comrie 1977, Comrie 1989:156). Cross-linguistically relative clauses may be classified as either embedded or adjoined. If a language uses embedded relative clauses, they may be pre-nominal, post-nominal, or circum-nominal. If a language uses adjoined relative clauses, they are either sentence initial or sentence final. There are generally three strategies for encoding the coreferential noun in a relative clause: the gap strategy, the pronoun retention strategy, and the relative pronoun strategy. The relative clause rules in LA enable a linguist to describe what types of relative clauses are employed in his target language, and which strategies are used at the various positions in the Accessibility Hierarchy.

Collocation Correction Rules: Collocation deals with how certain words go together, and how words and phrases co-occur with certain grammatical choices. Every word in every language has its own collocational range and restrictions. Therefore collocation correction rules are used to change one target word to another target word in a particular environment. For example, in English a king *wears* his crown, but in Korean, a king 쓰다 [sseu da] *uses* his crown. So a collocation correction rule will change the Korean verb 입다 [ip da] 'to wear' to 쓰다 [sseu da] 'to use' whenever the agent is a *king* or *queen* and the patient is a *crown.*

Theta Grid Adjustment Rules: Every verb in every language has an associated theta grid which describes its argument structure. The theta grids for the events in the semantic representations are very similar to the theta grids for the equivalent English verbs. However, the verbs in other languages have different argument structures, so the theta grid adjustment rules enable a linguist to easily restructure an event's arguments according to the theta grid of the target language's equivalent verb. The Korean theta grid adjustment rule for the concept *walk* is shown in Figure 4. That rule inserts the appropriate Korean postpositions into the source and destination phrases.

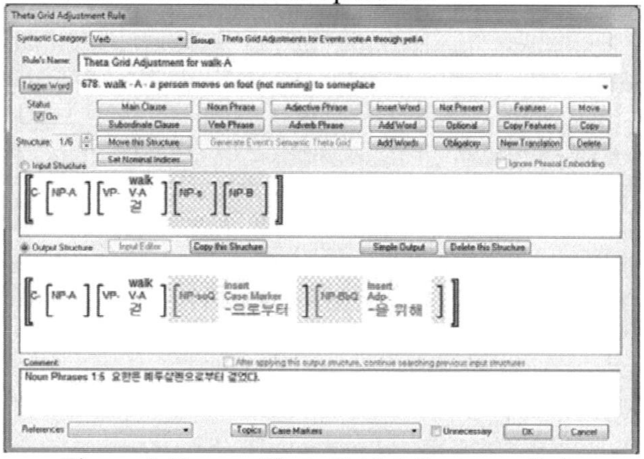

Figure 4. Korean Theta Grid Adjustment Rule

Structural Adjustment Rules: The structural adjustment rules are used to restructure the semantic representations in any way that's necessary in order to construct an appropriate underlying representation for the target language. These rules may be used to handle lexical mismatch, convert predicate adjective constructions to verbal constructions, build clause chains from coranking propositions, make adjustments for various views of time, etc. The structural adjustment rules look identical to the theta grid adjustment rule shown in Figure 4, but they are grouped separately because they perform a variety of tasks.

The final product of the transfer grammar is a new underlying representation that is appropriate for the target language. This underlying representation consists of the target language's words, structures, and features. This underlying representation serves as the input to the synthesizing grammar.

6 LA's Synthesizing Grammar

LA's synthesizing grammar is responsible for synthesizing the final surface forms of the target text.

LA's synthesizing grammar was designed to resemble as closely as possible the descriptive grammars that field linguists routinely write. Before developing this grammar, dozens of descriptive grammars written by field linguists were examined in order to observe the capabilities that are required to synthesize surface text. A model of the final result is shown in Figure 5, and several of these rule types will be briefly described below.

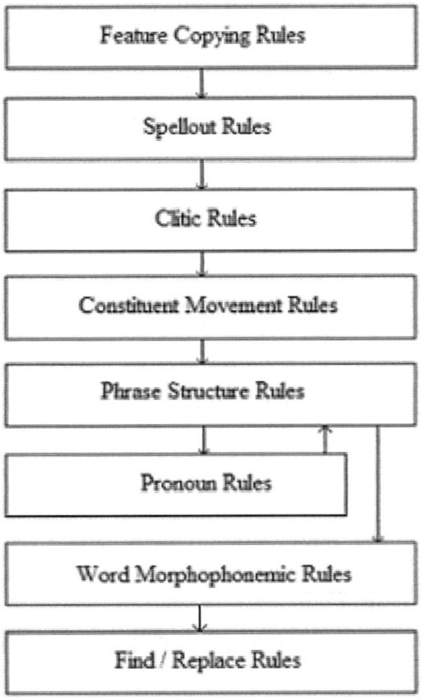

Figure 5. Model of LA's Synthesizing Grammar

Feature Copying Rules: The feature copying rules copy features from one constituent to another constituent so that the spellout rules can add the necessary morphology to indicate appropriate agreement. For example, certain Jula nouns agree in person and number with their object nouns, so a feature copying rule copies the person and number of the object noun to the verb. Then a spellout rule adds the appropriate morphology to the verb.

Spellout Rules: The spellout rules add contextual morphology in order to synthesize the final form of each target word. There are four basic types of spellout rules: (i) simple spellout rules which add a prefix, suffix, infix, circumfix, or a new word to an existing word, or they provide a new translation of a particular target word in a given context; (ii) form selection rules which select a form of a target word from the target lexicon; (iii) morphophonemic rules which perform morphophonemic operations on the affixes that were added to the stem; and (iv) table spellout rules which group a common set of affixes together into a single rule. After these spellout rules have been executed, each target word is in its final surface form. A table spellout rule that adds tense suffixes to Kewa verbs is shown in Figure 6.

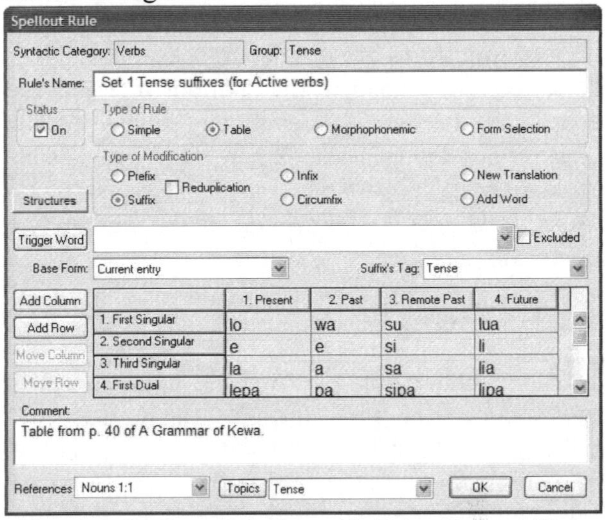

Figure 6. Spellout Rule that adds Kewa Tense Affixes

Clitic Rules: Linguists have found that languages employ three different types of clitics (Payne, 1997): (i) pre-clitics which attach to the beginning of the first word in a phrase, (ii) second position clitics which attach to the end of the first word in a phrase, and (iii) post-clitics which attach to the end of the last word in a phrase. A clitic rule that adds the post-clitic *–me* to Kewa subjects is shown in Figure 7.

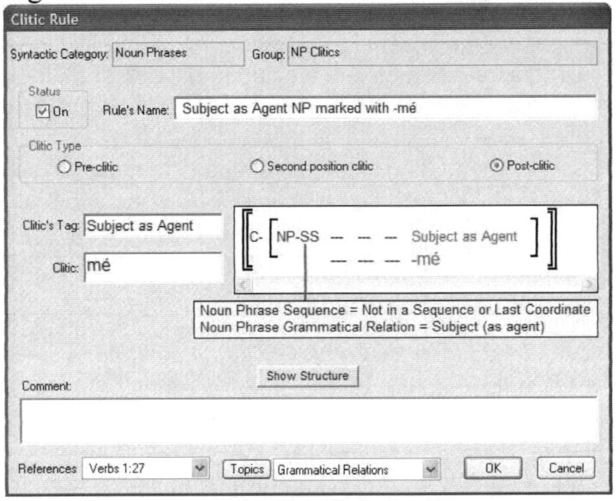

Figure 7. A Clitic Rule for Kewa

Pronoun Rules: There are no pronouns in the semantic representations because each language has its own rules for determining when and where pronouns are appropriate. Therefore, after the phrase structure rules have moved each constituent into its final position, the pronoun rules identify the nominals that should be realized with pronouns, and then supply the appropriate surface forms.

Word Morphophonemic Rules: The word morphophonemic rules are similar to the morphophonemic rules described in the spellout rule section above, but these morphophonemic rules operate across word boundaries rather than morpheme boundaries. For example, the English indefinite article *a* changes to *an* whenever the next word begins with a vowel.

7 LA's Target Text

After the synthesizing grammar has been executed and produced the final form of the target text, mother-tongue speakers edit the text to improve the naturalness and information flow. Samples of English and Korean texts generated by LA are shown in Figure 8. The texts in that figure have not been edited; they are the actual texts that were generated by LA. These texts occur at the beginning of a story that describes how to prevent the spread of Avian Influenza.

One day a doctor named Paulus returned from the market to his village named Terpen. While Paulus had been at the market, some people had told him about a certain disease. So when Paulus returned to his village, he said to Isak, who was the village chief, and the other people who lived in Terpen, "A new disease named Avian Influenza has killed most of the birds that are at the market. This disease has killed many chickens and many ducks.	어느 날 팔러스라는 의사가 시장에서 터펜이라는 자기 마을로 돌아왔다. 팔러스가 시장에 있는 동안 사람들이 팔러스에게 어떤 병에 대해서 말하였다. 그래서 팔러스는 자기 마을로 돌아왔을 때 마을 이장인 아이작과 터펜에 사는 다른 사람들에게 말하였다. "조류 인플루엔자라는 새 병이 시장에 있는 대부분 새들을 죽였습니다. 이 병은 닭들과 오리들을 많이 죽였습니다.

Figure 8. Examples of LA's English and Korean Texts

8 LA's Results

Extensive grammars and lexicons were developed for English, Korean, Kewa, and Jula. We began each project by working through a set of sentences called the Grammar Introduction. The Grammar Introduction consists of approximately 500 basic sentences, each illustrating a particular feature or construction of the semantic representational system. For example, the Grammar Introduction includes a series of propositions dealing with the various tenses, aspects, and moods, there's a set of propositions dealing with relative clauses, object complement clauses, and adverbial clauses, another set of propositions dealing with pronouns, etc. After completing the Grammar Introduction[2], a very thorough foundation has been developed for the lexicon and grammar, but the Grammar Introduction is intentionally restricted to a very small set of concepts. Therefore rules that deal with concept-specific issues must be dealt with while working through actual texts. While working through the semantic representations of these texts, a very clear trend developed for each of the test languages: the number of new grammatical rules required per chapter of text decreased very quickly as seen in Figures 9 through 12.

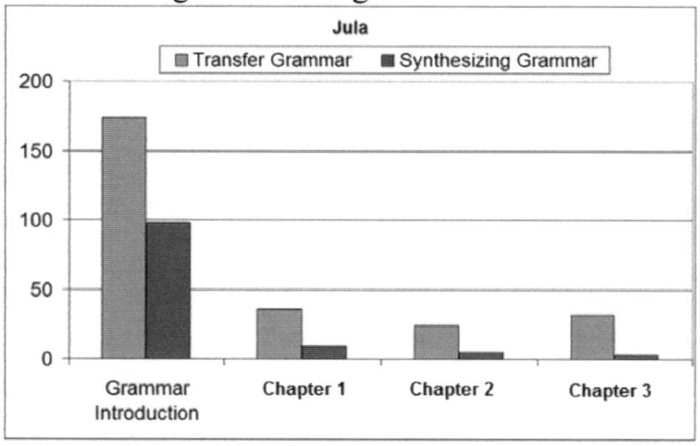

Figure 9. Graph of New Rules for Jula

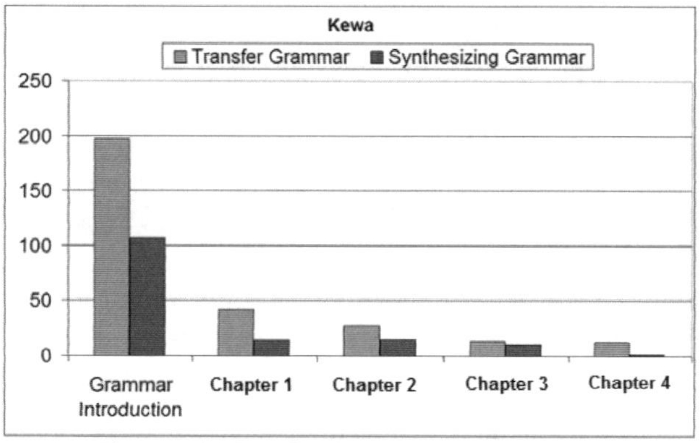

Figure 10. Graph of New Rules for Kewa

[2] For each test language, working through the Grammar Introduction took approximately 40 to 50 hours.

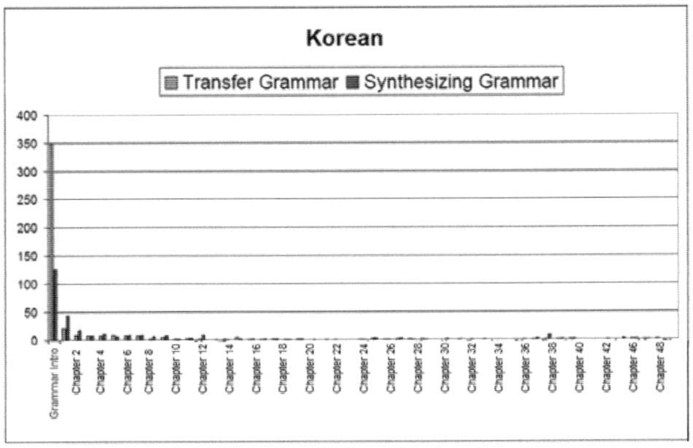

Figure 11. Graph of New Rules for Korean

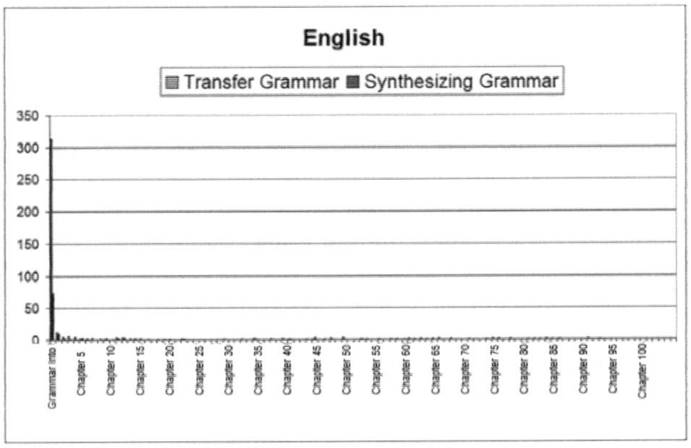

Figure 12. Graph of New Rules for English

The graphs shown above conclusively demonstrate that the grammars developed in LA are accurately capturing the significant generalizations of these four languages.

9 Quality of Generated Texts

After generating texts in Korean, Kewa, and Jula, experiments were performed to determine whether or not the drafts generated by LA are of sufficient quality that they improve the productivity of experienced mother-tongue translators. Two sets of experiments were performed: the first set tested for increased productivity, and the second set tested for quality. The first set compared the quantity of text an experienced translator could translate in a given period of time with the quantity of text generated by LA that the same person could edit in the given time. Eight professional mother-tongue translators participated in the Jula experiment, one translator participated in the Kewa experiment, and eighteen translators participated in the Korean experiment. In these experiments, quantity was determined by word count. Table 2 summarizes the results of these productivity experiments.

Language	Ratio of Edited Words to Manually Translated Words
Jula	4.3
Kewa	6.7
Korean	4.6

Table 2. Summary of Productivity Experiments

The table shown above indicates that in each test language, the drafts generated by LA were of such high quality that they more than quadrupled the productivity of experienced mother-tongue translators. The results of these experiments were certainly encouraging, but at this point we didn't know whether or not the editors had done a thorough job of editing the generated texts. Therefore we performed another set of experiments to determine whether or not the edited texts were comparable in quality with professionally translated texts.

10 Quality of Edited Texts

The second set of experiments was performed with Jula and Korean speakers in order to determine the quality of the edited LA drafts. Speakers of these languages were asked to compare the edited LA texts with the manually translated texts. These evaluations were performed by people who did not know how either of the texts had been produced. Forty evaluations were performed by Jula speakers, and 192 evaluations were performed by Korean speakers. Although no evaluations were performed by Kewa speakers, the edited Kewa draft was ultimately published. Table 3 summarizes the Jula and Korean evaluations.

Language	LA Texts	Manual Texts	Equal
Jula	12	11	17
Korean	88	71	33

Table 3. Summary of the Evaluation Experiments

In Table 3, the column labeled "LA Texts" indicates the number of evaluators who said that the edited LA text was better[3] than the manually translated text, the column labeled "Manual Texts" indicates the number of evaluators who said the manually translated text was better than the edited LA text, and the column labeled "Equal" indicates the number of evaluators who said that the edited LA text was equal in quality to the manually trans-

[3] The term "better" is intentionally very generic. We didn't want to ask the evaluators which text was more natural, or was easier to read, etc. Instead we let the evaluators choose whichever text they thought was better for any reason.

lated text. In both languages the evaluation experiments indicate that the edited LA texts are considered as good as the manually translated texts.

11 Conclusions

LA is a tool which drastically reduces the amount of time and effort required to produce an initial draft of a translation of a text. This tool enables linguists to build large scale lexicons and grammars for a very wide variety of languages, particularly minority and endangered languages. After a lexicon and grammar have been completed, LA generates drafts of texts which are at approximately a sixth grade reading level. We hope to eventually have a large library of community development texts which will describe how to prevent the spread of various diseases such as AIDS, Avian Influenza, etc. This tool works equally well for languages that are thoroughly studied, languages that have only slightly been studied, and languages that are endangered. Similarly, this tool works equally well for languages that are typologically diverse with respect to their morphological and syntactic features. It is hoped that this tool will empower speakers of minority languages around the world by providing them with translations of vital information, which will not only enable them to live longer, healthier, and more productive lives, but will also enable them to participate in the larger world.

References

Allman, Tod. 2010. The Translator's Assistant: A Multilingual Natural Language Generator based on Linguistic Universals, Typologies, and Primitives. Arlington, TX: University of Texas dissertation.

Allman, Tod, and Stephen Beale. 2006. A Natural Language Generator for Minority Languages. In Proceedings of Speech and Language Technology for Minority Languages (SALTMIL). Genoa, Italy.

Beale, Stephen. In print. Documenting Endangered Languages using Linguist's Assistant. Language Documentation and Conservation. Draft available at http:/onyxcons.com/LA/

Beale, Stephen, and Tod Allman. 2011. Linguist's Assistant: a Resource for Linguists. In Proceedings of 5th International Joint Conference on Natural Language Processing (IJCNLP-11), The 9th Workshop on Asian Language Resources, Chiang Mai, Thailand.

Cann, Ronnie. 1993. *Formal Semantics.* Cambridge: Cambridge University Press.

Givón, Talmy. 1990. *Syntax: A Functional-Typological Introduction,* 2 vols. Amsterdam: John Benjamins.

Goddard, Cliff, and Anna Wierzbicka. 1994. *Semantic and Lexical Universals: Theory and Empirical Findings.* Amsterdam: John Benjamins.

Jackendoff, Ray. 1990. *Semantic Structures.* Cambridge, Massachusetts: The MIT Press.

Lakoff, George. 1987. *Women, Fire, and Dangerous Things.* Chicago: University of Chicago Press.

Longacre, Robert. 1996. *The Grammar of Discourse.* 2nd ed. New York: Plenum Press.

Payne, Thomas. 1997, *Describing Morphosyntax.* Cambridge: Cambridge University Press.

Wierzbicka, Anna. 1996. *Semantics: Primes and Universals.* Oxford: Oxford University Press.

"Hidden semantics": what can we learn from the names in an ontology?*

Allan Third
Computing Department, Open University, UK
a.third@open.ac.uk

Abstract

Despite their flat, semantics-free structure, ontology identifiers are often given names or labels corresponding to natural language words or phrases which are very dense with information as to their intended referents. We argue that by taking advantage of this information density, NLG systems applied to ontologies can guide the choice and construction of sentences to express useful ontological information, solely through the verbalisations of identifier names, and that by doing so, they can replace the extremely fussy and repetitive texts produced by ontology verbalisers with shorter and simpler texts which are clearer and easier for human readers to understand. We specify which axioms in an ontology are "defining axioms" for linguistically-complex identifiers and analyse a large corpus of OWL ontologies to identify common patterns among all defining axioms. By generating texts from ontologies, and selectively including or omitting these defining axioms, we show by surveys that human readers are typically capable of inferring information implicitly encoded in identifier phrases, and that texts which do not make such "obvious" information explicit are preferred by readers and yet communicate the same information as the longer texts in which such information is spelled out explicitly.

1 Introduction

There has been increasing interest in recent years in the generation of natural language texts from, or using, ontologies ((Cregan et al., 2007; Kaljurand and Fuchs, 2007; Smart, 2008), for example). Such "verbalisations" – translations of the logic of, for example, OWL (W3C Consortium, 2012), into human-readable natural language – can be useful for a variety of purposes, such as communicating the results of ontology inference, generating custom texts to suit a particular application domain or assisting non-ontology-experts in authoring, reviewing and validating ontologies. This paper takes as its starting point an observation about ontology structure and use. The purpose of an ontology (specifically, the so-called "T-box"[1]) is to define the terms of a particular domain in order to allow automated inference of the semantics of that domain. Given that machines are essentially *tabulae rasae* with regard to nearly any kind of world knowledge, it is therefore necessary to spell out the meanings of most terms in what (to a human) would be excruciating detail. In most, if not all, ontology languages, and certainly in OWL, identifiers – the "names" for individual entities, classes and relations[2] – are atomic units. That is to say, every identifier is treated by the machine as simply a flat string, with no internal structure or semantics. The corresponding natural language constructions – noun and verb phrases – by contrast have a very rich internal structure which can communicate very subtle semantic distinctions. Best practice for human ontology developers recommends that for every entity in an ontology, either its identifier should be a meaningful simple or complex term, or it should have a (localised) label which is a meaningful simple or complex natural language

*Many thanks to Richard Power and Sandra Williams for their help and comments. This work was supported by Engineering and Physical Sciences Research Council Grant Ref. G033579/1.

[1] "Terminology box"

[2] "Property" is the OWL terminology for a relation between two entities

term. For example, in the domain of education, a class intended to represent the real-world class of junior schools ought to have (in English) an identifier such as `junior_school` or a label such as "junior school". Ontology developers who follow this best practice (and, according to (Power, 2010), the vast majority do) produce ontologies in which the entities are easily recognisable and understood by human readers who can parse these identifiers, to infer, for example, that "junior school" is a subclass of the class "school". As it stands, however, a machine will *not* make this inference. In order for the machine to comprehend the semantics of this example, there must additionally be an axiom equivalent to "a junior school is a school".

The motivation for this work is the desire to identify which kinds of identifier or label are "obvious" in this way. That is to say, if we treat an OWL identifier as if it were in fact a multi-word natural language expression, can we infer at least some of its semantics from its properties as a noun phrase, for example? This has two overall purposes: given an existing ontology, definitional axioms for "obvious" identifiers can be omitted when verbalising for a human user, in order to shorten the text and make it more relevant, and, conversely, during the process of ontology creation, if a human uses an obvious identifier, a reasonable guess can be made as to its definitional axiom(s), and these can be presented to the user for confirmation, thus saving the user the need to spend time and energy spelling out the obvious for the machine's purposes. This paper addresses the first of these two purposes. Note that the aim of this work is not particular to consider how best to *realise* entity names in a verbalisation, but rather, how to use the names of entities to *guide* the choice and construction of sentences.

This work was undertaken in the context of the SWAT (Semantic Web Authoring Tool) project, which is investigating the application of NLG/NLP to ontology authoring and editing (Williams et al., 2011),(Williams and Power, 2010),(Power and Third, 2010),(Stevens et al., 2011), (Power, 2010),(The SWAT Project, 2012).

2 Existing work

Other researchers have attempted to take advantage of the internal structure of ontology identifiers to infer semantics, but these have exclusively been concerned with the question of checking or improving an ontology's coverage of its domain. Examples include (Wroe et al., 2003; Fernandez-Breis et al., 2010; Egaña Aranguren et al., 2008). To the best of our knowledge, our current research is the first to take advantage of identifier structure to infer semantics in order to improve verbalisation and produce more human-focused texts.

3 Hypothesis

Informal feedback from existing work indicates that many readers are dissatisfied with the kinds of text produced by ontology verbalisers, feeling them to be somewhat fussy and unnatural. Some of this can no doubt be put down to the verbalisations themselves – it is very difficult to find a natural way to express that one property is the inverse of another without resorting to mathematical variables – but, as with other generation tasks, the problem is not necessarily just how things are said, but also in the selection of which things to say at all. Our hypothesis takes two parts:

1. linguistically-complex identifiers/labels are often defined by "obvious" axioms in the OWL ontologies containing them, and
2. ontology verbalisations which omit such "obvious" axioms lead to a better reading experience for users without sacrificing content.

A prerequisite for these is also the claim that linguistically-complex identifiers are reasonably common in ontologies. (Power, 2010) demonstrated very clearly that recommended best-practice is in fact followed very well in much ontology development, and entities do tend to be given meaningful names.

One caveat is necessary here. We are talking about what an average human reader might reasonably expect to follow from a given use of language. However, observing that a black horse is a horse, a grey horse is a horse, a brown horse is a horse, and so on, does not guarantee the truth of any inferences we might make on encountering a reference to a clothes-horse. There will always be situations in which ordinary uses of language will need to be made more precise. An interesting future direction of this work would be to investigate whether it is possible to detect exactly when such clarification is necessary, in the context of ontology verbalisation, at least.

4 Definitions

Of course, "complex", "obvious", and so on can be loaded terms, and it is necessary to make them precise before continuing.

4.1 Simple and complex identifiers

Identifiers[3] may consist of a single natural language word, in which case we call it *simple*, or multiple words, in which case it is *complex*. The words in a complex identifier may be separated by spaces ("junior school"), punctuation (`junior_school`) or capitalisation (`juniorSchool`). In any case, it is trivial to separate these words into a list automatically.

4.2 Content words

In looking for "defining" axioms, we often need to ignore words occurring in complex identifiers which have some grammatical function. For example, if comparing "has as father" to other identifiers in the same ontology, we may ignore "has" and "as" and consider only the *content word* "father". "Has" occurs far too frequently to be of any use in identifying axioms relating to the semantics of "has as father", although it is of course relevant to what those semantics actually are in any one of such axioms.

4.3 Constructed identifiers

A complex identifier is *constructed* if its component words (or just its content words) are themselves simple identifiers in the containing ontology. For example, if an ontology contains identifiers corresponding to "French", "woman" and "French woman", then "French woman" is a constructed identifier. We may wish to relax this definition slightly to consider constructed identifiers where *most* of the component (content) words are also identifiers, or where component words are morphological variants of other identifiers.

[3]Henceforth, for brevity, "identifier" may mean "OWL identifier", if that is human-meaningful, or it may mean "label", otherwise.

4.4 Defining axioms

The meaning of a constructed identifier can be *defined* in an ontology by axioms in which all, or most, of its component or content words occur as, or in, other identifiers. For example, if there is an identifier `van_driver`, there is likely to be an axiom similar to

A van driver drives a van.

So, for a complex identifier I, we take an axiom A to be a *defining axiom* if:

- A contains at least two distinct identifiers,
- I occurs in A, and either
- for each identifier $J \neq I$ in A, the content words in J are a subset of the content words in I, OR
- the content words in I are a subset of the union of the content words of at least two other identifiers in A.

The third condition is relatively straightforward – a phrase such as "white van man" can be defined in OWL using at most terms corresponding to "white", "van" and "man", but not every word in a complex phrase must appear in its defining axiom. Adjectives often work like this: we accept "a junior school is a school" as being a defining axiom of "junior school", but "junior" only appears in the definiendum. It is worth noting here that a defining axiom need not be the whole of the definition of its definiendum; a complex identifier may have more than one defining axiom associate with it, in which case its definition would be the set of all of its defining axioms.

The fourth condition perhaps seems stranger. The intention here is to capture defining axioms such as

A French woman is a woman whose nationality is French

where "nationality" is *not* a content word of "French woman", and yet there is an underlying relationship between this "extra" word/phrase and one of the content words of "French woman", namely in this case that "French" is a nationality. One goal of future work might be to look into ways to identify such underlying relationships from OWL semantics in order to use them in new contexts.

5 Corpus study

So far, we have given criteria for which identifiers we consider to be linguistically-complex and for which axioms we believe serve as definitions for such identifiers. The immediately obvious question is whether these criteria are useful. To test this, we evaluate them against a corpus of 548 OWL ontologies collected from a variety of sources, include the Tones repository (TONES, 2012), the Swoogle semantic web search engine (Finin et al., 2004) and the Ontology Design Patterns corpus (ODP, 2012). The corpus includes ontologies on a wide range of topics and featuring a variety of authoring styles.

By using the OWL API (OWL API, 2012), a Java program was written to scan through the corpus for identifiers matching the definition of "complex" above, and for each such identifier found, look for defining axioms for it. Of the logical entity types possible in OWL – Named Individuals, Classes, Data- and Object-Properties – it was decided to omit Named Individuals from the current study. Much as with proper nouns in natural language, the names of individuals typically have less internal structure than other kinds of entity or relation names, and those which do have such structure (such as, e.g., "Lake Windermere") are usually very simple. Individuals are also not really "defined" as such. One may state what are deemed to be highly-salient features about them, such as that Lake Windermere is a lake, but this is not a definition. Had we included individuals in this study, it was thought that the large number of non-defined names would artificially depress the statistics and give an inaccurate view of the phenomena being studied. Re-running the analysis including Named Individuals confirmed this hypothesis: less than 10 ontologies in the whole corpus contained any defining axioms for named individuals, with the most common pattern having only 77 occurrences in the whole corpus – a negligible frequency. It would be interesting to look at these cases in more detail, however, to examine what kinds of individual are defined in this way.

Having identified defining axioms across the corpus, the results were then abstracted, by replacing the occurrences of content words of each identifier in an axiom with alphabetic variables, so that

```
SubClassOf(junior_school school)
```

and

```
SubClassOf(domestic_mammal mammal)
```

both become

```
SubClassOf(AB B).
```

The occurrences of each abstracted axiom pattern could then be counted and tabulated. Table 1 shows the most frequent 10 patterns, comprising 43% of all results. Across the whole corpus, 69% of all identifiers were complex, according to our definition, and of those, 45% had at least one defining axiom. These figures indicate that the phenomenon we are investigating is in fact a very common one, and hence that any improvements to ontology verbalisation based on taking advantage of identifier semantics are likely to be significantly useful.

Of all the patterns identified, 64% involve the SubClassOf axiom type ("A junior school is a school"). A further 14% involve InverseObjectProperties ("Bill is father of John if and only if John has father Bill"), and another 14% involve ObjectPropertyDomain or ObjectPropertyRange ("If something has as segment X, then X is a segment"). Collectively, then, these axiom types cover 92% of all defining axioms. An informal glance at the results involving SubClassOf axioms shows that what appears to be the case in Table 1 is generally true – the bulk of the SubClassOf axioms involve some form of adjective construction.

It should be noted here that the intention was to use the absolute bare minimum of linguistic knowledge in identifying these axioms – almost everything is done by matching substrings – in order to avoid influencing the results with our own intuitions about how we think it ought to look. It is reassuring to see nonetheless how far it is possible to get without involving linguistic knowledge. Indeed, one of the ontologies in the test corpus has identifiers in Italian, and it was confirmed by a bilingual English/Italian speaker that the axiom patterns our software identified for that ontology were just as "obvious" in Ital-

Table 1: 10 most frequent patterns of defining axiom

No. of occurrences	Pattern	Example
1430	`SubClassOf(AB B )`	`SubClassOf(representation-activity activity)`
1179	`SubClassOf(ABC BC )`	`SubClassOf(Quantified set builder Set builder)`
455	`InverseObjectProperties(hasA isAof )`	`InverseObjectProperties(HasInput IsInputOf)`
387	`SubClassOf(ABCD BCD )`	`SubClassOf(Continental-Statistical-Water-Area Statistical-Water-Area)`
348	`SubClassOf(ABCD CD )`	`SubClassOf(NonWikipediaWebPage WebPage)`
240	`SubClassOf(ABC AC )`	`SubClassOf(Process-Resource-Relation Process-Relation)`
229	`ObjectPropertyRange(hasA A )`	`ObjectPropertyRange(hasAnnotation Annotation)`
192	`ObjectPropertyRange(hasAB AB )`	`ObjectPropertyRange(hasTrustValue TrustValue)`
188	`InverseObjectProperties(AB ABof )`	`InverseObjectProperties(situation-place situation-place-of)`
179	`InverseObjectProperties(Aof hasA )`	`InverseObjectProperties(contentOf hasContent)`

ian as they are in English. There are limitations, of course. A defining axiom such as "a pet owner is a person who owns a pet" would *not* be picked up by this software, as "owner" and "owns" do not match each other as strings. To bypass this particular limitation, the software has been modified to allow the optional use of a (language-specific) stemming algorithm before substring matching, so that both "owner" and "owns" would be matched as "own", for example. The current work, however, focuses on the non-stemmed results for reasons of simplicity and time; we intend to carry out further research using the stemmed results in future.

6 Generation study

6.1 Design

A core part of our claim for these defining axioms is that their semantics are in some sense "obvious". A human reading a phrase such as "junior school" is unlikely to need to be told explicitly that a junior school is a school. This claim needs to be tested. Furthermore, it was suggested above that ontology verbalisations would be improved in quality for human readers if such "obvious" sentences were omitted and the semantics implied by the internal structure of noun and verb phrases were used to improve verbalisation. Again, it is necessary to test whether any improvement does occur.

In order to test the first of these claims, a survey was designed, in which each question would consist of a (verbalised) identifier phrase, followed by three sentences containing that identifier phrase. Respondents were asked to indicate which of those sentences, if any, they were able to deduce from the phrase itself, without relying on any domain knowledge. The questions were based on the top 8 patterns of defining axiom from Table 1, and the containing ontology of each was verbalised using the SWAT ontology verbalisation tool ((The SWAT Project, 2012)). The choice of 8 was motivated by an intended survey size of 10 to 14 questions allowing for some duplication of patterns in order to vary, e.g., the order of elements in sentences, and to minimise the effects of possible domain knowledge on behalf of respondents.

Figure 1 shows an example of a question from the first survey. The prediction was that respondents would be more likely to select sentences based on a defining axiom pattern than sentences which are not based on any such pattern.

The second claim required a more involved test. It was decided to present respondents with two paragraphs of text, both verbalised from the same set of axioms "about" the same class or property. One paragraph of each pair contains verbalisations of every initial axiom, possibly with common subjects or objects aggregated between sentences (the "full" paragraph). The other omitted the verbalisations of any defining axioms, and allowed aggregation of common elements from *within* identifiers where that was justified by one of the omitted defining axiom. For example, the already-aggregated (in the full paragraph) sentence

The following are kinds of atrium cavity: left atrium cavity, right atrium cavity

was further aggregated to

The following are kinds of atrium cavity: left, right.

because of the defining axioms

A left (right) atrium cavity is an atrium cavity.

This second paragraph is the "simplified" paragraph. Both paragraphs were checked in each case to ensure that the original set of axioms could be

Choose all the sentence(s) which you can deduce from the phrase itself, without relying on any knowledge of the physical or natural world.

*** 6. Posterior booklung spiracle**

- [ ] A posterior booklung spiracle is part of a respiratory system.
- [ ] A posterior booklung spiracle is a booklung spiracle.
- [ ] A posterior booklung spiracle is a booklung.
- [ ] None of the above.

Figure 1: Sample question from survey 1

inferred without any external information, providing an objective guarantee that both carried the same semantic content even if one only did so implicitly. Respondents were asked to judge whether each pair of paragraphs expressed the same information, to express a preference (or lack of preference) for one paragraph over the other, and to select those sentences from each paragraph which conveyed information which was not conveyed by the other paragraph. Figure 2 shows an example survey question.

Three hypotheses were tested simultaneously by this survey. The first was that respondents would be able to detect when two paragraphs contained the same information at a probability significantly greater than chance and the second that respondents would tend to prefer the simplified paragraphs. The third hypothesis was that respondents would be unlikely to label information as being "missing" from a paragraph when that information was implicitly expressed.

Our initial survey design also included pairs of paragraphs which genuinely did contain different information, to serve as a control, and so respondents' ability to judge pairs of paragraphs as carrying the same information would be compared to their ability to judge when the presence of different information. However, in piloting that design, nearly every respondent reported such examples as being highly confusing and distracting. This is perhaps not surprising; the task of telling when two texts express the same content is not symmetrical with the task of telling when they express different content. The latter is considerably easier, by virtue of the fact that different content will involve different words or phrases, or noticably different sentence structures. Because of this, the decision was taken only to test texts which objectively did contain the same logical content, and to compare the results to chance. Each paragraph pair was controlled to minimise the effects of ordering of information and, where possible, of length.

To maximise take-up and completion, it was decided to try to keep the length of time taken to complete each survey down to around five minutes. Consequently, survey 1 had 14 of the relatively simple identifier inference questions and survey 2 had 4 of the more complex paragraph-comparison questions. Both surveys were published via SurveyMonkey (Monkey, 2012) and were publicised via the social networking sites Twitter (Twitter, 2012), Facebook (Facebook, 2012) and Google+ (Google+, 2012).

6.2 Results and evaluation

The first survey attracted 30 respondents, the second 29. The data collected from the first survey are summarised in Table 2, where S is "sentence predicted to be obvious by a defining axiom pattern" and J is "sentence judged inferrable from the given identifier". Applying a 2×2 χ^2 contingency test results in $\chi^2 = 342.917$, $df = 1$ and $P < 0.0001$, indicating an extremely significant association between the predicted obviousness of a sentence and respondent judgement of that sentence as following from the given identifier.

It is interesting, however, to note the top row of Table 2: for sentences which are predicted to hold, human judges are ambivalent as to whether to judge it as definitely true or not. One interpretation of this result is that, while it is very clear that *non*-defining axioms can *not* be inferred from identifier phrases, people are hesitant to commit to *asserting* these axioms in an unfamiliar domain, perhaps for fear of an unknown exception to the general rule. For example,

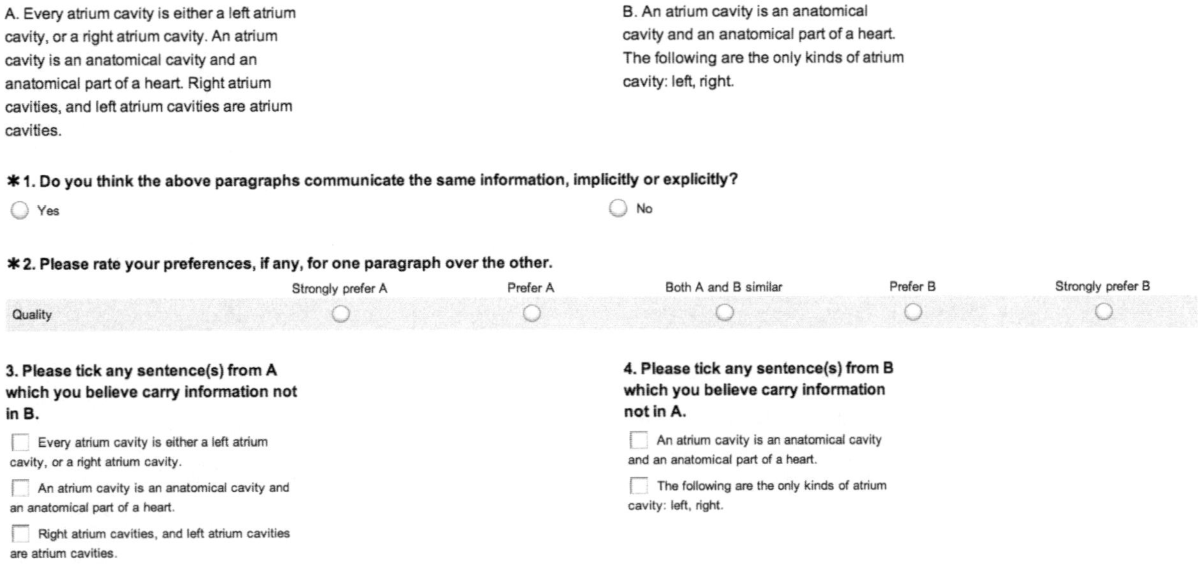

Figure 2: Sample question from survey 2

while "a Qualifier Noun is a Noun" is usually a good rule of thumb, "a clothes-horse is a horse" is a clear counterexample. So perhaps the better interpretation of these results would be to say that, presented for example with a phrase of the form "Qualifier Noun", a reader would not be surprised if it turned out that the entity referred to is also a "Noun". Either way, these statistics suggest that it could well be safe, when generating texts, to omit defining axioms and allow readers' default assumptions to apply. A simple improvement suggests itself. In the situation where a particular defining axiom pattern would be predicted, but its negation is in fact present, the said negation is automatically highly-salient. It is always likely to be worthwhile verbalising "a clothes-horse is not a horse."

Table 2: Results of the survey on identifier inference.

	J	not J
S	224	211
not S	44	739

It is also interesting to separate out the results of this survey by type of axiom. There were three general families of defining axiom type tested – SubClassOf ("A junior school is a school"), InverseObjectProperties ("Bill is father of John if and only if John has father Bill") and ObjectPropertyRange ("If something has as segment X, then X is a segment"). Table 3 shows the results broken down by these categories, where "SC" is SubClassOf, "IOP" is InverseObjectProperties" and "OPR" is ObjectPropertyRange.

Table 3: Breakdown of identifier inference results by axiom type.

	J	not J
SC	152	109
IOP	52	64
OPR	20	38

A 3×2 χ^2 test results in $\chi^2 = 13.54$, $df = 2$ and $P = 0.001148$, indicating that the judgement of a sentence as obvious or not varies to a significant degree with the type of sentence it is. This is perhaps to be expected, given that not all axiom-types can be verbalised by sentences of similar linguistic complexities. In particular, it is very difficult to see how to verbalise ObjectPropertyRange sentences without appealing to the use of variables such as X and Y, which tend to lead to rather clunky sentences. Sentences corresponding to SubClassOf axioms are most likely to be judged as obvious. Further work is necessary to determine the reasons for these differences empirically.

Table 4: Results of paragraph comparison survey (I)

	Yes	No
Same info	74	22
Prefer simplified paragraph	61	24

Table 4 summarises the results of the "same information" and "preference" questions from the paragraph-comparison survey, aggregated across questions. Comparing each of these to a random distribution of Yes/No answers gives, in turn, $\chi^2 = 15.198$, $df = 1$ and $P < 0.0001$ (same information) and $\chi^2 = 8.498$, $df = 1$ and $P = 0.0036$ (preference), indicating an extremely significant likelihood of judging two paragraphs containing the same information as in fact doing so, and a significant likelihood of preferring the more concise of such paragraphs.

More interesting are the results shown in Table 5. Here, taken across all paragraph-pairs, E denotes that the information expressed by a sentence in one paragraph is explicitly expressed in the other paragraph, and J denotes the judgement as to whether each sentence was judged to express information *not* also expressed in the other paragraph. These distributions of observations need to be compared, for explicit and implicit in turn, to the expected distributions of judgements as to whether the information is missing or not. For explicit information, the expected distribution is zero judgements of "missing" – where sentences were explicit in both paragraphs, they were in fact identical in both paragraphs and so should never have been judged missing – and 696 judgements of "not missing". It scarcely needs a statistical test to show that the actual observations of 3, and 693, respectively, do not differ significantly from these expectations. Nonetheless, Fisher's exact test (since one of the expected values is 0, ruling out χ^2) gives P=0.2495. For implicit information, the null hypothesis is that implicit information is indistinguishable from absent information, and so the expected distribution is 290 judgements of "missing" and zero judgements of "not missing", compared to observations of 33, and 257, respectively. Applying Fisher's exact test gives P less than 0.0001, indicating an extremely significant difference. In other words, implicit information is readily distinguishable from absent information, as predicted.

Table 5: Results of paragraph comparison survey (II)

	J	not J
E	3	693
not E	33	257

7 Conclusion and further work

Beginning from some observations about identifier use and semantics in ontologies, we posed two hypotheses, that linguistically-complex identifiers are often defined by "obvious" axiom patterns in terms of the content words contained in those identifiers, and that these "obvious" axiom patterns could be omitted from ontology verbalisations in order to produce clearer texts without significant information loss. By means of an ontology corpus study, and the survey evaluation of generated NL texts with human readers, we have confirmed these hypotheses. As a result, these generation strategies have already been incorporated into the SWAT ontology verbaliser and ontology authoring tool and are already being evaluated in use by ontology developers as those tools progress.

Of course, there are many avenues along which this work could be taken further. We have barely scratched the surface when it comes to using underlying logical formalisms, and the information "hidden" in identifiers to improve generated text. Further investigation of the possibilities of language-specific stemming algorithms in defining-axiom-pattern detection, the interactions between multiple defining axioms for the same entities to form whole definitions, and exploitation of the logical contents of an ontology to determine the salience of "usual" or "unusual" features in order to aid text organisation, all offer rich opportunities to improve natural-language generation from ontologies. We look forward to being able to look further into these areas, and to identifying which of these phenomena can perhaps be generalised to other NLG applications by means of ontologies.

References

Anne Cregan, Rolf Schwitter, and Thomas Meyer. 2007. Sydney owl syntax - towards a controlled natural language syntax for owl 1.1. In *OWLED*.

M. Egaña Aranguren, C. Wroe, C. Goble, and R. Stevens. 2008. In situ migration of handcrafted ontologies to reason-able forms. *Data & Knowledge Engineering*, 66(1):147–162.

Facebook. 2012. Facebook. http://www.facebook.com. Last checked: 10th February 2012.

J. Fernandez-Breis, L. Iannone, I. Palmisano, A. Rector, and R. Stevens. 2010. Enriching the gene ontology via the dissection of labels using the ontology pre-processor language. *Knowledge Engineering and Management by the Masses*, pages 59–73.

Tim Finin, Yun Peng, R. Scott, Cost Joel, Sachs Anupam Joshi, Pavan Reddivari, Rong Pan, Vishal Doshi, and Li Ding. 2004. Swoogle: A search and metadata engine for the semantic web. In *In Proceedings of the Thirteenth ACM Conference on Information and Knowledge Management*, pages 652–659. ACM Press.

Google+. 2012. Google+. http://plus.google.com, February. Last checked: 10th February 2012.

Kaarel Kaljurand and Norbert E. Fuchs. 2007. Verbalizing owl in attempto controlled english. In *Proceedings of Third International Workshop on OWL: Experiences and Directions, Innsbruck, Austria (6th–7th June 2007)*, volume 258.

Survey Monkey. 2012. Survey monkey. http://www.surveymonkey.com. Last checked: 10th February 2012.

ODP. 2012. Ontology design patterns. http://ontologydesignpatterns.org. Last checked: 10th February 2012.

OWL API. 2012. The OWL API. http://owlapi.sourceforge.net. Last checked: 10th February 2012.

Richard Power and Allan Third. 2010. Expressing OWL axioms by English sentences: dubious in theory, feasible in practice. In *23rd International Conference on Computational Linguistics*.

Richard Power. 2010. Complexity assumptions in ontology verbalisation. In *48th Annual Meeting of the Association for Computational Linguistics*.

Paul R Smart. 2008. Controlled natural languages and the semantic web. July.

R. Stevens, J. Malone, S. Williams, R. Power, and A. Third. 2011. Automating generation of textual class definitions from owl to english. *Journal of Biomedical Semantics*, 2(Suppl 2):S5.

The SWAT Project. 2012. Last checked: 10th February 2012.

TONES. 2012. The TONES ontology repository. http://owl.cs.manchester.ac.uk/repository/browser. Last checked: 10th February 2012.

Twitter. 2012. Twitter. http://twitter.com. Last checked: 10th February 2012.

W3C Consortium. 2012. Last checked: 10th February 2012.

Sandra Williams and Richard Power. 2010. Grouping axioms for more coherent ontology descriptions. In *6th International Natural Language Generation Conference*, pages 197–202.

Sandra Williams, Allan Third, and Richard Power. 2011. Levels of organisation in ontology verbalisation. In *Proceedings of the 13th European Workshop on Natural Language Generation (forthcoming)*.

CJ Wroe, R. Stevens, CA Goble, and M. Ashburner. 2003. A methodology to migrate the gene ontology to a description logic environment using. In *Pacific Symposium on Biocomputing*, volume 8, pages 624–635.

On generating coherent multilingual descriptions of museum objects from Semantic Web ontologies

Dana Dannélls
Språkbanken
Department of Swedish
University of Gothenburg, Sweden
dana.dannells@svenska.gu.se

Abstract

During the last decade, there has been a shift from developing natural language generation systems to developing generic systems that are capable of producing natural language descriptions directly from Web ontologies. To make these descriptions coherent and accessible in different languages, a methodology is needed for identifying the general principles that would determine the distribution of referential forms. Previous work has proved through cross-linguistic investigations that strategies for building coreference are language dependent. However, to our knowledge, there is no language generation methodology that makes a distinction between languages about the generation of referential chains. To determine the principles governing referential chains, we gathered data from three languages: English, Swedish and Hebrew, and studied how coreference is expressed in a discourse. As a result of the study, a set of language specific coreference strategies were identified. Using these strategies, an ontology-based multilingual grammar for generating written natural language descriptions about paintings was implemented in the Grammatical Framework. A preliminary evaluation of our method shows language-dependent coreference strategies lead to better generation results.

createdBy (Guernica, PabloPicasso) currentLocation (Guernica, MuseoReinaSofía) hasColor (Guernica, White) hasColor (Guernica, Gray) hasColor (Guernica, Black)
Guernica is created by Pablo Picasso. **Guernica** has as current location the Museo Reina Sofía. **Guernica** has as color White, Gray and Black.

Figure 1: A natural language description generated from a set of ontology statements.

1 Introduction

During the last decade, there has been a shift from developing natural language generation systems to developing generic systems that are capable of producing natural language descriptions directly from Web ontologies (Schwitter and Tilbrook, 2004; Fuchs et al., 2008; Williams et al., 2011). These systems employ controlled language mechanisms and Natural Language Generation (NLG) technologies such as discourse structures and simple aggregation methods to verbalise Web ontology statements, as exemplified in figure 1.

If we want to adapt such systems to the generation of coherent multilingual object descriptions, at least three language dependent problems must be faced, viz. lexicalisation, aggregation and generation of referring expressions. The ontology itself may contain the lexical in-

Guernica is created by Pablo Picasso. **It** has as current location the Museo Reina Sofía. **It** has as color White, Gray and Black.
Guernica målades av Pablo Picasso. **Den** finns på Museo Reina Sofía. **Den** är målad i vitt, svart och grått.

Figure 2: A museum object description generated in English and Swedish.

formation needed to generate natural language (McCrae et al., 2012) but it may not carry any information either about the aggregation of semantic concepts or the generation of a coherent discourse from referring expressions. Halliday and Hasan (1976), and other well known theories such as Centering Theory (Grosz et al., 1995), propose establishing a coherent description by replacing the entity referring to the Main Subject Reference (MSR) with a pronoun – a replacement which might result in simple descriptions such as illustrated in figure 2. Although these descriptions are coherent, i.e. they have a connectedness that contributes to the reader's understanding of the text, they are considered non-idiomatic and undeveloped by many readers because of consecutive pronouns – a usage which in this particular context is unacceptable.

Since previous theories do not specify the types of linguistic expressions different entities may bear in different languages or domains, there remain many open questions that need to be addressed. The question addressed here is the choice of referential forms to replace a sequence of pronouns, which makes the discourse coherent in different languages. Our claim is that different languages use different linguistic expressions when referring to a discourse entity depending on the semantic context. Hence a natural language generator must employ language dependent coreferential strategies to produce coherent descriptions. This claim is based on cross-linguistic investigations into how coreference is expressed, depending on the target language and the domain (Givón, 1983; Hein, 1989; Ariel, 1990; Prince, 1992; Vallduví and Engdahl, 1996).

In this paper we present a contrasting study conducted in English, Swedish and Hebrew to learn how coreference is expressed. The study was carried out in the domain of art, more specifically focusing on naturally-occurring museum object descriptions. As a result of the study, strategies for generating coreference in three languages are suggested. We show how these strategies are captured in a grammar developed in the Grammatical Framework (GF).[1] We evaluated our method by experimenting with lexicalised semantic web ontology statements which were structured according to particular organizing principles. The result of the evaluation shows language-dependent coreference strategies lead to better generation results.

2 Related work

Also Prasad (2003) employed a corpus-based methodology to study the usage of referring expressions. Based on the results of the analysis, he developed an algorithm to generate referential chains in Hindi. Other algorithms for characterizing referential expressions based on corpus studies have been proposed and implemented in Japanese (Walker et al., 1996), Italian (Di Eugenio, 1998), Catalan and Spanish (Potau, 2008), and Romanian (Harabagiu and Maiorano, 2000).

Although there has been computational work related to Centering for generating a coherent text (Kibble and Power, 2000; Barzilay and Lee, 2004; Karamanis et al., 2009), we are not aware of any methodology or NLG system that employs ontologies to guide the generation of referential chains depending on the language considered.

3 Data collection, annotations and analysis

3.1 Material

To study the domain-specific conventions and the ways of signalling linguistic content in En-

[1] http://www.grammaticalframework.org/

glish, Swedish and Hebrew, we collected object descriptions written by native speakers of each language from digital libraries that are available through on-line museum databases. The majority of the Swedish descriptions were taken from the World Culture Museum.[2] The majority of the English descriptions were collected from the Metropolitan Museum.[3] The majority of the Hebrew descriptions were taken from Artchive.[4] Table 1 gives an overview of the three text collections. In addition, we extracted 40 parallel texts that are available under the sub-domain *Painting* from Wikipedia.

Number of	Eng.	Swe.	Heb.
Descriptions	394	386	110
Tokens	42792	27142	5690
Sentences	1877	2214	445
Tokens/sentence	24	13	13
Sentences/description	5	6	4

Table 1: Statistics of the text collections.

3.2 Syntactic annotation

All sentences in the reference material were tokenised, part-of-speech tagged, lemmatized, and parsed using open-source software. We used Hunpos, an open-source Hidden Markov Model (HMM) tagger (Halácsy et al., 2007) and Maltparser, version 1.4 (Nivre et al., 2007). The English model for tagging was downloaded from the Hunpos web page.[5] The model for Swedish was trained on the Stockholm Umeå Corpus (SUC) and is available to download from the Swedish Language Bank web page.[6] The Hebrew tagger and parsing models are described in Goldberg and Elhadad (2010).

3.3 Semantic annotation

The texts were semantically annotated by the author. The annotation schema for the semantic annotation is taken from the CIDOC Conceptual Reference Model (CRM) (Crofts et al., 2008).[7] Ten of the CIDOC-CRM concepts were employed to annotate the data semantically. These are given in table 2. Examples of semantically annotated texts are given in figure 3.[8]

Actor	Man-Made_Object
Actor Appellation	Material
Collection	Place
Dimension	Time-span
Legal Body	Title

Table 2: The semantic concepts for annotation.

3.4 Referential expressions annotation

The task of identifying referential instances of a painting entity, which is our main subject reference, requires a meaningful semantic definition of the concept *Man-Made Object*. Such a fine-grained semantic definition is available in the ontology of paintings (Dannélls, 2011),[9] which was developed in the Web Ontology Language (OWL) to allow expressing useful descriptions of paintings.[10] The ontology contains specific concepts of painting types, examples of the hierarchy of concepts that are specified in the ontology are listed below.

subClassOf(Artwork, E22_Man-Made_Object)

subClassOf(Painting, Artwork)

subClassOf(PortraitPainting, Painting and
depicts(Painting, AnimateThing))

subClassOf(OilPainting, Painting and
hasMaterial(Painting, OilPaint))

When analysing the corpus-data, we look closer at two linguistic forms of reference expressions: definite noun phrases and pronouns, focusing on three semantic relations: direct hypernym (for example *Painting* is direct hypernym of *Portrait Painting*), higher hypernym (for example, both *Artwork* and *Man-Made Object* are higher hypernyms of *Portrait Painting*) and

[2] http://collections.smvk.se/pls/vkm/rigby.welcome
[3] http://www.metmuseum.org
[4] http://www.artchive.com/
[5] http://code.google.com/p/hunpos/downloads/list
[6] http://spraakbanken.gu.se/
[7] http://cidoc.ics.forth.gr/
[8] In the Hebrew examples we use a Latin transliteration instead of the Hebrew alphabet.
[9] http://spraakdata.gu.se/svedd/painting-ontology/painting.owl
[10] http://www.w3.org/TR/owl-features/

Eng: (1) [[The Starry Night]$_{Man-Made\_Object}$]$_i$ is [[a painting]$_{Man-Made\_Object}$]$_i$ by [[Dutch Post-Impressionist artist]$_{Actor\_Appellation}$]$_j$ [[Vincent van Gogh]$_{Actor}$]$_j$. (2) Since [1941]$_{Time-Span}$ [[it]$_{Man-Made\_Object}$]$_i$ has been in the permanent collection of [the Museum of Modern Art]$_{place}$, [New York City]$_{Place}$. (3) Reproduced often, [[the painting]$_{Man-Made\_Object}$]$_i$ is widely hailed as his magnum opus.
Swe: (1) [[Stjärnenatten]$_{Man-Made\_Object}$]$_i$ är [[en målning]$_{Man-Made\_Object}$]$_i$ av [[den nederländske postimpressionistiske konstnären]$_{Actor\_Appellation}$]$_j$ [[Vincent van Gogh]$_{Actor}$]$_j$ från [1889]$_{Time-Span}$. (2) Sedan [1941]$_{Time-Span}$ har [[den]$_{Man-Made\_Object}$]$_i$ varit med i den permanenta utställningen vid [det moderna museet]$_{place}$ i [New York]$_{Place}$. (3) [[Tavlan]$_{Man-Made\_Object}$]$_i$ har allmänt hyllats som [[hans]$_{Actor}$]$_j$ magnum opus och har reproducerats många gånger och är [en av [[hans]$_{Actor}$]$_j$ mest välkända målningar]$_{Man-Made\_Object}$]$_i$.
Heb: (1) [[lila 'ohavim]$_{Man-Made\_Object}$]$_i$ hyno [[stiyor śhemen]$_{Man-Made\_Object}$]$_i$ śel [[hastayar haholandi]$_{Actor\_Appellation}$]$_j$ [[vincent van gogh]$_{Actor}$]$_j$, hametoharac lesnat [1889]$_{Time-Span}$. (2) [[hastiyor]$_{Man-Made\_Object}$]$_i$ mostag kayom [bemozehon lehomanot modernit]$_{place}$ [sebahir new york]$_{Place}$. (3) [[ho]$_{Man-Made\_Object}$]$_i$ exad hastiyorim hayedoyim beyoter sel [[van gogh]$_{Actor}$]$_j$.

Figure 3: A comprehensive semantic annotation example.

synonym, i.e. two different linguistic units of reference expressions belonging to the same concept.

3.5 Data analysis and results

The analysis consisted of two phases: (1) analyse the texts for discourse patterns, and (2) analyse the texts for patterns of coreference in the discourse.

Discourse patterns A discourse pattern (DP) is an approach to text structuring through which particular organizing principles of the texts are defined through linguistic analysis. The approach follows McKeown (1985) to formalize principles of discourse for use in a computational process. Following this approach, we have identified three discourse patterns for describing paintings that are common in the three languages. These are summarised below.

- **DP1** Man-Made_Object, Object-Type, Actor, Time-span, Place, Dimension
- **DP2** Man-Made_Object, Time-span, Object-Type, Actor, Dimension, Place
- **DP3** Man-Made_Object, Actor, Time-span, Dimension, Place

Patterns of coreference In the analysis for coreference, we only considered entities appearing in subject positions. Below follows examples of the most common types of coreference found in the corpus-data.

As seen in (1b) and in many other examples, the first reference expressions are the definite noun phrase *the painting*, i.e. coreference is build through the direct hypernym relation. The choice of the reference expression in the following sentence (1c) is the definite noun phrase *the work*, which is a higher hypernym of the main subject of reference *The Old Musician*.

(1) a. The Old Musician is an 1862 painting by French painter, Édouard Manet.
b. **The painting** shows the influence of the work of Gustave Courbet.
c. **This work** is one of Manet's largest paintings and **Ø** is now conserved at the National Gallery of Art in Washington.

Sentence (2b) shows a noun is avoided; the linguistic unit of the reference expression is a pronoun preceding a conjunction, followed by an ellipsis.

(2) a. The Birth of Venus is a painting by the French artist Alexandre Cabanel.
b. **It** was painted in 1863, and **Ø** is now in the Musée d'Orsay in Paris.

In the Swedish texts we also find occurrences of pronouns in the second sentence of the discourse, as in (3b). We learn that the most common linguistic units of the reference expressions also are definite noun phrases given by the direct hypernym relation.

(3) a. Stjärnenatten är en målning av den nederländske postimpressionistiske konstnären Vincent van Gogh från 1889.
b. Sedan 1941 har **den** varit med i den permanenta utställningen vid det moderna museet i New York.
c. **Tavlan** har allmänt hyllats som hans magnum opus och har reproducerats många gånger.

((a) The Starry Night is a painting by the dutch artist Vincent van Gogh, created in 1889. (b) Since 1941 **it** was in the permanent exhibition of the museum in New York. (c) **The picture** is widely hailed as his magnum opus and has been reproduced many times.)

Similar to English, the most common linguistic units of the reference expressions are definite noun phrases, as in (4b). However, the relation of these phrases with respect to the main subject of reference is either a direct hypernym or a synonym, such as *tavlan* in (3c) and (5b).

(4) a. Wilhelm Tells gåta är en målning av den surrealistiske konstnären Salvador Dalí.
b. **Målningen** utfördes 1933 och **Ø** finns idag på Moderna museet i Stockholm.

((a) Wilhelm Tell's Street is a painting by the artist Salvador Dali. (b) **The painting** was completed in 1933 and today it is stored in the modern museum in Stockholm.)

(5) a. Baptisterna är en målning av Gustaf Cederström från 1886, och **Ø** föreställer baptister som samlats för att förrätt dop.
b. **Tavlan** finns att beskåda i Betel folkhögskolas lokaler.

((a) The Baptists is a painting by Gustaf Cederström from 1886, and depicts baptists that have gathered for a bad. (b) **The picture** can be seen in Betel at the people's high school premises.)

The Hebrew examples also include definite noun phrases determined by the direct hypernym relation, as *hastiyor* in (6b). Pronouns only occur in a context that contains a comparison, for example (6c). In other cases, e.g. (7b), (7c), the relation selected for the reference expression is higher-hypernym.

(6) a. lila 'ohavim hyno stiyor ŝhemen ŝel hasayar haholandi vincent van gogh, hametoharac lesnat 1889.
b. **hastiyor** mosag kayom bemozehon lehomanot modernit sebahir new york.
c. **ho exad hastiyorim** hayedoyim beyoter sel van gogh.

((a) The Starry Night is an oil painting by the dutch painter Vincent van Gogh, created in 1899. (b) **The painting** is stored in the Museum of Modern Art in New York. (c) **It** is one of the most famous works of Vincent van Gogh.)

(7) a. hahalmon nehaviyon ho stiyor sel pablo picasso hametaher hames zonot.
b. **hayestira** sestzoyra ben ha sanyim 1906-1907 nehsevet lehahat min heyestirot hayedohot sel picasso vesel hahomanot hamodernit.
c. **hayestira** mosteget kayom bemostehon lehomanot modernitt sebe new york.

((a) The Young Ladies of Avignon is a painting by Pablo Picasso that portrays five prostitutes. (b) **The artwork** that was painted during 1906-1907 is one of the most known works by Picasso in the modern art. (c) **The artwork** can today be seen in the Museum of Modern Art in New York City.)

The synonym relation occurs when giving the dimensions of the painting, as in (8b).

(8) a. Soded haken (1568) ho stiyor semen al luax est meet hastayar hapalmi peter broigel haav.

b. **hatmona** hi begodel 59 al 68 centimeter, ve **Ø** motseget bemozeon letoldot haaomanot bevina.

((a) The Nest thief (1568) is an oil painting made on wood by the painter Peter Brogel Hav. (b) **The picture** measures 59 x 68 cm, and is displayed in the art museum in Vienna.)

3.6 The results of the analysis

The above examples show a range of differences in the way chains of coreference are constructed. Table 3 summarizes the results the analysis revealed. 1st, 2nd and 3rd correspond to the first, second and third reference expression in the discourse. In summary, we found:

- Pronoun is common in Swedish and English, and rare in Hebrew
- Direct-hypernym is common in English, Swedish and Hebrew
- Higher-hypernym is rare in English and Swedish, and common in Hebrew
- Synonym is common in Swedish, less frequent in English, and rare in Hebrew

DP	English			Swedish			Hebrew		
	1st	2nd	3rd	1st	2nd	3rd	1st	2nd	3rd
1	DH	P		DH	P		DH	Ø	
1	DH	HH	Ø	DH	Ø		DH		
1	P	Ø		P	Ø				
1	P	P	Ø	Ø	DH				
1				Ø	P	DH			
1,2	P	DH		P	S	Ø			
2							HH	HH	
2							HH	Ø	HH
3	P	DH		P	DH				

Table 3: Coreference strategies for a painting object realisation. Pronoun (P), Synonym (S), Direct Hypernym (DH), Higher Hypernym (HH), Ellipsis (Ø).

Although the identified strategies are constrained by a relatively simple syntax and a domain ontology, they show clear differences between the languages. As table 3 shows, consecutive pronouns occur commonly in English, while consecutive higher hypernym noun phrases are common in Hebrew.

4 Generating referential chains from Web ontology

4.1 Experimental data

We made use of the data available in the painting ontology presented in section 3.4 to generate multilingual descriptions by following the domain discourse patterns. The data consists of around 1000 ontology statements and over 250 lexicalised entities extracted from the Swedish National Museums of World Culture and the Gothenburg City Museum.

4.2 The generation grammar

The grammar was implemented in GF, a grammar formalism oriented toward multilingual grammar development and generation (Ranta, 2004). It is a logical framework based on a general treatment of syntax, rules, and proofs by means of a typed λ-calculus with dependent types (Ranta, 1994). Similar to other logical formalisms, GF separates between abstract and concrete syntaxes. The abstract syntax reflects the type theoretical part of a grammar. The concrete syntax is formulated as a set of linearization rules that can be superimposed on an abstract syntax to generate words, phrases, sentences, and texts of a desirable language. In addition, GF has an associated grammar library (Ranta, 2009); a set of parallel natural language grammars that can be used as a resource for various language processing tasks.

Our grammar consists of one abstract module that reflects the domain knowledge and is common to all languages, plus three concrete modules, one for each language, which encode the language dependent strategies. Rather than giving details of the grammatical formalism, we will show how GF captures the constraints presented in section 3.6. The examples include the following GF constructors: `mkText` (Text), `mkPhr` (Phrase), `mkS` (Sentence), `mkCl` (Clause), `mkNP` (Noun Phrase), `mkVP` (Verb Phrase), `mkAdv` (Verb Phrase modifying adverb), `passiveVP` (Passive Verb Phrase), `mkN` (Noun).

English

```
painting paintingtype painter
                year museum = let
str1 : Phr = mkPhr
(mkS (mkCl (mkNP painting) (mkVP
(mkVP  (mkNP
(mkNP a_Art paintingtype) make_V2))
(mkAdv by8agent_Prep
(mkNP (mkNP  painter)
(mkAdv in_Prep year.s)))))));
str2 : Phr = mkPhr (mkS
(mkCl (mkNP the_Art paintingtype)
(mkVP (passiveVP display_V2)
(mkAdv at_Prep  museum.s))))
in mkText str1 (mkText str2) ;
```

Swedish

```
painting paintingtype painter
                year museum = let
str1 : Phr = mkPhr
(mkS (mkCl (mkNP  painting)
(mkVP (mkVP
(mkNP a_Art paintingtype))
(mkAdv by8agent_Prep
(mkNP (mkNP painter)
(mkAdv from_Prep (mkNP year)))))));
str2 :  Phr = mkPhr
(mkS (mkCl (mkNP the_Art
(mkN "tavla" "tavla"))
(mkVP (mkVP (depV  finna_V))
(mkAdv on_Prep (mkNP museum)))) )
in mkText str1 (mkText str2) ;
```

Hebrew

```
painting paintingtype painter
                year museum = let
str1 : Str = ({s =  painting.s ++
paintingtype.s ++  "sl " ++
painter.s ++ "msnt " ++ year.s}).s;
str2 : Str = ({s = artwork_N.s ++
(displayed_V ! Fem) ++ at_Prep.s ++
museum.s}).s in
ss (str1 ++ " ." ++ str2 ++ " ." );
```

The above extracts from the concrete modules follow the observed organization principles concerning the order of semantic information in a discourse and the generation of language-dependent referential chains (presented in the right-hand column of table 4). In these extracts, variations in referential forms are captured in the noun phrase of *str2*. In the English module, the *paintingtype* that is the direct hypernym of the painting object is coded, while in the Swedish module, a synonym word of the painting concept is coded, e.g *tavla*. In the Hebrew module, a higher concept in the hierarchy of paintings, *artwork_N.s* is coded.

4.3 Experiments and results

A preliminary evaluation was conducted to test how significant is the approach of adapting language-dependent coreference strategies to produce coherent descriptions. Nine human subjects participated in the evaluation, three native speakers of each language.

The subjects were given forty object description pairs. One description containing only pronouns as the type of referring expressions and one description that was automatically generated by applying the language dependent coreference strategies. Examples of the description pairs the subjects were asked to evaluate are given in table 4. We asked the subjects to choose the description they find most coherent based on their intuitive judgements. Participant agreement was measured using the kappa statistic (Fleiss, 1971). The results of the evaluation are reported in table 5.

	Pronouns	Pronouns/NPs	$\mathcal{K}$
English	17	18	0.66
Swedish	9	29	0.78
Hebrew	6	28	0.72

Table 5: A summary of the human evaluation.

On average, the evaluators approved at least half of the automatically generated descriptions, with a considerably good agreement. A closer look at the examples where chains of pronouns were preferred revealed that these occurred in English when a description consisted of two or three sentences and the second and third sentences specified the painting dimensions or a date. In Swedish, these were preferred whenever a description consisted of two sentences. In Hebrew, the evaluators preferred a description containing a pronoun over a description containing the higher hypernym *Man-made object*, and also preferred the pronoun when a description consisted of two sentences,

English	
The Long Winter is an oil-painting by Peter Kandre from 1909. **It** is displayed in the Museum Of World Culture.	The Long Winter is an oil-painting by Peter Kandre from 1909. **The painting** is displayed in the Museum Of World Culture.
The Little White Girl is a painting by James Abbott McNeill Whistler. **It** is held in the Gotheburg Art Museum.	The Little White Girl is a painting by James Abbott McNeill Whistler. **The painting** is held in the Gotheburg Art Museum.
The Long Winter is a painting by Peter Kandre from 1909. **It** measures 102 by 43 cm. **It** is displayed in the Museum Of World Culture.	The Long Winter is a painting by Peter Kandre from 1909. **It** measures 102 by 43 cm. **The painting** is displayed in the Museum Of World Culture.
Swedish	
Den långa vintern är en oljemålning av Peter Kandre från 1909. **Den** återfinns på Världskulturmuseet.	Den långa vintern är en oljemålning av Peter Kandre från 1909. **Tavlan** återfinns på Världskulturmuseet.
Den lilla vita flickan är en målning av James Abbott McNeill Whistler. **Den** återfinns på Göteborgs Konstmuseum.	Den lilla vita flickan är en målning av James Abbott McNeill Whistler. **Målningen** återfinns på Göteborgs Konstmuseum.
Den långa vintern målades av Peter Kandre 1909. **Den** är 102 cm lång och 43 cm bred. **Den** återfinns på Världskulturmuseet.	Den långa vintern målades av Peter Kandre 1909. **Målningen** är 102 cm lång och 43 cm bred. **Tavlan** återfinns på Världskulturmuseet.
Hebrew	
hHwrP hArwK hnw Zywr smN sl pyTr qndrh msnt 1909. **hyA** mwZg bmwzAwN sl OlM htrbwt.	hHwrP hArwK hnw Zywr smN sl pyTr qndrh msnt 1909. **hZywr** mwZg bmwzAwN sl OlM htrbwt.
hyaldh hktnh alevmh hi tmona sl abut mcnil wistl. **hyA** mwZgt bmwzAwN homanot sl gwTnbwrg.	hyaldh hktnh alevmh hi tmona sl abut mcnil wistl. **hyZyrh** mwZgt bmwzAwN homanot sl gwTnbwrg.
HwrP ArwK tzoyar el–yedy pyTr qndrh b–1909. **hyA** bgwdl 102 Ol 43 Sg2m. **hyA** mwZgt bmwzAwN sl OlM htrbwt.	HwrP ArwK tzoyar el–yedy pyTr qndrh b–1909. **hyZyrh** bgwdl 102 Ol 43 Sg2m. **hyZyrh** mwZgt bmwzAwN sl OlM htrbwt.

Table 4: Examples of object description pairs that were used in the evaluation.

the second of which concerned the painting dimensions.

5 Conclusions and future work

This paper has presented a cross-linguistic study and demonstrated some differences in how coreference is expressed in English, Swedish and Hebrew. As a result of the investigation, a set of language-specific coreference strategies were identified and implemented in GF. This multilingual grammar was used to generate object descriptions which were then evaluated by native speakers of each language. The evaluation results, although performed with a small number of descriptions and human evaluators, indicate that language-dependent coreference strategies lead to better output. Although the data used to compare the co-referential chains was restricted in size, it was sufficient to determine several differences between the languages for the given domain.

Future work aims to extend the grammar to cover more ontology statements and discourse patterns. We will consider conjunctions and ellipsis in these patterns. We intend to formalize and generalize the strategies presented in this paper and test whether there exist universal co-referential chains, which might result in coherent descriptions in more than three languages.

Acknowledgments

The research presented in this paper was supported in part by MOLTO European Union Seventh Framework Programme (FP7/2007-

2013) under grant agreement FP7-ICT-247914.[11] I would like to thank the Centre for Language Technology (CLT) in Gothenburg and the anonymous INLG reviewers.[12]

References

Mira Ariel. 1990. *Accessing Noun Phrase Antecedents*. Routlege, London.

Regina Barzilay and Lillia Lee. 2004. Catching the drift: Probabilistic content models, with applications to generation and summarization. In *Proc. of HLT-NAACL*, pages 113–120.

Nick Crofts, Martin Doerr, Tony Gill, Stephen Stead, and Matthew Stiff, 2008. *Definition of the CIDOC Conceptual Reference Model*.

Dana Dannélls. 2011. An ontology model of paintings. *Journal of Applied Ontologies*. Submitted.

B. Di Eugenio, 1998. *Centering in Italian*, pages 115–137. Oxford: Clarendon Press.

Joseph L. Fleiss. 1971. Measuring nominal scale agreement among many raters. *Psychological Bulletin*, 76(5):378–382.

Norbert E. Fuchs, Kaarel Kaljurand, and Tobias Kuhn. 2008. Attempto Controlled English for Knowledge Representation. In *Reasoning Web, Fourth International Summer School*. Springer.

T. Givón, editor. 1983. *Topic continuity in discourse: A quantitative cross-language study*. Amsterdam and Philadelphia: John Benjamins.

Yoav Goldberg and Michael Elhadad. 2010. An efficient algorithm for easy-first non-directional dependency parsing. In *Proc. of NAACL 2010*.

Barbara J. Grosz, Scott Weinstein, and Aravind K. Joshi. 1995. Centering: A framework for modeling the local coherence of discourse. *Computational Linguistics*, 21(2).

Péter Halácsy, András Kornai, and Csaba Oravecz. 2007. HunPos: an open source trigram tagger. In *Proc. of ACL on Interactive Poster and Demonstration Sessions*, pages 209–212, Morristown, NJ, USA.

Michael A. K. Halliday and R. Hasan. 1976. *Cohesion in English*. Longman Pub Group.

S. Harabagiu and S. Maiorano. 2000. Multilingual coreference resolution. In *Proc. of ANLP*.

Anna Sågvall Hein. 1989. Definite NPs and background knowledge in medical text. *Computer and Artificial Intelligence*, 8(6):547–563.

[11]http://www.molto-project.eu/

[12]http://www.clt.gu.se/

Nikiforos Karamanis, Massimo Poesio, Chris Mellish, and Jon Oberlander. 2009. Evaluating Centering for Information Ordering using Corpora. *Computational Linguistics*, 35(1).

Rodger Kibble and Richard Power. 2000. Optimizing Referential Coherence in Text Generation. *Computational Linguistics*, 30(4).

J. McCrae, G. Aguado-de Cea, P. Buitelaar, P. Cimiano, T. Declerck, A. Gomez-Perez, J. Gracia, L. Hollink, E. Montiel-Ponsoda, D. Spohr, and T. Wunner. 2012. Interchanging lexical resources on the semantic web. *Language Resources and Evaluation*.

Kathleen R. McKeown. 1985. *Text generation : using discourse strategies and focus constraints to generate natural language text*. Cambridge University Press.

Joakim Nivre, Johan Hall, Jens Nilsson, Atanas Chanev, Gülsen Eryigit, Sandra Kübler, Svetoslav Marinov, and Erwin Marsi. 2007. Maltparser: A language-independent system for data-driven dependency parsing. *Natural Language Engineering*, 13(2):95–135.

Marta Recasens Potau. 2008. *Towards Coreference Resolution for Catalan and Spanish*. Ph.D. thesis, University of Barcelona.

Rashmi Prasad. 2003. *Constraints on the generation of referring expressions, with special reference to hindi*. Ph.D. thesis, University of Pennsylvania.

Ellen F. Prince. 1992. The ZPG letter: Subjects, definiteness, and information-status. In *Discourse description. diverse linguistic analyses of a fund-raising text*, volume 10, pages 159–173.

Aarne Ranta. 1994. *Type-theoretical grammar: A Type-theoretical Grammar Formalism*. Oxford University Press, Oxford, UK.

Aarne Ranta. 2004. Grammatical Framework, a type-theoretical grammar formalism. *Journal of Functional Programming*, 14(2):145–189.

Aarne Ranta. 2009. The GF resource grammar library. *The on-line journal Linguistics in Language Technology (LiLT)*, 2(2).

R. Schwitter and M. Tilbrook. 2004. Controlled Natural Language meets the Semantic Web. In *Proceedings of the Australasian Language Technology Workshop*, pages 55–62, Macquarie University.

Enric Vallduví and Elisabet Engdahl. 1996. The linguistic realization of information packaging. *Linguistics*, (34):459–519.

M. A. Walker, M. Iida, and S. Cote. 1996. Centering in Japanese Discourse. *Computational Linguistics*.

Sandra Williams, Allan Third, and Richard Power. 2011. Levels of organisation in ontology verbalisation. In *Proc. of ENLG*, pages 158–163.

Extractive email thread summarization: Can we do better than He Said She Said?

Pablo Ariel Duboue
Les Laboratoires Foulab
999 du College
Montreal, Quebéc
pablo.duboue@gmail.com

Abstract

Human-written, good quality extractive summaries pay great attention to the text intermixing the extracts. In this work, we focused on the lexical choice for verbs introducing quoted text. We analyzed 4000+ high quality summaries for a high traffic mailing list and manually assembled 39 quotation-introducing verb classes that cover the majority of the verb occurrences. A significant amount of the data is covered by on-going work on e-mail "speech acts." However, we found that one third of the "tail" is composed by "risky" verbs that most likely will be beyond the state of the art for longer time. We used this fact to highlight the trade-offs of risk taking in NLG, where interesting prose might come at the cost of unsettling some of the readers.

1 Introduction

High traffic mailing lists pose a challenge to an extended audience laterally interested on the subject matter but unable or unwilling to follow them on everyday minutiae. In this context, high-level summaries are of great help and in certain cases there are people or companies that step into the plate to provide such service. In recent years, there has been an ever increasing interest (Muresan et al., 2001; Nenkova and Bagga, 2003; Newman and Blitzer, 2003; Rambow et al., 2004; Wan and McKeown, 2004; McKeown et al., 2007; Ulrich, 2008; Wang et al., 2009) in automating this task, with many works focusing on selectively extracting quotes from key e-mail exchanges.

In this work, we focus on finding appropriate and varied ways to cite selected quotes from the email threads. A seemingly simple task, this problem touches: speech act detection (Searle, 1975) (question vs. announcement vs. reply), opinion mining (Pang and Lee, 2008) (complained vs. thanked) and citation polarity analysis (Teufel, 1999): (agreed vs. disagreed vs. added).

At this stage, we will show training data we have acquired for the task and a set of manually assembled verb clusters that show the richness of the problem. Moreover, we have used these clusters to highlight a trade-off of "risk taking" in NLG, where generating interesting prose might lead to text that can upset some readers in the presence of errors.

This paper is structured as follows: in the next section we discuss the data from where we obtained the raw verbs and then proceed to describe the manual analysis to cluster and identify "risky" verbs. We then present the whole set of clusters and conclude with a discussion of risk taking in NLG.

2 Data

This work is part of a larger effort to build automatic tools to replace a key resource that the Linux Kernel development community enjoyed for five years: the Kernel Traffic summaries of the activities in the Linux Kernel mailing list (LKML).

The LKML is of extremely high traffic (300 mails a day on average). For five years (since 1999), Jack Brown hand-picked the most newsworthy threads in a week time and published a summary for each thread. The summaries were made available (under a Free Software license) in a rich XML-based format

```
<p>Gregory Maxwell replied, <quote who="George␣Maxwell">Do you
see the "(sic)" That usually stands for "Spelling␣is␣Correct".
</quote></p>
<p>Oliver Xymoron rejoined:</p>
<quote who="Oliver␣Xymoron">
<p>I think what we have here is an ironic double typo. The
message is actually indicating the drive is not feeling very
good:</p>
<p>+         { 0xb900, "Play␣operation␣aborted␣(sick)" },</p>
<p>Hopefully this very important change will make it into
2.2.2.</p>
</quote>
<p>Brendan Cully kafloogitated:</p>
<quote who="Brendan␣Cully">
<p>"sic" doesn't␣stand␣for␣"spelling␣is␣correct",␣or␣even
"stated␣in␣context"␣(yech!).</p>
<p>In␣fact,␣it␣stands␣for␣"yes,␣I␣know␣it␣looks␣funny,␣but
that's how I want it".␣But␣people␣got␣tired␣of␣typing
Y,IKILF,BTHIWI␣so␣they␣abbreviated␣it␣to␣SIC.</p>
```

Figure 1: Kernel Traffic #6, Feb. 18th 1999 (excerpt).

(Figure 1) that included, among many other things, explicit marking of all quoted text, with attribution.

These summaries were in general followed by a much larger audience than the mailing list itself due to a number of factors including the fact that they make for quite an entertaining read. Mr. Brown's prose was high quality and quite consistent in style,[1] which highlights its potential as training material for NLG. As Reiter and Sripada (2002) pointed out, learning tasks in NLG profit from training data of the highest possible quality in terms of prose and consistency (as compared with training data for NLU, where robustness comes from exposing the system to a variety of malformed texts).

In our journey to approximate Mr. Brown's work by automatic means, we decided to start on a relatively unstudied problem: introducing quoted references in a rich manner. In the 4,253 hand written summaries by Mr. Brown (made available in 344 newsletter issues) 95% contain a quote, with an average of 3.28 quotes per summary. Moreover, 72% of the total characters in the summaries are inside quotes (including markup).

2.1 Processing

We employed a processing pipeline implemented in the UIMA framework (Ferrucci and Lally, 2004) to extract the verbs immediately before a quotation. We used annotators from the OpenNLP project (Apache, 2011) implementing Maximum Entropy models for NLP (Ratnaparkhi, 1998). For the sentence before a quotation we extracted the word marked with the POS tag 'VBD' closer to the quotation. Processing the 334 issues available for Kernel Traffic resulted in 11,634 verb occurrences extracted for 344 verbs (and verb-like errors). These verbs are the ones we employ for the analysis and inferences drawn in the next section.

3 Analysis

From the grand-total of 344 verbs (including typos and POS-tagger errors), we took all the verbs that appeared at least a hundred times (the top 55 verbs) and expanded them from the larger list (plus WordNet synsets (Miller, 1995)), grouping them into classes. The grouping captures synonyms *for the particular task of introducing quoted text in summaries*. The resulting 39 classes (Table 1) contain 127 verbs accounting for 96% of the cases (the table contains an "other" class with the remaining 217 verbs that account for 4% of the occurrences). The verbs included from WordNet do not appear in the corpus and thus have a count of zero. This large set of verbs highlights the many possibilities a system that chooses to go just with 's/he said' will be missing. Moreover, such a system can be immediately enriched with 17 different variations with associated likelihoods.

We determined whether or not generation errors for a given verb class would be "dangerous" using the following criteria:

> *If the automatic determination of whether the original quote fell into a particular verb class fails, would the original author take issue with the summary upon reading the misclassified verb?*

That is, if the system decides that Brendan Cully (from the example in the introduction) has indeed kafloogitated[2] with his reply but such decision was made in error (and Mr. Cully was just remarking or explaining), would Mr. Cully take issue with the summary? As with any automated system, the possibility of automated mistakes should make its designers err on the side of making more conservative decisions. Under such desiderata, we think the 10

[1] A quality of prose that continues with his editorial contributions to Linux Journal and Linux Magazine.

[2] That word has been invented by Mr. Brown and was used only once within the five years of Kernel Traffic.

classes highlighted in Table 1 are thus too "dangerous" to be addressed currently by automated means.

Initially, that might not appear such a big loss, as none of them account for more than 1% of the total occurrences. However, as with many other phenomena in NLP, a few cases account for most occurrences: the clusters for "said," "asked," and "replied" account for 2/3 of the total occurrences and, overall, the top 9 classes account for 93% of the cases. From the rich tail that encompasses Mr. Brown prose, the "dangerous" classes account for 35% of the cases from position 10 and onward. It is our opinion that such cases were the reason Mr. Brown's summaries were enjoyable to read and are only a small example of the humor and piquancy behind his prose. Now, it might be the case such quality will be beyond the state of the art of NLG for quite some time.

In that sense, we consider the prevalence of risky classes as a negative result that highlights a problem for NLG well beyond the task at hand: we, as humans, enjoy text that takes a stand, that argues its points in an opinionated manner.[3] Such is the distinction between dull reports and flourish summaries. Even in the highly technical domain of operating system kernel discussions, Mr. Brown felt the need to use words such as 'groused' and 'chastised.'

The problem might as well be cultural, with opinionated prose paradigmatic to the Western world. It might also be related to our culture as NLG practitioners, where we always thrive for perfect output. Our data shows that to go beyond 'He Said She Said' in a truly interesting manner we will have to be ready to make mistakes which could make some people unhappy, a trade-off that it would be interesting to see explored more often in NLG.

4 Related Work

Since the seminal work by Muresan et al. (2001), email summarization and in particular email thread summarization has spanned full dissertations (Ulrich, 2008). Existing resources for email summarization (Ulrich et al., 2008), however, do not emphasize explicitly the type of quotes being used.

Understandingly, most of the work has been devoted to selecting the particular words, sentences or paragraphs to extract from the original e-mails. either by distilling terms or topics (Muresan et al., 2001; Newman and Blitzer, 2003) or finding a representative example (Nenkova and Bagga, 2003; Rambow et al., 2004; Wang et al., 2009).

The issue of choosing how to introduce the extracted text has only been studied in the context of speech act detection (Cohen et al., 2004; Wan and McKeown, 2004) within emails or within threaded discussions (Feng et al., 2006), which is limited to questions, replies and the like (a very important case which covers 2/3 of our available data). The problem of detecting question / answer pairs in e-mails is by far the one who has received the most attention in the field (Bickel and Scheffer, 2004; Shrestha and McKeown, 2004; McKeown et al., 2007).

The verbs in each of the classes in Table 1 have a near-synonym relation:[4] even though "recommended" and "urged" share most of their meaning, the differences in style, color and subtle meaning need to be further elucidated for successful lexical choice. This topic has started to be explored in detail recently (Edmonds and Hirst, 2002).

Our work falls in the larger field of summarization by using NLG means, a discipline that has received significant attention of late (Belz et al., 2009).

5 Conclusion

In this paper, we have brought to the attention of NLG practitioners the rich resource embodied in five years of Kernel Traffic newsletters. We had also highlighted the richness of the problem of lexical choice for verbs introducing quotations in extractive email summarization.

Moreover, we contributed 39 clusters manually assembled from naturally occurring verbs extracted from 4000+ high quality summaries. These clusters can enrich even the most straightforward existing systems. Finally, we argued that, while useful summaries might be around the corner, entertaining summaries will be well beyond the state of the art until the field is willing to take the risk involved in standing behind automatically generated prose with intrinsic value-judgments.

In our ongoing work, we are targeting the creation

[3]Not unlike this discussion.

[4]Thanks to an anonymous reviewer for bringing this fact into our attention.

Table 1: Quotation introducing verb classes, with counts. The "other" class appears in row 7. Lines in bold are considered "dangerous." The last column is the author's opinion about which type of technology is more relevant for choosing that class (speech act detection (A), opinion mining (O) or citation link analysis (C)). Verbs missing due to space restrictions are in the appendix.

#	Top Verbs	# verbs	Total Counts		Accum.	Type
1	said (2726) remarked (361) posted (163) pointed out (148)	17	3531	(30.35%)	30.35%	A
2	replied (3476) responded (21) answered (11)	3	3508	(30.15%)	60.50%	A
3	added (1059) included (13) followed (10)	3	1082	(9.30%)	69.80%	C
4	announced (902) declared (1)	2	903	(7.76%)	77.56%	A
5	asked (509) inquired (0)	2	509	(4.37%)	81.94%	A
6	explained (427)	1	427	(3.67%)	85.61%	A
7	FELT (21) MADE (21) WANTED (8) BROKE (8)	217	403	(3.46%)	89.07%	-
8	reported (254) detailed (1)	2	255	(2.19%)	91.26%	A
9	suggested (188) proposed (35)	2	223	(1.91%)	93.18%	O
10	**objected (90) protested (5)**	**2**	**95**	**(0.81%)**	**94.00%**	**O**
11	concluded (48) ended (5) finished (4) closed (2)	5	59	(0.50%)	94.50%	C
12	offered (52) volunteered (6)	2	58	(0.49%)	95.00%	O
13	confirmed (44) supported (4) affirmed (3) reasserted (1)	7	52	(0.44%)	95.45%	C
14	summed up (21) summarized (18)	2	39	(0.33%)	95.78%	A
15	agreed (37) concurred (1) concorded (0)	3	38	(0.32%)	96.11%	C
16	described (33)	1	33	(0.28%)	96.39%	A
17	**took issue (17) disagreed (11) dissented (2) differed (1)**	**4**	**31**	**(0.26%)**	**96.66%**	**O**
18	**complained (22) sounded off (2) kicked (1) groused (1)**	**7**	**29**	**(0.24%)**	**96.91%**	**O**
19	**argued (28) contended (0) debated (0)**	**3**	**28**	**(0.24%)**	**97.15%**	**O**
20	listed (27) enumerated (0)	2	27	(0.23%)	97.38%	A
21	continued (25) kept (1)	2	26	(0.22%)	97.61%	A
22	clarified (25) elucidated (0)	2	25	(0.21%)	97.82%	C
23	recommended (17) urged (4) advised (2) advocated (1)	4	24	(0.20%)	98.03%	C
24	**speculated (16) mused (2) guessed (2) supposed (1)**	**6**	**22**	**(0.18%)**	**98.22%**	**O**
25	elaborated (11) expanded (7) expounded (2)	3	20	(0.17%)	98.39%	C
26	**corrected (18) chastised (1) rectified (0) righted (0)**	**4**	**19**	**(0.16%)**	**98.55%**	**O**
27	**exclaimed (6) called out (5) cried out (4) shouted (2)**	**5**	**18**	**(0.15%)**	**98.71%**	**O**
28	quoted (15) cited (2)	2	17	(0.14%)	98.85%	C
29	**warned (8) cautioned (6) admonished (2)**	**3**	**16**	**(0.13%)**	**98.99%**	**O**
30	interjected (11) sprung (1) interposed (1)	3	13	(0.11%)	99.10%	O
31	**quipped (10) joked (1) chuckled (1) cracked (1)**	**4**	**13**	**(0.11%)**	**99.21%**	**O**
32	requested (12)	1	12	(0.10%)	99.32%	A
33	tried (9) attempted (2) tested (1)	3	12	(0.10%)	99.42%	O
34	acknowledged (8) admitted (3) recognized (0)	3	11	(0.09%)	99.51%	A
35	countered (10)	1	10	(0.08%)	99.60%	C
36	found (7) discovered (2) launched (1)	3	10	(0.08%)	99.69%	A
37	reiterated (9) repeated (1)	2	10	(0.08%)	99.77%	C
38	started (9) began (1)	2	10	(0.08%)	99.86%	A
39	**rejoined (6) retorted (2) returned (1)**	**3**	**9**	**(0.07%)**	**99.93%**	**O**
40	chimed (7)	1	7	(0.06%)	100%	O

of a systemic fragment for the quotation-introducing verbs, in the style of KPML (Bateman, 1995).

Acknowledgments

The author would like to thank the anonymous reviewers as well as Annie Ying for valuable feedback and insights. He will also like to thank the Debian NYC group for bringing the Kernel Traffic summaries to his attention.

Appendix

The verbs omitted for reasons of space in Table 1 are the following: for the "said" cluster, mentioned (34), commented (25), wrote (20), noticed (17), spoke (9), expressed (6), showed (5), observed (5), stated (5), asserted (4), referred (1), noted (1), declared (1); for the "concluded" cluster, resolved (0); for the "confirmed" cluster, corroborated (0), sustained (0), substantiated (0); for the "complained" cluster, hollered (1), ranted (1), kvetched (1); for the "speculated" cluster, theorized (1), conjectured (0); for the "exclaimed" cluster, sputtered (1).

References

Apache. 2011. OpenNLP *http://incubator.apache.org/opennlp*.

John A. Bateman. 1995. KPML: The KOMET–Penman multilingual linguistic resource development environment. In *Proc. of EWNLG*, pages 219–222.

Anja Belz, Roger Evans, and Sebastian Varges, editors. 2009. *Proc. of the 2009 Workshop on Language Generation and Summarisation (UCNLG+Sum 2009)*. ACL, Suntec, Singapore, August.

Steffen Bickel and Tobias Scheffer. 2004. Learning from message pairs for automatic email answering. In *ECML*, volume 3201 of *LNCS*, pages 87–98. Springer.

William W. Cohen, Vitor R. Carvalho, and Tom M. Mitchell. 2004. Learning to classify email into "speech acts". In *Proc. of EMNLP*, volume 4.

Philip Edmonds and Graeme Hirst. 2002. Near-synonymy and lexical choice. *Computational Linguistics*, 28(2):105–144.

Donghui Feng, Erin Shaw, Jihie Kim, and Eduard Hovy. 2006. Learning to detect conversation focus of threaded discussions. In *Proc. HLT-NAACL*, pages 208–215.

David Ferrucci and Adam Lally. 2004. UIMA: an architectural approach to unstructured information processing in the corporate research environment. *Natural Language Engineering*, 10(3-4):327–348.

Kathleen McKeown, Lokesh Shrestha, and Owen Rambow. 2007. Using question-answer pairs in extractive summarization of email conversations. In *CICLing*, volume 4394 of *LNCS*, pages 542–550. Springer.

G.A. Miller. 1995. Wordnet: a lexical database for english. *Communications of the ACM*, 38(11):39–41.

Smaranda Muresan, Evelyn Tzoukermann, and Judith L. Klavans. 2001. Combining linguistic and machine learning techniques for email summarization. In *Proc. of the 2001 workshop on Computational Natural Language Learning-Volume 7*, page 19. ACL.

Ani Nenkova and Amit Bagga. 2003. Facilitating email thread access by extractive summary generation. In *RANLP*, volume 260 of *Current Issues in Linguistic Theory (CILT)*, pages 287–296.

Paula S. Newman and John C. Blitzer. 2003. Summarizing archived discussions: a beginning. In *IUI*, pages 273–276. ACM.

Bo Pang and Lillian Lee. 2008. Opinion mining and sentiment analysis. *Foundations and Trends in Information Retrieval*, 2(1-2):1–135.

Owen Rambow, L. Shrestha, J. Chen, and C. Lauridsen. 2004. Summarizing email threads. In *Proc. of HLT-NAACL 2004: Short Papers*, pages 105–108. ACL.

Adwait Ratnaparkhi. 1998. *Maximum Entropy Models for Natural Language Ambiguity Resolution*. Ph.D. thesis, University of Pennsylvania, Philadelphia, PA.

Ehud Reiter and S. Sripada. 2002. Should corpora texts be gold standards for NLG? In *Proceedings of Second International Conference on Natural Language Generation INLG-2002*, pages 97–104, Arden House, NY.

John R. Searle. 1975. A taxonomy of illocutionary acts. In *Language, Mind and Knowledge*, pages 344–369. University of Minnesota Press.

Lokesh Shrestha and Kathleen McKeown. 2004. Detection of question-answer pairs in email conversations. In *Proc. of ACL*, page 889. ACL.

Simone Teufel. 1999. *Argumentative zoning: Information extraction from scientific text*. Ph.D. thesis, University of Edinburgh, England.

Jan Ulrich, Gabriel Murray, and Giuseppe Carenini. 2008. A publicly available annotated corpus for supervised email summarization. In *AAAI08 EMAIL Workshop*, Chicago, USA. AAAI.

Jan Ulrich. 2008. Supervised machine learning for email thread summarization. Master's thesis, Computer Science.

Stephen Wan and Kathleen McKeown. 2004. Generating overview summaries of ongoing email thread discussions. In *Proc. of ACL*, page 549. ACL.

Baoxun Wang, Bingquan Liu, Chengjie Sun, Xiaolong Wang, and Bo Li. 2009. Adaptive maximum marginal relevance based multi-email summarization. In *AICI*, volume 5855 of *LNCS*, pages 417–424. Springer.

Rich Morphology Generation Using Statistical Machine Translation

Ahmed El Kholy and **Nizar Habash**
Center for Computational Learning Systems, Columbia University
475 Riverside Drive New York, NY 10115
{akholy,habash}@ccls.columbia.edu

Abstract

We present an approach for generation of morphologically rich languages using statistical machine translation. Given a sequence of lemmas and *any* subset of morphological features, we produce the inflected word forms. Testing on Arabic, a morphologically rich language, our models can reach 92.1% accuracy starting only with lemmas, and 98.9% accuracy if all the gold features are provided.

1 Introduction

Many natural language processing (NLP) applications, such as summarization and machine translation (MT), require natural language generation (NLG). Generation for morphologically rich languages, which introduce a lot of challenges for NLP in general, has gained a lot of attention recently, especially in the context of statistical MT (SMT). The common wisdom for handling morphological richness is to reduce the complexity in the internal application models and then generate complex word forms in a final step.

In this paper,[1] we present a SMT-based approach for generation of morphologically rich languages. Given a sequence of lemmas and *any* subset of morphological features, we produce the inflected word forms. The SMT model parameters are derived from a parallel corpus mapping lemmas and morphological features to the inflected word forms.

As a case study, we focus on Arabic, a morphologically rich language. Our models can reach 92.1% accuracy starting only with tokenized lemmas and predicting some features, up from 55.0% accuracy without inflecting the lemmas. If all of the gold morphological features are provided as input, our best model achieves 98.9% accuracy.

[1]This work was funded by a Google research award.

2 Related Work

In the context of morphological generation for MT, the state-of-the-art factored machine translation approach models morphology using generation factors in the translation process (Koehn et al., 2007). One of the limitations of factored models is that generation is based on the word level not the phrase level and the context is only captured through a language model. Minkov et al. (2007) and Toutanova et al. (2008) model translation and morphology independently for English-Arabic and English-Russian MT. They use a maximum entropy model to predict inflected word forms directly. Clifton and Sarkar (2011) use a similar approach for English-Finnish MT where they predict morpheme sequences. Unlike both approaches, we generate the word forms from the deeper representation of lemmas and features.

As for using SMT in generation, there are many previous efforts. Wong and Mooney (2007) use SMT methods for tactical NLG. They learn through SMT to map meaning representations to natural language. Quirk et al. (2004) apply SMT tools to generate paraphrases of input sentences in the same language. Both of these efforts target English, a morphologically poor language. Our work is conceptually closer to Wong and Mooney (2007), except that we focus on the question of morphological generation and our approach includes an optional feature prediction component. In a related publication, we integrate our generation model as part of end-to-end English-Arabic SMT (El Kholy and Habash, 2012). In that work, we make use of English features in the Arabic morphology prediction component, e.g., English POS and parse trees.

3 Arabic Challenges

Arabic is a morphologically complex language. One aspect of Arabic's complexity is its orthography which often omits short vowel diacritics. As a result, ambiguity is rampant. Another aspect is the various attachable clitics which include conjunction proclitics, e.g., +و *w*+ 'and', particle proclitics, e.g., +ل *l*+ 'to/for', the definite article +ال *Al*+ 'the', and the class of pronominal enclitics, e.g., هم+ +*hm* 'their/them'. Beyond these clitics, Arabic words inflect for person (PER), gender (GEN), number (NUM), aspect (ASP), mood (MOD), voice (VOX), state (STT) and case (CAS). Arabic inflectional features are realized as affixes as well as templatic changes, e.g., *broken plurals*.[2]

These three phenomena, optional diacritics, attachable clitics and the large inflectional space, lead to thousands of inflected forms per lemma and a high degree of ambiguity: about 12 analyses per word, typically corresponding to two lemmas on average (Habash, 2010). The Penn Arabic Treebank (PATB) tokenization scheme (Maamouri et al., 2004), which we use in all our experiments, separates all clitics except for the determiner clitic *Al*+ (DET). As such we consider the DET as an additional morphological feature.

Arabic has complex morpho-syntactic agreement rules in terms of GEN, NUM and definiteness. Adjectives agree with nouns in GEN and NUM but plural irrational nouns exceptionally take feminine singular adjectives. Moreover, verbs agree with subjects in GEN only in VSO order while they agree in GEN and NUM in SVO order (Alkuhlani and Habash, 2011). The DET in Arabic is used to distinguish different syntactic constructions such as the possessive or adjectival modification. These agreement rules make the generation of correctly inflected forms in context a challenging task.

4 Approach

In this section, we discuss our approach in generating Arabic words from Arabic lemmas (LEMMA) using a pipeline of three steps.

1. **(Optional) Morphology Prediction** of linguistic features to inflect LEMMAS.

[2]The Arabic NLP tools we use in this paper do not model all templatic inflectional realizations.

Tokens	*w+*	*s+*	*yktbwn*	*+hA*
POS	conj	fut_part	verb	pron
Lemma	wa	sa	katab	hA
Features	na,na,na, na,na,na, na,na,na,	na,na,na, na,na,na, na,na,na,	3rd,masc,pl, imp,act,ind, na,na,na,	3rd,fem,sg, na,na,na, na,na,na,

Figure 1: An example و+سـ+يكتبون+ها *w+s+yktbwn +hA* 'and they will write it'. Features' order of presentation is: PER, GEN, NUM, ASP, VOX, MOD, DET, CAS, and STT. The value 'na' is for 'not-applicable'.

2. **Morphology Generation** of inflected Arabic tokens from LEMMAS and any subset of Arabic linguistic features.
3. **Detokenization** of inflected Arabic tokens into surface Arabic words.

Morphology generation is the main contribution of this paper which in addition to detokenization represents an end-to-end inflection generator. The morphology prediction step is an optional step that complements the whole process by enriching the input of the morphology generation step with one or more predicted morphological features.

We follow numerous previously published efforts on the value of tokenization for Arabic NLP tasks (Badr et al., 2008; El Kholy and Habash, 2010). We use the best performing tokenization scheme (PATB) in machine translation in all our experiments and focus on the question of how to generate Arabic inflected words from LEMMAS and features. Figure 1 shows an example of a tokenized word and its decomposition into a LEMMA and morphological features.

Morphology Prediction This optional step takes a sequence of LEMMAS and tries to enrich them by predicting one or more morphological features. It is implemented using a supervised discriminative learning model, namely Conditional Random Fields (CRF) (Lafferty et al., 2001). Table 1 shows the accuracy of the CRF module on a test set of 1000 sentences compared to using the most common feature value baseline. Some features, such as CAS and STT are harder to predict but they also have very low baseline values. GEN, DET and NUM have a moderate prediction accuracy while ASP, PER, VOX and MOD have high prediction accuracy (but also very high baselines). This task is similar to POS tagging

Predicted Feature	Baseline Accuracy %	Prediction Accuracy %
Case (CAS)	42.87	70.39
State (STT)	42.85	76.93
Gender (GEN)	67.42	84.17
Determiner (DET)	59.71	85.41
Number (NUM)	70.61	87.31
Aspect (ASP)	90.38	92.10
Person (PER)	85.71	92.80
Voice (VOX)	90.38	93.70
Mood (MOD)	90.38	**93.80**

Table 1: Accuracy (%) of feature prediction starting from Arabic lemmas (LEMMA). The second column shows the baseline for prediction using the most common feature value. The third column is the prediction accuracy using CRF.

except that it starts with lemmas as opposed to inflected forms (Habash and Rambow, 2005; Alkuhlani and Habash, 2012). As such, we expect it to perform worse than a comparable POS tagging task. For example, Habash and Rambow (2005) report 98.2% and 98.8% for GEN and NUM, respectively, compared to our 84.2% and 87.3%.

In the context of a specific application, the performance of the prediction could be improved using information other than the context of provided LEMMAs. For example, in MT, source language lexical, syntactic and morphological information could be used in the prediction module (El Kholy and Habash, 2012).

The morphology prediction step produces a lattice with all the possible feature values each having an associated confidence score. We filter out options with very low confidence scores to control the exponential size of the lattice when combining more than one feature. We tried some experiments using only one or two top values but got lower performance. The morphology generation step takes the lattice and decides on the best target inflection.

Morphology Generation This step is implemented using a SMT model that translates from a deeper linguistic representation to a surface representation. The model parameters are derived from a parallel corpus mapping LEMMAs plus morphological features to Arabic inflected forms. The model is monotonic and there is neither reordering nor word deletion/addition. We plan to consider these variations in the future. The main advantage of this approach is that it only needs monolingual data which is abundant.

The morphology generation step can take a sequence of LEMMAs and a subset of morphological features directly or after enriching the sequence with one or more morphological features using the morphology prediction step.

Detokenization Since we work on tokenized Arabic, we use a detokenization step which simply stitches the words and clitics together as a post-processing step after morphology generation. We use the best detokenization technique presented by El Kholy and Habash (2010).

5 Evaluation

Evaluation Setup All of the training data we use is available from the Linguistic Data Consortium (LDC).[3] For SMT training and language modeling (LM), we use 200M words from the Arabic Gigaword corpus (LDC2007T40). We use 5-grams for all LMs implemented using the SRILM toolkit (Stolcke, 2002).

MADA+TOKAN (Habash and Rambow, 2005; Habash et al., 2009) is used to preprocess the Arabic text for generation and language modeling. MADA+TOKAN tokenizes, lemmatizes and selects all morphological features in context.

All generation experiments are conducted using the Moses phrase-based SMT system (Koehn et al., 2007). The decoding weight optimization is done using a set of 300 Arabic sentences from the 2004 NIST MT evaluation test set (MT04). The tuning is based on tokenized Arabic without detokenization. We use a maximum phrase length of size 4. We report results on the Arabic side of the 2005 NIST MT evaluation set (MT05), our development set. We use the Arabic side of MT06 NIST data set for blind test. We evaluate using BLEU-1 and BLEU-4 (Papineni et al., 2002). BLEU is a precision-based evaluation metric commonly used in MT research. Given the way we define our generation task to exclude reordering and word deletion/addition, BLEU-1 can be interpreted as a measure of word accuracy. BLEU-4 is the geometric mean of unigram, bigram, trigram and 4-gram precision.[4] Since Arabic text

[3] http://www.ldc.upenn.edu

[4] n-gram precision is the number of test n-word sequences that appear in the reference divided by the number of all possible n-word sequences in the test.

is generally written without diacritics, we evaluate on undiacritized text only. In the future, we plan to study generation into diacritized Arabic, a more challenging goal.

Baseline We conducted two baseline experiments. First, as a degenerate baseline, we only used detokenization to generate the inflected words from LEMMAs. Second, we used a generation step before detokenization to generate the inflected tokens from LEMMAs. The BLEU-1/BLEU-4 scores of the two baselines on the MT05 set are 55.04/24.51 and 91.54/82.19. We get a significant improvement (~35% BLEU-1 & ~58% BLEU-4) by using the generation step before detokenization.

Generation with Gold Features We built several SMT systems translating from LEMMAs plus one or more morphological features to Arabic inflected tokens. We then use the detokenization step to recombine the tokens and produce the surface words.

Table 2 shows the BLEU scores for MT05 set as LEMMAs plus different morphological features and their combinations. We greedily combined the features based on the performance of each feature separately. Features with higher performance are combined first. As expected, the more features are included the better the results. Oddly, when we add the POS to the feature combination, the performance drops. That could be explained by the redundancy in information provided by the POS given all the other features and the added sparsity.

Although STT and MOD features hurt the performance when added incrementally to the feature combination, removing them from the complete feature set led to a drop in performance. We suspect that there are synergies in combining different features. We plan to investigate this point extensively in the future. BLEU scores are very high because the input is golden in terms of word order, lemma choice and features. These scores should be seen as the upper limit of our model's performance. Most of the errors are detokenization and word form underspecification errors.

Generation with Predicted Features We compare results of generation with a variety of predicted features (see Table 3). The results show that using predicted features can help improve the generation quality over the baseline in some cases, e.g., when the LEMMAs are enriched with CAS, ASP, PER, VOX or MOD features. Our best performer is LEMMA+MOD. Unlike gold features, greedily combining predicted features hurts the performance and the more features added the worse the performance. One explanation is that each feature is predicted independently which may lead to incompatible feature values. In the future, we plan to investigate ways of combining features that could help performance such predicting more than one feature together and filtering out bad feature combinations. The feature prediction accuracy (Table 1) does not always correlate with the generation performance, e.g., CAS has lower accuracy than GEN, but has a relatively higher BLEU score. This may be due to the fact that some features are mostly realized as diacritics (CAS) which are ignored in our evaluation.

Gold Generation Input	BLEU-1%	BLEU-4%
LEMMA	91.54	82.19
LEMMA+MOD	91.70	82.44
LEMMA+ASP	92.09	83.26
LEMMA+PER	92.09	83.34
LEMMA+VOX	92.33	83.70
LEMMA+CAS	92.71	84.34
LEMMA+STT	93.92	86.55
LEMMA+DET	93.97	86.62
LEMMA+NUM	93.91	86.89
LEMMA+GEN	94.33	87.32
LEMMA+GEN+NUM	95.67	91.16
++DET	97.88	95.76
++STT	97.73	95.39
++CAS	98.13	96.35
++VOX	98.19	96.47
++PER	98.24	96.59
++ASP	**98.85**	**98.08**
++MOD	**98.85**	98.06
LEMMA + *All Features* + POS	98.82	98.01

Table 2: Results of generation from gold Arabic lemmas (LEMMA) plus different sets of morphological features. Results are in (BLEU-1 & BLEU-4) on our MT05 set. "++" means the feature is added to the set of features in the previous row.

Blind Test Set To validate our results, we applied different versions of our system to a blind test set (MT06). Our results are as follows (BLEU-1/BLEU-4): detokenization without inflection (55.64/24.92), generation from LEMMAs only (86.70/72.69), generation with gold MOD feature (87.00/73.31), and generation with predicted MOD feature (86.96/73.29). These numbers are generally

Generation Input	BLEU-1%	BLEU-4%
Baseline (LEMMA)	91.54	82.19
LEMMA+GEN	89.23	78.37
LEMMA+NUM	91.14	81.35
LEMMA+STT	91.16	81.70
LEMMA+DET	91.18	81.78
LEMMA+CAS	91.60	82.43
LEMMA+ASP	91.94	83.07
LEMMA+PER	91.97	83.10
LEMMA+VOX	91.99	83.18
LEMMA+MOD	**92.05**	**83.26**
LEMMA+MOD+VOX	91.76	82.73
++PER	91.57	82.32
++ASP	91.07	81.32
++CAS	89.71	78.68

Table 3: Results of generation from LEMMA plus different sets of predicted morphological features. Results are in (BLEU-1 & BLEU-4) on our MT05 set. "++" means the feature is added to the set of features in the previous row.

lower than our development set, but the trends and conclusions are consistent.

6 Conclusion and Future Work

We present a SMT-based approach to generation of morphologically rich languages. We evaluate our approach under a variety of settings for Arabic. In the future, we plan to improve the quality of feature prediction and test our approach on other languages.

References

Sarah Alkuhlani and Nizar Habash. 2011. A Corpus for Modeling Morpho-Syntactic Agreement in Arabic: Gender, Number and Rationality. In *Proc. of ACL'11*, Portland, OR.

Sarah Alkuhlani and Nizar Habash. 2012. Identifying Broken Plurals, Irregular Gender, and Rationality in Arabic Text. In *Proc. of EACL'12*, Avignon, France.

Ibrahim Badr, Rabih Zbib, and James Glass. 2008. Segmentation for English-to-Arabic Statistical Machine Translation. In *Proc. of ACL'08*, Columbus, OH.

Ann Clifton and Anoop Sarkar. 2011. Combining morpheme-based machine translation with post-processing morpheme prediction. In *Proc. of ACL'11*, Portland, OR.

Ahmed El Kholy and Nizar Habash. 2010. Orthographic and Morphological Processing for English-Arabic Statistical Machine Translation. In *Proc. of TALN'10*, Montréal, Canada.

Ahmed El Kholy and Nizar Habash. 2012. Translate, Predict or Generate: Modeling Rich Morphology in Statistical Machine Translation. In *Proc. of EAMT'12*, Trento, Italy.

Nizar Habash and Owen Rambow. 2005. Arabic Tokenization, Part-of-Speech Tagging and Morphological Disambiguation in One Fell Swoop. In *Proc. of ACL'05*, Ann Arbor, MI.

Nizar Habash, Owen Rambow, and Ryan Roth. 2009. MADA+TOKAN: A toolkit for Arabic tokenization, diacritization, morphological disambiguation, pos tagging, stemming and lemmatization. *Proc. of MEDAR*, Cairo, Egypt.

Nizar Habash. 2010. *Introduction to Arabic Natural Language Processing*. Morgan & Claypool Publishers.

Philipp Koehn, Hieu Hoang, Alexandra Birch, Christopher Callison-Burch, Marcello Federico, Nicola Bertoldi, Brooke Cowan, Wade Shen, Christine Moran, Richard Zens, Christopher Dyer, Ondrej Bojar, Alexandra Constantin, and Evan Herbst. 2007. Moses: open source toolkit for statistical machine translation. In *Proc. of ACL'07*, Prague, Czech Republic.

J. Lafferty, A. McCallum, and F.C.N. Pereira. 2001. Conditional random fields: Probabilistic models for segmenting and labeling sequence data. In *Proc. of the International Conference on Machine Learning*.

Mohamed Maamouri, Ann Bies, Tim Buckwalter, and Wigdan Mekki. 2004. The Penn Arabic Treebank: Building a Large-Scale Annotated Arabic Corpus. In *Proc. of NEMLAR'04*, Cairo, Egypt.

Einat Minkov, Kristina Toutanova, and Hisami Suzuki. 2007. Generating complex morphology for machine translation. In *Proc. of ACL'07*, Prague, Czech Republic.

Kishore Papineni, Salim Roukos, Todd Ward, and Wei-Jing Zhu. 2002. BLEU: a Method for Automatic Evaluation of Machine Translation. In *Proc. of ACL'02*, Philadelphia, PA.

Chris Quirk, Chris Brockett, and William Dolan. 2004. Monolingual machine translation for paraphrase generation. In Dekang Lin and Dekai Wu, editors, *Proc. of EMNLP'04*, Barcelona, Spain.

Andreas Stolcke. 2002. SRILM - an Extensible Language Modeling Toolkit. In *Proc. of ICSLP'02*, Denver, CO.

Kristina Toutanova, Hisami Suzuki, and Achim Ruopp. 2008. Applying morphology generation models to machine translation. In *Proc. of ACL'08*, Columbus, OH.

Yuk Wah Wong and Raymond Mooney. 2007. Generation by inverting a semantic parser that uses statistical machine translation. In *Proc. of NAACL'07*, Rochester, NY.

Reformulating student contributions in tutorial dialogue*

Pamela Jordan[1]
pjordan@pitt.edu

Sandra Katz[1]
katz@pitt.edu

Patricia Albacete[1]
palbacet@pitt.edu

Michael Ford[2]
mjford@pitt.edu

Christine Wilson[1]
clwilson@pitt.edu

University of Pittsburgh
Learning Research & Development Center[1]
School of Education[2]
Pittsburgh PA 15260, USA

Abstract

While some recent work in tutorial dialogue has touched upon tutor reformulations of student contributions, there has not yet been an attempt to characterize the intentions of reformulations in this educational context nor an attempt to determine which types of reformulation actually contribute to student learning. In this paper we take an initial look at tutor reformulations of student contributions in naturalistic tutorial dialogue in order to characterize the range of pedagogical intentions that may be associated with these reformulations. We further outline our plans for implementing reformulation in our tutorial dialogue system, Rimac, which engages high school physics students in post problem solving reflective discussions. By implementing reformulations in a tutorial dialogue system we can begin to test their impact on student learning in a more controlled way in addition to testing whether our approximation of reformulation is adequate.

1 Introduction

In the current study of tutorial dialogue we describe here, we seek to identify the most pedagogically valuable ways in which a tutor incorporates a student's contribution into his turn so that we can implement these in a tutorial dialogue system. In educational research, two teaching techniques that have been shown to benefit students, Accountable Talk (O'Connor and Michaels, 1993) and Questioning the Author (Beck et al., 1996), both train teachers to make use of a number of discussion moves that react to student contributions. One such move that is shared by both teaching techniques is *revoicing*. Revoicing is characterized as a reformulation of what the student said with the intention of expressing it in a way that most of the student's fellow classmates will be able to make sense of it and elaborate upon it. In the case of Accountable Talk it also includes the intent that the teacher attempt to relinquish authority on the topic under discussion. This is done by not evaluating the student contribution and instead inviting the student to assess the teacher's reformulation. In tutorial dialogue, the pedagogical intention of revoicing cannot be exactly the same. However, a reformulation that invites the student to assess it may retain some of the benefits of classroom revoicing. This is something we intend to test as part of our research. A step we are taking towards such a test is to look at what reformulations appear in tutorial dialogue and then attempt to characterize the tutor intentions that may be associated with them.

In some applied contexts, such as second language learning, reformulations are more narrowly defined as using different words while keeping the content semantically equivalent. However, research in pragmatics takes a broader view of reformulation. In a corpus study of lectures that examined reformulation markers such as "in other words," "that is" and "i.e." and also endeavored to consolidate the findings from previous linguistics studies, the range of

*The research reported here was supported by the Institute of Education Sciences, U.S. Department of Education, through Grant R305A100163 to the University of Pittsburgh. The opinions expressed are those of the authors and do not represent the views of the Institute or the U.S. Department of Education.

intentions identified include, among others, definition, denomination, specification, explanation, correction and consequence (Murillo, 2008). In our preliminary characterization of reformulations in naturalistic tutorial dialogue, we will use this broader definition and will test whether a tutor contribution is a reformulation of what the student said by checking the felicity of inserted reformulation markers such as "in other words."

Two recent studies of tutorial dialogue specifically recognize revoicing. The first study (Chi and Roy, 2010) examines face to face naturalistic tutorial dialogue in which a tutor is helping a student work through a physics problem. They suggest that when the tutor repeats part of what the student said, it is often done with the intention of providing positive feedback for correct answers and call this revoicing as with the excerpt below which is repeated from (Chi and Roy, 2010) .

> S: First the gravity is pulling down
> T: Pulling it down. [Tutor revoiced.]
> S: Weight is..the mass times..acceleration due to gravity and that's force.
> T: Right. Right.
> S: Ok.
> T: So weight is the force. [Tutor revoiced.]

Given the limited context of these transcribed excerpts it is difficult to argue that these are revoicings in the sense of Accountable Talk (AT). There are no implicit or explicit invitations, such as a question mark, to assess the tutor's contributions.

While it is possible in the first example that the tutor understood the student to be making a generic statement and was adding "it" to apply it to the particular problem under discussion, it is also possible they have the shared goal of identifying and summing all the forces on a particular object and the tutor is just acknowledging understanding.

The second example seems to draw attention to what is most important in what the student just said. In AT and Questioning the Author (QtA), this type of move is called *marking* instead of *revoicing*. A marking is a reformulation that emphasizes what is most important in what the student said and attempts to direct the student to focus his/her continued discussion on the reformulation.

Although neither of these examples are revoicings in the sense of AT and the first seems more like a repetition to acknowledge rather than reformulate, both are still important to consider for tutorial dialogue. They may help lessen the student's cognitive load (Walker, 1996) by drawing attention to what is most important in what the student said (Becker et al., 2011).

The other recent study of tutorial dialogue that considers revoicing collected a corpus using human tutors who were trained to use QtA and who fill in for a conversational virtual tutor in a science education system (Becker et al., 2011). This corpus has been annotated along multiple dimensions. Two discussion moves from QtA, revoicing and marking, which are noted to be frequent in this corpus, are included in the dialogue act dimension along with other more general speech acts. However, there is no stated goal to annotate other reformulations. So we do not know what other intentions associated with reformulations may appear in the corpus.

In addition, the authors' description of revoicing differs from that used in AT. Here, it is a reformulation that is meant to help a student who is struggling with a particular concept. As shown in the annotated example of revoicing repeated below from (Becker et al., 2011), authority is not relinquished and the student is not invited to assess the reformulation.

> S33: well when you scrub the the paperclip to the magnet the paperclip is starting to be a magnet [Answer/Describe/Process]
> T34: very good, so if the magnet gets close to the paperclip it picks it up [Feedback/Positive/None, Revoice/None/None]

A range of reformulations are recognized in other work on tutorial dialogue and have been incorporated into tutorial dialogue systems. In AutoTutor (Person et al., 2003), elaboration and summary involve reformulation. In Circsim-Tutor (Freedman, 2000), student answers that are close to correct except for terminology trigger a reformulation. Finally, in Beetle II (Dzikovska et al., 2008), restatements of correct and near correct answers involve reformulations. In our work we wish to identify a more comprehensive set of reformulation types and intentions and determine which of these types are most beneficial to emulate.

In this paper we examine a corpus of naturalistic human tutorial dialogues for tutor reformulations. We further outline our plans for implementing revoicing and reformulation in our tutorial dialogue system, Rimac (Katz et al., 2011), which engages high school physics students in post problem solving reflective discussions. By implementing reformulations and revoicings we can begin to test their impact on student learning in a more controlled way in addition to testing whether our approximations of them are adequate.

First, we will describe the corpus of human tutorial dialogues we are analyzing and then we will present examples of some of the reformulations we have found in the corpus and speculate upon possible tutor intentions for these reformulations. We will then outline our plans for implementing certain types of reformulation by first describing the current tutorial dialogue system and the planned modifications for implementing tutor reformulations.

2 The Corpus

The corpus of human tutorial dialogues we are analyzing was collected during a study (Katz et al., 2003) on the effectiveness of reflection questions after a physics problem-solving session with the Andes physics tutoring system (VanLehn et al., 2005). The tutors in this corpus were graduate teaching assistants who had experience in tutoring physics. The students were recruited from introductory undergraduate physics courses.

The students first solved a problem using the Andes system and afterwards they were presented with a deep-reasoning reflection question which they needed to answer. After typing their answer, they then engaged in a typed dialogue with a human tutor to follow up on their answer. This dialogue continued until the tutor was satisfied that the student understood the correct answer. Three to eight reflection questions were asked per problem solved in Andes. There were 12 Andes problems in all.

3 Characterizing Reformulations in Reflective Tutorial Dialogue

As part of our analysis of the corpus described in the previous section, we have been annotating cases of repetition and reformulation across immediately adjacent tutor-student and student-tutor turns (Katz et al., 2011). While this effort is still ongoing and we cannot yet fully characterize the reformulations found, we can show examples of some of the reformulations we have identified and speculate upon what the tutor's intentions may have been. Our goal in this section is to show the variety of intentions one can attribute to these reformulations. Due to space limitations we cannot include examples of the full range of intentions we have found.

The first example, shown below, reformulates what the student said (in italics) by using terminology that is typical to mathematics/physics (in bold). Arguably, "I would call that" may act as a reformulation marker in this example. At the end of a reformulation, we list in square brackets the pragmatics labels we believe best characterize the reformulation.

> T: what direction (in words) is the displacement?
> S: *downwards/towards the negative y-axis*
> T: right: **I would call that the -y direction** [denomination]

The next example, shown below, reformulates what the student said in terms of a more fully specified definition. Inserting "in other words" after "Right" seems felicitous.

> T: What is speed?
> S: *it is velocity without direction*
> T: Right, **The (instantaneous) speed is the magnitude of the (instantaneous) velocity**. [specification/definition]

The next example, shown below, reformulates some of what the student said so that it is correct. Here we can insert the marker "you mean" in front of "the mass and acceleration are related to forces" and arguably "as you point out" could be serving as an explicit reformulation marker. In this case the tutor seems to be correcting an implied "equated to" to "related to."

> S: *the mass and the acceleration push the man into the airbag*
> S: *so aren't they considered forces?*
> T: **the mass and acceleration are related to**

forces as you point out, but in Newtonian mechanics are not considered forces. [correction]

And finally, the example shown below is a reformulation that is a revoicing. In this case the student may be struggling to explain but seems to have a correct conceptual understanding. The tutor attempts to summarize in a clearer way what he thinks the student meant and invites a student assessment with "I think I see what you mean" and the question mark.

> S: no *gravity is no effecting x directly, but if it did not effect y, it would go on forever, and x would countinue to grow as well, but since y has a bound, so does the x*
> T: **I think I see what you mean. That when gravity pulls the ball back to the earth, that the earth then affects the horizontal motion (by direct contact), which wouldn't have happened without gravity?** [summary]
> S: gravity is needed to bring y back to 0 so that the d_x comp is = d

4 The Rimac Tutorial Dialogue System

To understand how we propose to implement reformulations, we must begin with a high level description of the current Rimac system. To build Rimac, we used the TuTalk (Jordan et al., 2007) natural language (NL) tutorial dialogue toolkit. This toolkit enables system developers to focus on developing the content to be presented to students and rapidly developing an end-to-end system for conducting experiments that determine what content and presentation is most pedagogically effective. Tutorial dialogue system developers can gradually transition towards a more principled dialogue system as questions of pedagogical effectiveness are answered, since core modules such as NL understanding and generation are designed to be replaced or supplemented as needed.

The simplest dialogue one can write using this toolkit can be represented as a finite state machine. Each state represents a tutor turn. The arcs leaving the state correspond to all classifications of a student's response turn. When creating a state, the author enters the NL text for a tutor's turn and enters the NL text that defines several classes of student responses as transition arcs, and indicates which state each arc leads to. An arc can also push to another finite state network.

In this toolkit, the NL text associated with a state or an arc is represented by a concept definition. In the simplest case, a concept is a set of NL phrases. For instance, the set for a concept labelled NEG-ACK might be "Not quite," "Well, not exactly," "No." When a student turn is received, the dialogue manager sends a request to the understanding module to determine what concepts it best represents and determines transitions on the basis of the concept labels returned. Likewise when a concept is to be expressed, the dialogue manager asks the generation module to determine how to best express it in NL.

In the next section we outline an initial approach for rapidly testing which reformulations matter to student learning.

5 Implementing Reformulation in Rimac and Future Work

In our preliminary approach for emulating some of the types of reformulation we have found in the corpus, if there is a more preferred phrasing for a matched concept, regardless of whether the student's response is considered correct or incorrect, then a reformulation with the preferred phrasing is presented to the student. How the reformulation is presented depends on the quality or confidence of the concept match. If the student turn is a poor match for a concept, but it is the best available match then the system will revoice the student response; e.g.:

> S: the *distance of the hailstone*
> T: **Are you saying 'distance the hailstone travels'**?

In this example, we assume that "distance of the hailstone" is a poor match for the expected correct concept and it does not match any other concepts that represent an incorrect response. Further, we assume that the author indicated "distance the hailstone travels" as one of the most highly ranked phrases for expressing the correct concept. So the tutor's response revoices using the preferred phrasing. In this example, the tutor's question invites the student to confirm the system's reformulation of her response or try again.

However, if the student's response is a high quality match for a concept but the author ranked this phrasing as a less preferred way of expressing the concept, then the system will reformulate using the most preferred phrasing for the concept; e.g.:

S: *the height of the cloud and the starting place for the hailstone*
T: Good. **You could have also said 'the magnitude of the displacement of the hailstone'**.

Note that we are not yet attempting to distinguish the intentions behind reformulations. Instead we are focusing on when to revoice vs. reformulate. Here, revoicing is similar to the confirmation/clarification questions used in spoken dialogue systems when recognition of the user's speech is uncertain.

We have also implemented a standalone prototype of simple repetitions using the XSLT approach described in (Wilcock, 2001). By this we mean that the system will incorporate part of a student's answer into correctness feedback; e.g. for positive feedback as found in (Chi and Roy, 2010; Dzikovska et al., 2008):

T: in which direction is the acceleration?
S: it is [to the right|eastward]
T: Yes, it is [to the right|eastward]

and, in addition, for negative feedback similar to splicing in (Person et al., 2003); e.g.:

T: in which direction is the acceleration?
S: it is [to the right|eastward]
T: No, if it were [to the right|eastward] then the velocity would be increasing instead of decreasing.

We are currently in the process of completing our analysis of reformulations and are just beginning to implement the approach for revoicing and reformulation we outlined for the Rimac system.

References

I. Beck, M. McKeown, C. Sandora, L. Kucan, and J. Worthy. 1996. Questioning the author: A yearlong classroom implementation to engage students with text. *The Elementary School Journal*, 96(4):385–413.

L. Becker, W. Ward, S. Van Vuuren, and M. Palmer. 2011. Discuss: A dialogue move taxonomy layered over semantic representations. In *IWCS 2011: The 9th International Conference on Computational Semantics*, Oxford, England, January.

M. T. H. Chi and M. Roy. 2010. How adaptive is an expert human tutor? In *Intelligent Tutoring Systems Conference, ITS 2010*, pages 401–412.

M. Dzikovska, G. Campbell, C. Callaway, N. Steinhauser, E. Farrow, J. Moore, L. Butler, and C. Matheson. 2008. Diagnosing natural language answers to support adaptive tutoring. In *Proc. of International FLAIRS Conference*.

R. Freedman. 2000. Using a reactive planner as the basis for a dialogue agent. In *Proc. of International FLAIRS Conference*.

P. Jordan, B. Hall, M. Ringenberg, Y. Cui, and C.P. Rosé. 2007. Tools for authoring a dialogue agent that participates in learning studies. In *Proc. of AIED 2007*.

S. Katz, D. Allbritton, and J. Connelly. 2003. Going beyond the problem given: How human tutors use post-solution discussions to support transfer. *International Journal of Artificial Intelligence and Education*, 13(1):79–116.

S. Katz, P. Albacete, P. Jordan, and D. Litman. 2011. Dialogue analysis to inform the development of a natural-language tutoring system. In *Proc. of SemDial 2011 (Los Angelogue) Workshop on the Semantics and Pragmatics of Dialogue*.

S. Murillo. 2008. The role of reformulation markers in academic lectures. In A.M. Hornero, M.J. Luzón, and S. Murillo, editors, *Corpus Linguistics: Applications for the Study of English*, pages 353–364. Peter Lang AG.

M.C. O'Connor and S. Michaels. 1993. Aligning academic task and participation status through revoicing: Analysis of a classroom discourse strategy. *Anthropology & Education Quarterly*, 24(4):318–335.

N. Person, A. Graesser, R. Kreuz, and V. Pomeroy. 2003. Simulating human tutor dialog moves in autotutor. *International Journal of Artificial Intelligence in Education*, 12(23-39).

K. VanLehn, C. Lynch, K. Schultz, J. A. Shapiro, R. H. Shelby, and L. Taylor. 2005. The Andes physics tutoring system: Lessons learned. *International Journal of Artificial Intelligence and Education*, 3(15):147–204.

M. A. Walker. 1996. The effect of resource limits and task complexity on collaborative planning in dialogue. *Artificial Intelligence Journal*, 85(1-2):181–243.

G. Wilcock. 2001. Pipelines, templates and transformations: Xml for natural language generation. In *1st NLP and XML Workshop*, page 18.

Working with Clinicians to Improve a Patient-Information NLG System

Saad Mahamood and Ehud Reiter
Department of Computing Science
University of Aberdeen
Aberdeen, Scotland, United Kingdom
{s.mahamood, e.reiter}@abdn.ac.uk

Abstract

NLG developers must work closely with domain experts in order to build good NLG systems, but relatively little has been published about this process. In this paper, we describe how NLG developers worked with clinicians (nurses) to improve an NLG system which generates information for parents of babies in a neonatal intensive care unit, using a structured revision process. We believe that such a process can significantly enhance the quality of many NLG systems, in medicine and elsewhere.

1 Introduction

Like other artificial intelligence (AI) systems, most Natural Language Generation (NLG) systems incorporate domain knowledge (and domain communication knowledge (Kittredge et al., 1991)), either implicitly or explicitly. Developers must work with domain experts to acquire such knowledge. Also like software systems in general, applied NLG systems must meet domain and application specific requirements in order to be useful; these again must come from domain experts.

Since very few domain experts are familiar with NLG, it is usually extremely difficult to acquire a complete set of requirements, domain knowledge, and domain communication knowledge at the beginning of an NLG project. Especially, if no pre-existing "golden standard" corpus of domain texts exists. Indeed, in many cases domain experts may find it difficult to give detailed requirements and knowledge until they can see a version of the NLG system working on concrete examples. This suggests that an iterative software development methodology should be used, where domain experts repeatedly try out an NLG system, revise underlying domain (communication) knowledge and request changes to the system's functionality, and wait for developers to implement these changes before repeating the process.

We describe how we carried out this process on BabyTalk-Family (Mahamood and Reiter, 2011), an NLG system which generates summaries of clinical data about a baby in a neonatal intensive care unit (NICU), for the babys parents. Over a 6 month period, this process enabled us to improve an initial version of the system (essentially the result of a PhD) to the point where the system was good enough to be deployable live in a hospital context. We also describe how the feedback from the clinicians changed over the course of this period.

2 Previous Research

Reiter et al. (2003) describe a knowledge acquisition strategy for building NLG systems which includes 4 stages: *directly asking domain experts for knowledge*, *structured knowledge acquisition activities with experts*, *corpus analysis*, and *revision with experts*. In this paper we focus on the last of these phases, revision with experts. Reiter et al. describe this process in high-level qualitative terms; in this paper our goal is to give a more detailed description of the methodology, and also concrete data about the comments received, and how they changed over time.

The most similar previous work which we are

aware of is Williams and Reiter (2005), who describe a methodology for acquiring content selection rules from domain experts, which is also based on an iterative refinement process with domain experts. Their process is broadly similar to what we describe in this paper, but they focus just on content selection, and do not give quantitative data about the revision process.

In the wider software engineering community, there has been a move to iterative development methodologies, instead of the classic "waterfall" pipeline. In particular, agile methodologies (Martin, 2002) are based on rapid iterations and frequent feedback from users; we are in a sense trying to apply some ideas from agile software engineering to the task of building NLG systems. Our methodology also can be considered to be a type of user-centred design (Norman and Draper, 1986).

3 BabyTalk-Family

BabyTalk-Family (Mahamood and Reiter, 2011) generates summaries of clinical data about babies in a neonatal intensive care unit (NICU) for parents. For more details about BabyTalk-Family, including example outputs, please see Mahamood and Reiter.

BabyTalk-Family (BT-Family) was initially developed as part of a PhD project (Mahamood, 2010). As such it was evaluated by showing output texts (based on real NICU data) to people who had previously had a baby in NICU; the texts did not describe the subject's own baby (i.e., the subjects read texts which summarised other people's babies; they had no previous knowledge of these babies). BT-Family was also not rigorously tested from a software quality assurance perspective. The work presented here arose from a followup project whose goal was to deploy BT-Family live in a NICU, where parents who currently had babies in NICU could read summaries of their baby's clinical data. Such a deployment required generated texts to be of much higher quality (in terms of both content and language); we achieved this quality using the revision process described in this paper.

BT-Family is part of the BabyTalk family of systems (Gatt et al., 2009). All BabyTalk systems use the same input data (NICU patient record), but they produce different texts from this data; in particular BT45 (Portet et al., 2009) produces texts which summarise short periods to help real-time decision making by clinicians, and BT-Nurse (Hunter et al., 2011) produces summaries of 12 hours of data for nurses, to support shift handover. BT-Nurse was also deployed in the ward, to facilitate evaluation by nurses who read reports about babies they were currently looking after. To support this deployment, the BT-Nurse developers spent about one month carrying out a revision process with clinicians, in a somewhat unstructured fashion. One outcome of the BT-Nurse evaluation was that the system suffered because the revision process was neither sufficiently well structured nor long enough; this was one of the motivations for the work presented here.

4 Revision Methodology

The revision process was carried out at the Neonatal Intensive Care Unit in conjunction with the hospital Principal Investigator (PI) of our project and two research nurses. We started with an initial familiarisation period for the nurses (the hospital PI was already familiar with BT-Family), where we explained the goals of the project and asked the nurses to examine some example BT-Family texts, which we then discussed.

After the nurses were familiar with the project, we conducted a number of revision cycles. Each cycle followed the following procedure:

1. The clinicians (either the hospital PI or the research nurses) choose between 3 and 11 scenarios (one day's worth of data from one baby). These scenarios were chosen to test the system against a diverse range of babies in different clinical conditions; scenarios were also chosen to check whether issues identified in previous cycles had been addressed.

2. The nurses examined the texts generated by BT-Family for the chosen scenarios. They both directly commented on the texts (by writing notes on hardcopy), and also (in some cases) edited the texts to show what they would have liked to see.

3. The NLG developers analysed the comments and revised texts; distilled from these a list of specific change requests; prioritised the change requests on the basis of importance and difficulty; and implemented as many change requests as possible given the time constraints of the cycle.

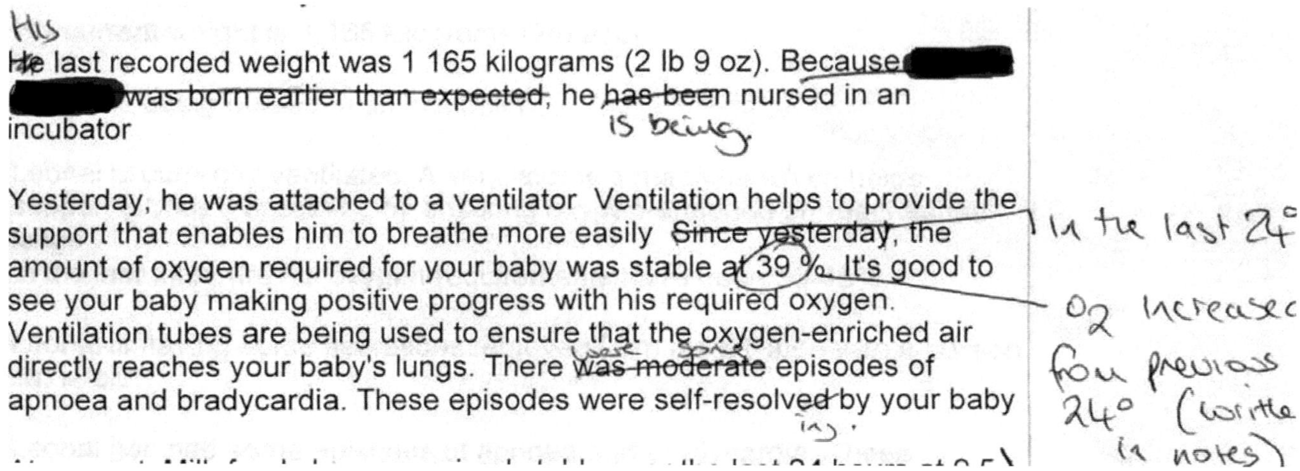
His
He last recorded weight was 1 165 kilograms (2 lb 9 oz). Because [redacted] was born earlier than expected, he has been nursed in an incubator
is being

Yesterday, he was attached to a ventilator Ventilation helps to provide the support that enables him to breathe more easily Since yesterday, the amount of oxygen required for your baby was stable at 39 %. It's good to see your baby making positive progress with his required oxygen. Ventilation tubes are being used to ensure that the oxygen-enriched air directly reaches your baby's lungs. There were some was moderate episodes of apnoea and bradycardia. These episodes were self-resolved by your baby
ing.

In the last 24°
O2 increased from previous 24° (written in notes)

Figure 1: Example of marked up text annotated by a research nurse. The baby's forename has been blacked out.

4. The scenarios were rerun through the updated system, and the NLG developers checked that the issues had been addressed. Clinicians did not usually look at the revised texts, instead they would check that the issues had been resolved in new scenarios in the next cycle.

The above process was carried out 14 times over a 6 month period with each cycle taking on average 11.28 days. A research fellow (Saad Mahamood) was assigned to implement these changes working full-time over this 6 month period. The length between each revision cycle was variable due to the availability of the domain experts and the variable level of complexity to implement identified changes to the BT-Family system.

Figure 1 shows a extract from an early BT-Family text generated in July 2011 that needed a lot of revision. In this example, the nurse has identified the following issues:

- Incorrect pronoun: *He* instead of *His*.
- Unnecessary phrase: *Because XXXX was born earlier than expected.*
- Change in tense: *is being* instead of *has been*.
- Change in wording of time phrase: *In the last 24 hours* instead of *Since yesterday*.
- Incorrect content: incubator oxygen has increased, it is not stable.
- Grammar mistake: *were* instead of *was*.
- Change in content: *some* (frequency) instead of *moderate* (severity).
- Change in wording: *self-resolving* instead of *self-resolved*.

5 Analysis of Feedback over Time

We extracted hand-written comments on BT-Family texts (of the type shown in Figure 1) and annotated the comments using a scheme similar to that used by Hunter et al (2011) for analysing comments on BT-Nurse texts. Two annotators were used with the first annotating the entire set of 75 reports using a pre-agreed classification scheme. The classification scheme that was used consisted of three types of categories: *Content Errors*, *Language Errors*, and *Comments* with each containing specific categorisation labels as shown in Table 1. Content Errors labels were used to annotate comments when there were content based mistakes. Language error labels were used to categorise the different types of language based mistakes. Finally, comment labels were used to classify different types of comments made by the nurses. The second annotator annotated a random partial subset of the reports independently to check for the level of agreement between the first and second annotators. By using Cohen's kappa coefficient we found the level of inter-annotator agreement was $k=0.702$.

Content errors were the most predominate type of annotation (*50.54%*), followed by Language errors (*25.18%*), and comments (*24.27%*). Positive comments were unusual (only 5 in total), because the clinicians were explicitly asked to focus on prob-

Content Errors	Language Errors	Comment
unnecessary *(44.20%)*	spelling mistake *(8.14%)*	positive *(3.75%)*
missing *(28.26%)*	grammar mistake *(22.22%)*	negative *(0.75%)*
wrong *(22.82%)*	incorrect tense/aspect *(18.51%)*	no agreement *(1.50%)*
should-be-elsewhere *(4.71%)*	different word(s) required *(35.55%)*	reformulation *(12.78%)*
	unnecessary words *(3.70%)*	observation *(66.16%)*
	precision/vagueness *(11.85%)*	question *(15.03%)*

Table 1: List of annotation categories and the labels within each category that was used. The frequency for each label in it's category is given in brackets.

Month	Number of revision cycles	Avg. scenarios per cycle	Avg. number of content errors	Avg. number of language errors	Avg. number of comments
June	1	5	1.8	4.2	1.2
July	2	8	4.93	5.5	1.87
August	2	5	4.8	4	5.8
September	2	4	6.37	8.5	4
October	3	7	2.95	1.57	6.42
November	3	5	1.6	1.6	3.6
December	1	5	0.8	0	0.4
Overall	14	5.7	6.92	3.62	3.32

Table 2: Summary table showing the average number of content errors, language errors, and comments per scenario.

lems. Table 2 shows statistics for the revision process per month; the process started in the second half of June, and ended in the first half of December.

From a qualitative perspective, the data suggests that there were two phases to the revision process. In the first phase (June to September), the number of content and language errors in fact went up. We believe this is because during this phase we were adding around 16 new types of content to the reports (based on requests from the clinicians) as well as fixing problems with existing content (of the sort shown in Figure 1); this additional content itself often needed to be revised in subsequent revision cycles, which increased the error count for these cycles. These additional errors from the addition of new content may of arisen due to the complexity and variation of clinical data. Additionally, our 3-year old anonymised test set of clinical data may not of been as representative as the live data due to changes/additions in patient data. In the second phase (October to December), requests for new content diminished (around 4 requests) and we focused on fixing problems with existing content; in this phase, the number of content and language errors steadily decreased (that is, the system improved from the clinician's perspective), until we reached the point in mid December when the clinicians were satisfied that the quality of BT-Family texts was consistently good from their perspective.

When the revision process ended, we started evaluating BT-Family texts directly with parents, by showing parents texts about their babies. This work is ongoing, but initial pilot results to date indicate that parents are very happy with the texts, and do not see major problems with either the language or the content of the texts.

6 Discussion

The revision process had a major impact on the quality of BT-Family texts, as perceived by the clinicians. At the start of the process (June 2011), the texts had so many mistakes that they were unusable; the clinicians would not allow us to show parents BT-Family texts about their babies, even in the context of a pilot study. After 14 revision rounds over a 6 month period, text quality had improved dramatically, to the point where clinicians allowed us to start working directly with parents to get their feedback and comments on BT-Family texts.

The fact that a new set of scenarios was used in every iteration of the revision process was essential to giving clinicians confidence that text quality would be acceptable in new cases; they would not have had such confidence if we had focused on improving the same set of texts.

The revision process took 6 months, which is a considerable amount of time. This process would have been shorter if BT-Family had undergone a more rigorous testing and quality assurance (QA) process ahead of time, which would for example have addressed grammar mistakes, and (more importantly) tested the system's handling of boundary and unusual cases. The process probably could also have been further shortened in other ways, for example by performing 3 revision cycles per month instead of 2.

However, one reason the process took so long was that the functionality of the system changed; as the clinicians got a better idea of what BT-Family could do and how it could help parents, they requested new features, which we tried to add to the system whenever possible. We also had to accommodate changes in the input data (patient record), which reflected changes in NICU procedures due to new drugs, equipment, procedures, etc. So we were not just tweaking the system to make it work better, we were also enhancing its functionality and adapting it to changing input data, which is a time consuming process.

7 Conclusion

We have presented a methodology for improving the quality and appropriateness of texts produced by applied NLG systems, by repeatedly revising texts based on feedback from domain experts. As we have show in the results, the process is a time consuming one, but appears to be quite effective in bringing an NLG system to the required level of quality in a clinical domain.

Acknowledgements

This work is funded by the UK Engineering and Physical Sciences Council (EPSRC) and Digital Economy grant EP/H042938/1. Many thanks to Dr. Yvonne Freer, Alison Young, and Joanne McCormick of the Neonatal Intensive Care Unit at Simpson Centre for Reproductive Health, Royal Infirmary of Edinburgh Hospital, for their help.

References

Albert Gatt, Francois Portet, Ehud Reiter, Jum Hunter, Saad Mahamood, Wendy Moncur, and Somayajulu Sripada. 2009. From data to text in the neonatal intensive care unit: Using NLG technology for decision support and information management. *AI Communications*, 22(3):153–186.

James Hunter, Yvonne Freer, Albert Gatt, Ehud Reiter, Somayajulu Sripada, Cindy Sykes, and Dave Westwater. 2011. BT-Nurse: Computer generation of natural language shift summaries from complex heterogeneous medical data. *Journal of the Americal Medical Informatics Association*, 18(5):621–624.

Richard Kittredge, Tanya Korelsky, and Owen Rambow. 1991. On the need for domain communication language. *Computational Intelligence*, 7(4):305–314.

Saad Mahamood and Ehud Reiter. 2011. Generating affective natural language for parents of neonatal infants. In *Proceedings of the 13th European Workshop on Natural Language Generation*, pages 12–21, Nancy, France, September. Association for Computational Linguistics.

Saad Mahamood. 2010. *Generating Affective Natural Language for Parents of Neonatal Infants*. Ph.D. thesis, University of Aberdeen, Department of Computing Science.

Richard Martin. 2002. *Agile Software Development, Principles, Patterns, and Practices*.

Donald A. Norman and Stephen W. Draper. 1986. *User Centered System Design; New Perspectives on Human-Computer Interaction*. L. Erlbaum Associates Inc., Hillsdale, NJ, USA.

François Portet, Ehud Reiter, Albert Gatt, Jim Hunter, Somayajulu Sripada, Yvonne Freer, and Cindy Sykes. 2009. Automatic generation of textual summaries from neonatal intensive care data. *Artificial Intelligence*, 173(7-8):789–816.

Ehud Reiter, Somayajulu Sripada, and Roma Robertson. 2003. Acquiring correct knowledge for natural language generation. *Journal of Artificial Intelligence Research*, 18:491–516.

Sandra Williams and Ehud Reiter. 2005. Deriving content selection rules from a corpus of non-naturally occurring documents for a novel NLG application. In *Proceedings of Corpus Linguistics workshop on using Corpora for NLG*.

Sign Language Generation with Expert Systems and CCG

Alessandro Mazzei
Dipartimento di Informatica
Università degli Studi di Torino
Corso Svizzera 185, 10185 Torino Italy
mazzei@di.unito.it

Abstract

This paper concerns the architecture of a generator for Italian Sign Language. In particular we describe a microplanner based on an expert-system and a combinatory categorial grammar used in realization.

1 Introduction

In this paper we present the main features of the generator used into a translation architecture from Italian to Italian Sign Language (Lingua Italiana dei Segni, henceforth LIS), that is the sign language used by the Italian deaf (signing) community (Volterra, 2004). Our generator consists of two modules: (i) SentenceDesigner, that is a rule-based microplanner; (ii) OpenCCG, that is a chart realizer (White, 2006). There are two main issues in this work. The first issue concerns the use of an expert system for microplanning. Most of our knowledge about LIS linguistics derives from discussions with linguists: expert systems allow for sharp modularization of this human knowledge. Moreover, expert-system allow us for easily updateable knowledge organization in cases of conflict or contradiction. The second issue in our work concerns the design of a combinatory categorial grammar (CCG) used by the realizer. This CCG accounts for a number of specific LIS phenomena as spatial verb-arguments agreement and NP coordination.[1]

[1] In this paper we present a *grammatical* account for spatial verb-arguments agreement. A different approach, that we are exploring too, is to consider space allocation as separate process that takes as input the syntactic structure, similar to prosody in vocal languages.

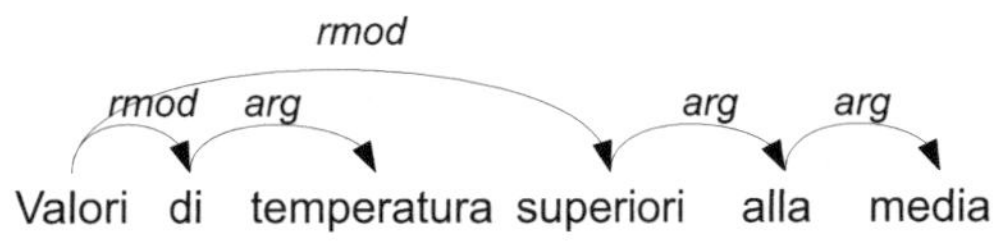

Figure 1: The (simplified) syntactic structure of the sentence "Valori di temperatura superiori alla media" (*Temperature values exceed the average*) produced by the TUP parser.

In order to reduce the difficulties of our project we concentrated on a specific application domain, i.e. weather forecasts: a group of linguists produced a small parallel corpus (300 sentences) of Italian-LIS sentences extracted from TV news and concerning weather forecasts. Building vocal-SL parallel corpora is a hard task: there are theoretical difficulties concerning the extra-video annotation. In particular, while there are standards for the representation of the phonological information of the signs, there are no standard ways to represent their morpho-syntactic inflections. The corpus has been used primarily to produce an electronic dictionary for the virtual interpreter consisting of about 1500 signs, that provides a lexicon for the realizer too. In contrast, most of the knowledge about LIS syntax comes from discussions with some linguists.

2 Parsing and Interpretation

Our interlingua translation system is a chain composed of four distinct modules, that are: (1) a dependency parser for Italian; (2) an ontology based semantic interpreter; (3) a generator; (4) a virtual actor that performs the synthesis of the final LIS sentence. In this Section we give some details about the parser and the semantic interpreter, in Sections 3 and 4 we describe the generator.

In the first step, the syntactic structure of the source language is produced by the TUP, a rule-based parser (Lesmo, 2007). The TUP is based on a morphological dictionary of Italian (about $25,000$ lemmata) and a rule-based grammar, and it produces a *dependency tree*, that makes clear the structural syntactic relationships occurring between the words of the sentence. Each word in the source sentence is associated with a node of the tree, and the nodes are linked via labeled arcs that specify the syntactic role of the dependents with respect to their head (the parent node). In Figure 1 we show the syntactic analysis for the sentence "Valori di temperatura superiori alla media" (rough translation: *Temperature values exceed the average*). The edge label "ARG" indicates an *ARG*ument relation, i.e. an obligatory relation between the head and its argument. The edge label "RMOD" indicates a *R*estricting *MODifier* relation, i.e. a non obligatory relation from the head and its dependent (Bosco and Lombardo, 2004).

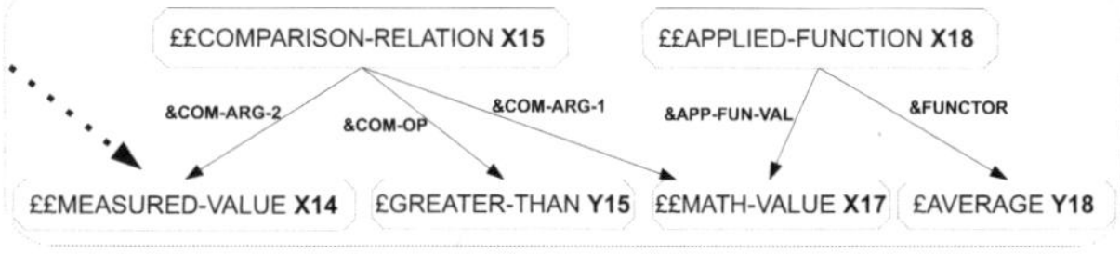

Figure 2: The fragment of the semantic network resulting from the interpretation of the sentence "Valori di temperatura superiori alla media".

The second step of the translation is the semantic interpretation: the syntax-semantics interface is based on ontologies (Lesmo et al., 2011). The knowledge in the ontology, which has been designed for this specific application, concerns the application domain, i.e. weather forecasts, as well as more general common knowledge about the world. Note that the ontology used by the semantic interpreter is not the same ontology used by the generator (microplanner and realizer): indeed, whilst the semantic interpreter ontology describes the linguistic knowledge of the Italian language, the generator describes the linguistic knowledge of the LIS. Starting from the lexical semantics of the words and on the basis of the dependency structure, a recursive function searches in the ontology providing a number of "connection paths" that represent the meaning. In fact, the final sentence meaning consists of a complex fragment of the ontology, i.e. a single connected semantic network (Lesmo et al., 2011). In Figure 2 we show a fragment of the semantic network resulting from the interpretation of the sentence "Valori di temperatura superiori alla media". The nodes of the network contain instances (prefix name £), concepts (prefix name ££) relations (prefix name &) from the ontology. In Figure 2 the nodes AVERAGE, GRATER-THAN are instances, the other nodes are concepts. Informally speaking, we can say that the semantic interpreter organizes the information of the semantic network as a number of "information chunks" that are weakly connected to the other parts of the network. In the network of Figure 2 we can distinguish two chunks. The paraphrase of these chuncks meanings is: there is a (temperature) value involved in a comparison (chunk 1) with a mathematical value that is the average (chunk 2). In the next section we describe how the microplanner manages this organization of the information.

3 The SentenceDesigner microplanner

In a previous version of our system we assumed that the semantic network encoded a single chunk of meaning expressing the semantics of the event only in terms of predicate-arguments. The working hypothesis was to assume a one-to-one sentence alignment between source and target sentences. This simplification assumption allowed for a trivial generation architecture that did not have a microplanning phase at all, and just delegated a simple form of lexicalization to the realizer. However, newer version of the semantic interpreter produced more complex semantic networks. Therefore, in our project we remove the previous assumption and in this Section we describe *SentenceDesigner*, a rule-based microplanner. SentenceDesigner basically performs the following three-steps algorithm:

```
1. Segmentation
   a. Split the semantic network
      into atomic messages
2. Lexicalization
   For each message:
   a. Introduce prelexical nodes
   b. Introduce syntactic relations
      between prelexical nodes
3. Simplification
```

```
For each message:
a. Extend syntactic relations
   among messages
b. Remove non-necessary
   prelexical nodes
c. Remove repetitions
   among messages
d. Remove semantic relations
   and reorder messages
```

In the first step SentenceDesigner split the semantic networks into a number of subgraphs: the idea is to recognize which parts of the network contain an atomic message, i.e. a complete information chunk, that can potentially be generated as a singular sentence. SentenceDesigner uses a very simple heuristic for this step: a message is a subtree of the network, i.e. a root-node together with all of its descendants in the network. We call root-node a node that does not have any parent: in Figure 2 the nodes COMPARISON-RELATION, APPLIED-FUNCTION are root-nodes. Note that some nodes belong to several distinct messages: for example the MATH-VALUE belongs to the messages rooted by COMPARISON-RELATION and APPLIED-FUNCTION respectively.

```
(defrule rule-COMPARISON-RELATION ()
  (semantic-state    (name ££COMPARISON-RELATION) (arg-1 ?X1))
  (semantic-relation (name &COMPAR-ARG1) (arg-1 ?X1) (arg-2 ?X2))
  (semantic-relation (name &COMPAR-ARG2) (arg-1 ?X1) (arg-2 ?X3))
  (semantic-relation (name &COMPAR-OP)    (arg-1 ?X1) (arg-2 ?X4))
   =>
  (assert (syntactic-relation (name SYN-SUBJ) (arg-1 ?X4) (arg-2 ?X2)))
  (assert (syntactic-relation (name SYN-OBJ)  (arg-1 ?X4) (arg-2 ?X3))))

(defrule rule-APPLIED-FUNCTION ()
  (semantic-state    (name ££APPLIED-FUNCTION) (arg-1 ?X1))
  (semantic-relation (name &FUNCTOR) (arg-1 ?X1) (arg-2 ?X2))
  (semantic-relation (name &APPLIED-FUNCTION-VALUE) (arg-1 ?X1)
                                                    (arg-2 ?X3))
   =>
  (assert (syntactic-relation (name SYN-RMOD)  (arg-1 ?X3) (arg-2 ?X2))))
```

Figure 3: Two rules of the knowledge-base used by the expert system for lexicalization.

In the second step, that corresponds to "lexicalization" (Reiter and Dale, 2000), SentenceDesigner performs two distinct procedures for each message. The procedure 2-a. introduces new prelexical nodes in the message that will be treated as lexical items in the realization phase. Also in this case we have a very simple heuristic that associates one-to-one prelexical nodes to concepts and instances. The prelexical nodes are organized into a lexical ontology that is shared with the realizer: in this way the microplanner informs the realizer of the selectional restrictions that the semantics imposes on the syntactic behaviour of lexical nodes (e.g. collocations). For example, the prelexical node value belonging to the class `evaluable-entity` is introduced in place to the concept MATH-VALUE. Note that currently we are not yet able to deal with referring expressions generation for instances, i.e. we uniformly treat concepts and instances: in future we plan to integrate into the system a specific module for this task. The procedure 2-b. concerns the introduction of syntactic relations between prelexical nodes. This is a very complex and critical task: on the one hand we need to encode the linguistic knowledge produced by the corpus analysis (see below) and by many discussions with linguists; on the other hand we need to account for the behaviour of these relations in the CCG used by the realizer. In order to manage this complexity we decided to use an expert system (Stefik et al., 1982).[2] Indeed, expert systems allow for a sharp modularization of the knowledge and allow for a clear resolution of conflicts: we needed several revisions of our formalization and expert systems speed-up this process. In Figure 3 we show two rules that are "fired" by SentenceDesigner during the microplanning of the semantic network in Figure 2: the first rule encodes the *comparison* semantic relation into one *subject* (SYN-SUBJ) and one *object* (SYN-OBJ) syntactic relations; the second rule encodes the semantic relation concerning a mathematical value as a *modifier* (SYN-RMOD) relation. The actual implementation of the system consists of about 50 rules and very complex rules are necessary for particular syntactic constructions as coordination or subordinate clauses, i.e. to manage aggregation.

The third step of the algorithm concerns the simplification of the messages built in the previous step. In 3-a. we "propagate" the syntactic relations among the various messages: if a prelexical node belongs to various messages, then all the syntactic relations starting from that node will be replicated in all the messages. For example, the prelexical node average is replicated in the message rooted by the node COMPARISON-RELATION, since value is connected to the prelexical node average by the syntactic re-

[2] In particular, since SentenceDesigner is written in lisp, we used the LISA expert system. This is an implementation of the RETE algorithm compliant with Common lisp Specifications (Young, 2007).

lation modifier in the message rooted by the node APPLIED-FUNCTION. In 3-b., we remove non necessary prelexical nodes: corpus analysis showed that LIS often is "lexically simpler" with respect to the corresponding Italian sentence, and in order to produce fluent LIS sentences we need to remove some prelexical nodes. For example, the Italian phrase "valori di temperatura" (*values of temperature*) is translated by omitting the sign for "valore". In 3-c., we remove messages that are properly included in other messages: this can happen as a consequence of the procedure 3-a. For example, at this stage the syntactic information of the message rooted by the node APPLIED-FUNCTION is properly contained in the message rooted by the node COMPARISON-RELATION. In 3-d., we remove the semantic relations and reorder the remaining messages on the basis of a simple heuristics: for example, temporal information will be passed first to the realizer. The final

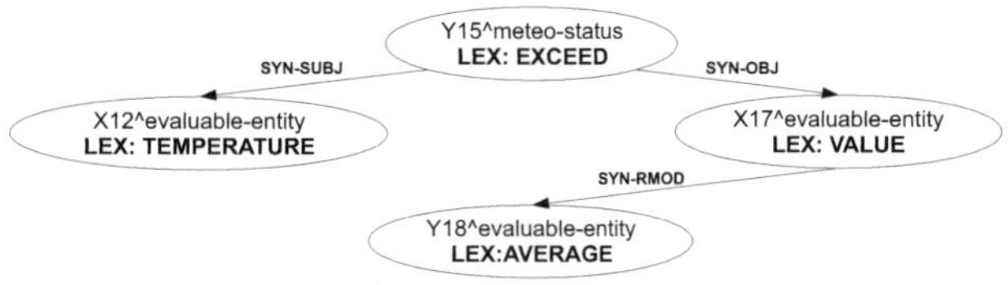

Figure 4: A fragment of the output of SentenceDesigner on the by the semantic network of Figure 2.

result of SentenceDesigner consists of a number of syntactic messages, i.e. a number of abstract syntax trees: each tree will be realized as single sentence (Reiter and Dale, 2000). In Figure 4 there are the abstract syntax tree produced by SentenceDesigner on the input given by the semantic network of Figure 2.

4 A CCG for LIS

In our architecture we use the OpenCCG realizer (White, 2006), an open source tool that is based on categorial grammars (CCG) (Steedman, 2000). Some previous works on translation to SL accounted for typical syntactic phenomena by using lexicalized grammars and feature unification too (Veale and Conway, 1994; Zhao et al., 2000; Huenerfauth, 2006). However we use the OpenCCG since it allows us to encode the LIS inflectional system by using features in the syntactic categories. The

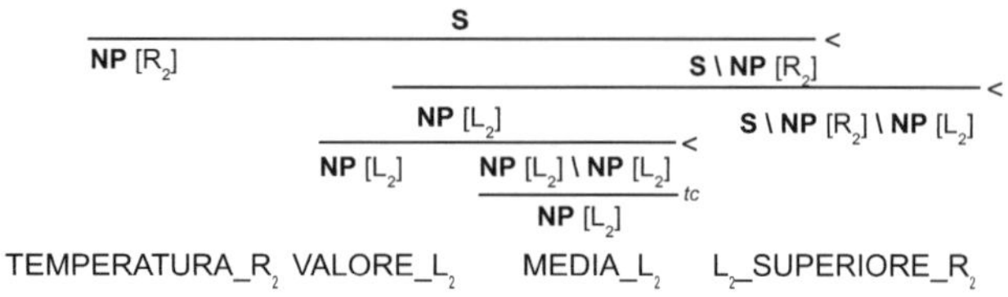

Figure 5: The realization of the LIS sentence "TEMPERATURA_R$_2$ VALORE_L$_2$ MEDIA_L$_2$ L$_2$_SUPERIORE_R$_2$".

integration in one single elementary structure of morphology-syntax-semantics is appealing for SLs, where the absence of function words increases the importance of morpho-syntactic features to express the correct meaning of the sentence.

A challenging requirement of our project is that the SLs do not have a *natural* written form. As a consequence we developed an *artificial* written form for LIS. Our electronic lexicon is stored into a database, such that an entry consists of a unique alphanumeric ID. However, for the sake of clarity here we write a LIS sentence just as a sequence of *glosses*. We use names (in uppercase) for the glosses that are related to their rough translation into Italian. The only feature that we explicitly represent in glosses is the *spatial position* of the sign (cf. (Zhao et al., 2000)). We assume a discrete horizontal dimension consisting of seven positions L_1 (the leftmost position), L_2, L_3, N (the neutral position), R_3, R_2, R_1 (the rightmost position).

Similarly to American SL, in LIS we can tell a number of verb classes on the basis of spatial accord (Volterra, 2004; Wright, 2008; Brentani, 2010). For instance the verb L_i_SUPERIORE_R_j (*exceed*) belongs to the class II-A, i.e. it is a transitive verb such that the starting position of the sign (L_i) coincides with the position of the subject, as well as the ending position of the sign (R_j) coincides with the position of the object (Volterra, 2004). Similarly to (Wright, 2008), we model LIS linguistic phenomenon in CCG by using a morphological feature. This feature encodes the position of the noun in the atomic category NP, as well as the starting and ending position of a verb in the complex category $S\backslash NP\backslash NP$ (in accord with (Geraci, 2004) and in contrast to (Volterra, 2004) we assume that LIS respects the SOV order). In Fig. 5 we show the realization of the LIS sentence "TEMPERATURA_R_2 VALORE_L_2 MEDIA_L_2 L_2_SUPERIORE_R_2" by using the abstract syntactic tree in Figure 4. The feature unification mechanism constraints the NP arguments to agree with the starting and ending position of the verb: the subject TEMPERATURA is signed in the position R_2, i.e. the starting position of the verb SUPERIORE, while the object MEDIA is signed in the position L_2, i.e. the ending position of the verb. More details about our formalization of verb-arguments and NP-coordination in LIS can be found in (Mazzei, 2011).

5 Conclusions

In this paper we have presented a generator for LIS adopted into a symbolic translation architecture. The generator is composed by a expert-system based microplanner and a CCG based realizer. The expert-system allows us to manage and update the knowledge provided by linguists and derived from corpus analysis. CCG allowed for a clear formalization of LIS syntax.

While the design of a quantitative evaluation of the system is still in progress, a preliminary qualitative evaluation provided us some information. In particular, two native LIS signers give a positive evaluation about the space allocation of the signs but give a negative feedback on modifiers word order.

Acknowledgments

This work has been partially supported by the ATLAS project, that is co-funded by Regione Piemonte within the "Converging Technologies - CIPE 2007" framework (Research Sector: Cognitive Science and ICT).

References

Cristina Bosco and Vincenzo Lombardo. 2004. Dependency and relational structure in treebank annotation. In *Proc. of the COLING'04 workshop on Recent Advances in Dependency Grammar*, Geneve, Switzerland.

Dana Brentani, editor. 2010. *Sign Languages*. Cambridge University Press.

Carlo Geraci. 2004. L'ordine delle parole nella LIS (lingua dei segni italiana). In *Convegno nazionale della Società di Linguistica Italiana*.

Matt Huenerfauth. 2006. *Generating American Sign Language classifier predicates for english-to-asl machine translation*. Ph.D. thesis, University of Pennsylvania.

Leonardo Lesmo, Alessandro Mazzei, and Daniele P. Radicioni. 2011. An ontology based architecture for translation. In *Proceedings of the Ninth International Conference on Computational Semantics (IWCS 2011)*, The University of Oxford.

Leonardo Lesmo. 2007. The Rule-Based Parser of the NLP Group of the University of Torino. *Intelligenza Artificiale*, 2(4):46–47, June.

Alessandro Mazzei. 2011. Building a generator for italian sign language. In *Proceedings of the 13th European Workshop on Natural Language Generation*, pages 170–175, Nancy, France, September. Association for Computational Linguistics.

Ehud Reiter and Robert Dale. 2000. *Building natural language generation systems*. Cambridge University Press, New York, NY, USA.

Mark Steedman. 2000. *The syntactic process*. MIT Press, Cambridge, MA, USA.

Mark Stefik, Jan Aikins, Robert Balzer, John Benoit, Lawrence Birnbaum, Frederick Hayes-Roth, and Earl D. Sacerdoti. 1982. The organization of expert systems, a tutorial. *Artif. Intell.*, 18(2):135–173.

Tony Veale and Alan Conway. 1994. Cross modal comprehension in zardoz an english to sign-language translation system. In *Proceedings of the Seventh International Workshop on Natural Language Generation*, INLG '94, pages 249–252, Stroudsburg, PA, USA. Association for Computational Linguistics.

Virginia Volterra, editor. 2004. *La lingua dei segni italiana*. Il Mulino.

Michael White. 2006. Efficient realization of coordinate structures in combinatory categorial grammar. *Research on Language and Computation*, 2006(4(1)):39—75.

Tony Wright. 2008. A combinatory categorial grammar of a fragment of american sign language. In *Proc. of the Texas Linguistics Society X Conference*. CSLI Publications.

David E. Young. 2007. The Lisa Project. http://lisa.sourceforge.net/.

Liwei Zhao, Karin Kipper, William Schuler, Christian Vogler, Norman I. Badler, and Martha Palmer. 2000. A machine translation system from english to american sign language. In *Proceedings of the 4th Conference of the Association for Machine Translation in the Americas on Envisioning Machine Translation in the Information Future*, AMTA '00, pages 54–67, London, UK, UK. Springer-Verlag.

Planning Accessible Explanations for Entailments in OWL Ontologies

Tu Anh T. Nguyen, Richard Power, Paul Piwek, Sandra Williams
The Open University
Milton Keynes, United Kingdom
{t.nguyen,r.power,p.piwek,s.h.williams}@open.ac.uk

Abstract

A useful enhancement of an NLG system for verbalising ontologies would be a module capable of explaining undesired entailments of the axioms encoded by the developer. This task raises interesting issues of content planning. One approach, useful as a baseline, is simply to list the subset of axioms relevant to inferring the entailment; however, in many cases it will still not be obvious, even to OWL experts, why the entailment follows. We suggest an approach in which further statements are added in order to construct a proof tree, with every step based on a relatively simple deduction rule of known difficulty; we also describe an empirical study through which the difficulty of these simple deduction patterns has been measured.

1 Introduction

A practical problem in developing ontologies for the semantic web is that mistakes are hard to spot. One reason for this lies in the opacity of the standard OWL formalisms, such as OWL/RDF, which are designed for efficient processing by computer programs and not for fast comprehension by people. Various tools have been proposed to address this problem, including not only graphical interfaces such as Protégé, but NLG (Natural Language Generation) programs that *verbalise* the axioms of an ontology as text (Kaljurand and Fuchs, 2007; Schwitter and Meyer, 2007; Hart et al., 2008). Using such a tool, a mistaken axiom presented through a sentence like 'Every person is a movie' immediately leaps to the eye.

Although there is evidence that verbalisation helps developers to check individual axioms (Stevens et al., 2011), there remains a more subtle problem of undesired *entailments*, often based on interactions among axioms. The difference between axioms and entailments is that whereas axioms are statements encoded by the developer, entailments are statements inferred from axioms by automated reasoners such as FaCT++ (Tsarkov and Horrocks, 2006). Because reasoning systems interpret statements absolutely literally, it is quite common for apparently innocuous axioms to lead to absurd conclusions such as 'Everything is a person', 'Nothing is a person', or indeed 'Every person is a movie'. The standard reasoning algorithms, based on tableau algorithms, will compute these entailments efficiently, but they provide no information that helps explain *why* an undesired conclusion was drawn, and hence which axiom or axioms need to be corrected.

To provide an explanation of an entailment, the first step is obviously to determine which axioms are relevant to the inference. A set of relevant axioms is known technically as a *justification* of the entailment, defined as any minimal subset of the ontology from which the entailment can be drawn (Kalyanpur, 2006). The minimality requirement here means that if any axiom is removed from a justification, the entailment will no longer be inferable.

Drawing on Kalyanpur's work, the most direct strategy for planning an explanation is simply to verbalise the axioms in the justification, followed by the entailment, with no additional content. This strategy serves as a useful baseline for comparison, and might even be effective for some simple justi-

Entailment	$Person \sqsubseteq Movie$	*Every person is a movie.*
Justification	1. $GoodMovie \equiv \forall hasRating.FourStars$ 2. $Domain(hasRating) = Movie$ 3. $GoodMovie \sqsubseteq StarRatedMovie$ 4. $StarRatedMovie \sqsubseteq Movie$	1. *A good movie is anything that only has ratings of four stars.* 2. *Anything that has a rating is a movie.* 3. *Every good movie is a star-rated movie.* 4. *Every star-rated movie is a movie.*

Table 1: An example justification that requires further explanation

fications; however, user studies have shown that in many cases even OWL experts are unable to work out how the conclusion follows from the premises without further explanation (Horridge et al., 2009). This raises two problems of content planning that we now address: (a) how we can ascertain that further explanation is needed, and (b) what form such explanation should take.

2 Explaining complex justifications

An example of a justification requiring further explanation is shown in Table 1. Statements are presented in mathematical notation in the middle column (rather than in OWL, which would take up a lot more space), with a natural language gloss in the right column. Since these sentences are handcrafted they should be more fluent than the output of a verbaliser, but even with this benefit, it is extremely hard to see why the entailment follows.

The key to understanding this inference lies in the first axiom, which asserts an equivalence between two classes: good movies, and things that only have ratings of four stars. The precise condition for an individual to belong to the second class is that all of its ratings should be four star, and this condition would be trivially satisfied *if the individual had no ratings at all*. From this it follows that people, parrots, parsnips, or in general things that cannot have a rating, all belong to the second class, which is asserted to be equivalent to the class of good movies. If individuals with no rating are good movies, then by axioms 3 and 4 they are also movies, so we are left with two paradoxical statements: individuals *with* a rating are movies (axiom 2), and individuals *without* a rating are movies (the intermediate conclusion just derived). Since everything that exists must either have some rating or no rating, we are driven to the conclusion that everything is a movie, from which it follows that any person (or parrot, etc.) must also be a movie: hence the entailment. Our target explanation for this case is as follows:

> Every person is a movie because the ontology implies that everything is a movie.
> Everything is a movie because (a) anything that has a rating is a movie, and (b) anything that has no rating at all is a movie.
> Statement (a) is stated in axiom 2 in the justification. Statement (b) is inferred because the ontology implies that (c) anything that has no rating at all is a good movie, and (d) every good movie is a movie.
> Statement (d) is inferred from axioms 3 and 4 in the justification. Statement (c) is inferred from axiom 1, which asserts an equivalence between two classes: 'good movie' and 'anything that has as rating only four stars'. Since the second class trivially accepts anything that has no rating at all, we conclude that anything that has no rating at all is a good movie.

Note that in this or any other intelligible explanation, a path is traced from premises to conclusion by introducing a number of intermediate statements, or *lemmas*. Sometimes a lemma merely unpacks part of the meaning of an axiom — the part that actually contributes to the entailment. This is clearly what we are doing when we draw from axiom 1 the implication that all individuals with no ratings are good movies. Alternatively a lemma could be obtained by combining two axioms, or perhaps even more. By introducing appropriate lemmas of either type, we can construct a *proof tree* in which the root node is the entailment, the terminal nodes are the axioms in the justification, and the other nodes are lemmas. An explanation based on a proof tree should be easier to understand because it replaces a single complex inference step with a number of simpler ones.

Assuming that some kind of proof tree is needed, the next question is how to construct proof trees that provide *effective* explanations. Here two conditions need to be met: (1) the proof tree should be correct, in the sense that all steps are valid; (2) it should be accessible, in the sense that all steps are understandable. As can be seen, one of these conditions is logical, the other psychological. Several research groups have proposed methods for producing logically correct proof trees for description logic (McGuinness, 1996; Borgida et al., 1999; Horridge et al., 2010), but explanations planned in this way will not necessarily meet our second requirement. In fact they could fail in two ways: either they might employ a single reasoning step that most people cannot follow, or they might unduly complicate the text by including multiple steps where a single step would have been understood equally well. We believe this problem can be addressed by constructing the proof tree from deduction rules for which the intuitive difficulty has been *measured* in an empirical study.[1]

3 Collecting Deduction Rules

For our purposes, a deduction rule consists of a conclusion (i.e., an entailment) and up to three premises from which the conclusion logically follows. Both conclusion and premises are generalised by using variables that abstract over class and property names, as shown in Table 2, where for example the second rule corresponds to the well-known syllogism that from 'Every A is a B' and 'Every B is a C', we may infer 'Every A is a C'.

Our deduction rules were derived through a corpus study of around 500 OWL ontologies. First we computed entailment-justification pairs using the method described in Nguyen et al. (2010), and collated them to obtain a list of deduction patterns ranked by frequency. From this list, we selected patterns that were simple (in a sense that will be explained shortly) and frequent, subsequently adding some further rules that occurred often as *parts* of more complex deduction patterns, but were not computed as separate patterns because of certain limitations of the reasoning algorithm.[2] The deduction rules required for the previous example are shown in Table 2. So far, 41 deduction rules have been obtained in this way; these are sufficient to generate proof trees for 48% of the justifications of subsumption entailments in the corpus (i.e., over 30,000 justifications).

As a criterion of *simplicity* we considered the number of premises (we stipulated not more than three) and also what is called the 'laconic' property (Horridge et al., 2008) — that an axiom should not contain information that is not required for the entailment to hold. We have assumed that deduction rules that are simple in this sense are more likely to be *understandable* by people; we return to this issue in section 5, which describes an empirical test of the understandability of the rules.

4 Constructing Proof Trees

A proof tree can be defined as any tree linking the axioms of a justification (terminal nodes) to an entailment (root node), in such a way that every local tree (i.e., every node and its children) corresponds to a deduction rule. This means that if the entailment and justification already correspond to a deduction rule, no further nodes (i.e., lemmas) need to be added. Otherwise, a proof can be sought by applying the deduction rules, where possible, to the terminal nodes, so introducing lemmas and growing the tree bottom-up towards the root. Exhaustive search using this method may yield zero, one or multiple solutions — e.g., for our example two proof trees were generated, as depicted in Figure 1.[3]

5 Measuring understandability

To investigate the difficulty of deduction rules empirically, we have conducted a survey in which 43 participants (mostly university staff and students unfamiliar with OWL) were shown the premises of the rule, expressed as English sentences concerning fictitious entities, and asked to choose the correct conclusion from four alternatives. They were also asked to rate the difficulty of this choice on a five-point scale. For instance, in one problem the premises

[1] Deduction rules were previously used by Huang for reconstructing machine-generated mathematical proofs; however, these rules were not for description logic based proofs and assumed to be intuitive to people (Huang, 1994). The output proofs were then enhanced (Horacek, 1999) and verbalised (Huang, 1994).

[2] Reasoning services for OWL typically compute only some kinds of entailment, such as subclass and class membership statements, and ignore others.

[3] In the current implementation, the proof tree can also be developed by adding lemmas that unpack part of the meaning of an axiom, using the method proposed by Horridge et al.(2008). These steps in the proof are not always obvious, so their understandability should also be measured.

ID	Deduction Rule	Example	Success Rate
1	$\forall r.\bot \sqsubseteq C$ $\exists r.\top \sqsubseteq C$ $\rightarrow \top \sqsubseteq C$	*Anything that has no ratings at all is a movie.* *Anything that has a rating is a movie.* *→ Everything is a movie.*	65%
2	$C \sqsubseteq D$ $D \sqsubseteq E$ $\rightarrow C \sqsubseteq E$	*Anything that has no ratings at all is a good movie.* *Every good movie is a movie.* *→ Anything that has no ratings at all is a movie.*	88%
3	$C \equiv \forall r.D$ $\rightarrow \forall r.\bot \sqsubseteq C$	*A good movie is anything that only has ratings of four stars.* *→ Anything that has no ratings at all is a good movie.*	—

Table 2: Deduction rules for the example in Table 1

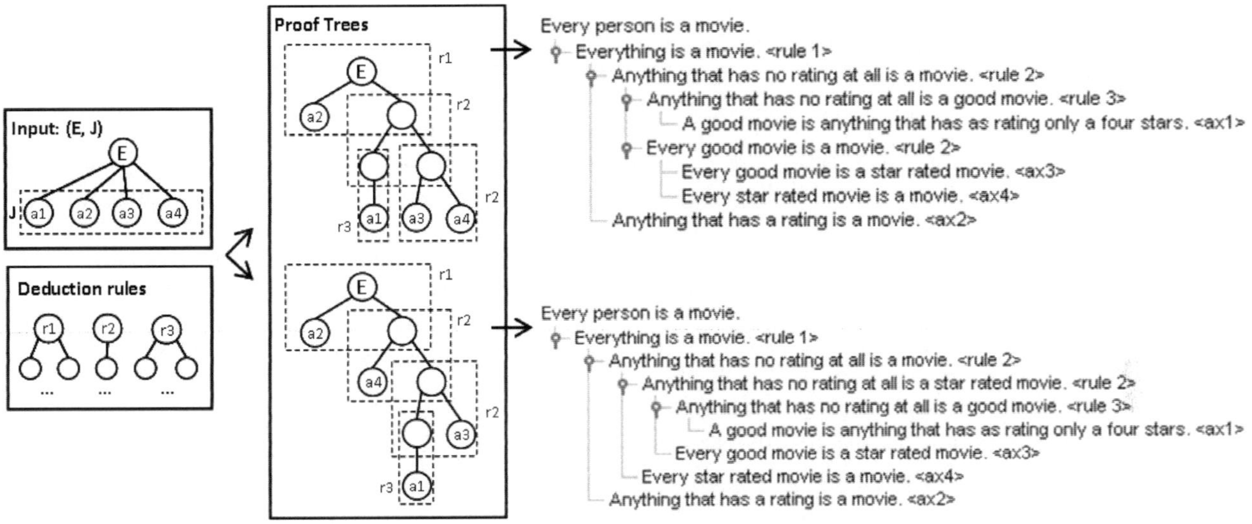

Figure 1: Proof trees generated by our current system

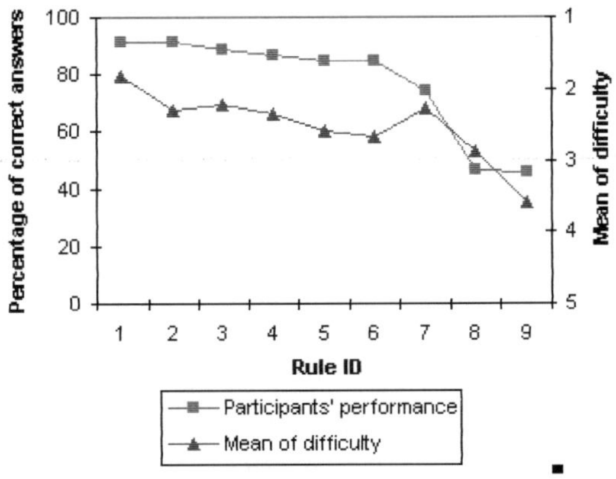

Figure 2: Results of the empirical study. In our difficulty scale, 1 means 'very easy' and 5 means 'very difficult'

were 'Every verbeeg is a giantkin; no giantkin is a verbeeg.'; to answer correctly, participants had to tick 'Nothing is a verbeeg' and not 'Nothing is a giantkin'.

So far 9/41 deduction rules have been measured in this way. Figure 2 shows the success rates and the means of difficulty of those rules. For most problems the success rates were around 80%, confirming that the rules were understandable, although in a few cases performance fell to around 50%, suggesting that further explanation would be needed. The study also indicates a statistically significant relationship between the accuracy of the participants' performance and their perceptions of difficulty ($r = 0.82$, $p < 0.01$). Two of the three rules in Table 2 were measured in this way. The third rule has not been tested yet; however, its success rate is expected to be very low as it was proved to be a very difficult inference (Horridge et al., 2009).

6 Conclusion

This paper has reported our work in progress on content planning for explanations of entailments. The main steps involved in the planning process are sum-

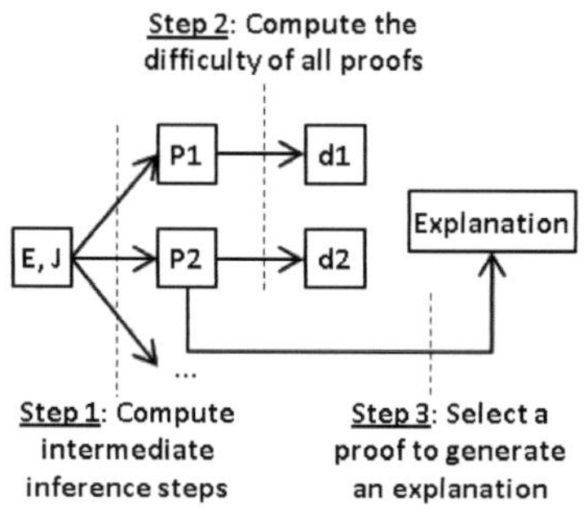

Figure 3: Our approach for the content planning. E, J, Pn are entailments, justifications and proofs respectively; d1 and d2 are difficulty scores and d2 $\leq$ d1

marised in Figure 3. We have focused on one aspect: the introduction of lemmas that mediate between premises and conclusion, so organising the proof into manageable steps. Lemmas are derived by applying deduction rules collected through a corpus study on entailments and their justifications. Through a survey we have measured the difficulty of some of these rules, as evidenced by performance on the task of choosing the correct conclusion for given premises. These measures should indicate which steps in a proof are relatively hard, and thus perhaps in need of further elucidation, through special strategies that can be devised for each problematic rule. Our hypothesis is that these measures will also allow an accurate assessment of the difficulty of a candidate proof tree, so providing a criterion for choosing among alternatives — e.g., by using the success rates as an index of difficulty, we can sum the index over a proof tree to obtain a simple measure of its difficulty. Our verbaliser currently translates OWL statements literally, and needs to be improved to make sure any verbalisations do not give rise to unwanted presuppositions and Gricean implicatures.

Acknowledgments

This research was undertaken as part of the ongoing SWAT project (Semantic Web Authoring Tool), which is supported by the UK Engineering and Physical Sciences Research Council (EPSRC). We thank our colleagues and the anonymous viewers.

References

Alexander Borgida, Enrico Franconi, Ian Horrocks, Deborah L. McGuinness, and Peter F. Patel-Schneider. 1999. Explaining $\mathcal{ALC}$ Subsumption. In *DL 1999, International Workshop on Description Logics*.

Glen Hart, Martina Johnson, and Catherine Dolbear. 2008. Rabbit: developing a control natural language for authoring ontologies. In *ESWC 2008, European Semantic Web Conference*, pages 348–360.

Helmut Horacek. 1999. Presenting Proofs in a Human-Oriented Way. In *CADE 1999, International Conference on Automated Deduction*, pages 142–156.

Matthew Horridge, Bijan Parsia, and Ulrike Sattler. 2008. Laconic and Precise Justifications in OWL. In *ISWC 2008, International Semantic Web Conference*, pages 323–338.

Matthew Horridge, Bijan Parsia, and Ulrike Sattler. 2009. Lemmas for Justifications in OWL. In *DL 2009, International Workshop on Description Logics*.

Matthew Horridge, Bijan Parsia, and Ulrike Sattler. 2010. Justification Oriented Proofs in OWL. In *ISWC 2010, International Semantic Web Conference*, pages 354–369.

Xiaorong Huang. 1994. *Human Oriented Proof Presentation: A Reconstructive Approach*. Ph.D. thesis, The University of Saarbrücken, Germany.

Kaarel Kaljurand and Norbert Fuchs. 2007. Verbalizing OWL in Attempto Controlled English. In *OWLED 2007, International Workshop on OWL: Experiences and Directions*.

Aditya Kalyanpur. 2006. *Debugging and repair of OWL ontologies*. Ph.D. thesis, The University of Maryland, US.

Deborah Louise McGuinness. 1996. *Explaining reasoning in description logics*. Ph.D. thesis, The State University of New Jersey, US.

Tu Anh T. Nguyen, Paul Piwek, Richard Power, and Sandra Williams. 2010. Justification Patterns for OWL DL Ontologies. Technical Report TR2011/05, The Open University, UK.

Rolf Schwitter and Thomas Meyer. 2007. Sydney OWL Syntax - towards a Controlled Natural Language Syntax for OWL 1.1. In *OWLED 2007, International Workshop on OWL: Experiences and Directions*.

Robert Stevens, James Malone, Sandra Williams, Richard Power, and Allan Third. 2011. Automating generation of textual class definitions from OWL to English. *Journal of Biomedical Semantics*, 2(S 2:S5).

Dmitry Tsarkov and Ian Horrocks. 2006. FaCT++ Description Logic Reasoner: System Description. In *IJCAR 2006, International Joint Conference on Automated Reasoning*, pages 292–297.

Interactive Natural Language Query Construction for Report Generation*

Fred Popowich
School of Computing Science
Simon Fraser University
Burnaby, BC, CANADA
popowich@sfu.ca

Milan Mosny
Response42 Inc
North Vancouver, BC, Canada
Milan.Mosny
@response42.com

David Lindberg
School of Computing Science
Simon Fraser University
Burnaby, BC, CANADA
dll4@sfu.ca

Abstract

Question answering is an age old AI challenge. How we approach this challenge is determined by decisions regarding the linguistic and domain knowledge our system will need, the technical and business acumen of our users, the interface used to input questions, and the form in which we should present answers to a user's questions. Our approach to question answering involves the interactive construction of natural language queries. We describe and evaluate a question answering system that provides a point-and-click, web-based interface in conjunction with a semantic grammar to support user-controlled natural language question generation. A preliminary evaluation is performed using a selection of 12 questions based on the Adventure Works sample database.

1 Introduction

There is a long history of systems that allow users to pose questions in natural language to obtain appropriate responses from information systems (Katz, 1988; El-Mouadib et al., 2009). Information systems safeguard a wealth of information, but traditional interfaces to these systems require relatively sophisticated technical know-how and do not always present results in the most useful or intuitive way for non-technical users. Simply put, people and computers do not speak the same language. The question answering challenge is thus the matter of developing a method that allows users with varying levels of technical proficiency to ask questions using natural language and receive answers in an appropriate, intuitive format. Using natural language to ask these questions may be easy for users, but is challenging due to the ambiguity inherent in natural language anaylsis. Proposals involving controlled natural language, such as (Nelken and Francez, 2000), can deal with some of the challenges, but the task becomes more difficult when we seek to answer natural language questions in a way that is domain portable.

Before we can attempt to design and implement a question answering system, we need to address several key issues. First, we need to decide what knowledge our system needs. Specifically, we must decide what *linguistic knowledge* is needed to properly interpret users' questions. Then we need to consider what kind of *domain-specific knowledge* the system must have and how that knowledge will be stored and accessed. We must address the challenges posed by *users* with varying levels of technical sophistication and domain knowledge. The sophistication of the user and the environment in which the system is used will also affect how users will give *input* to the system. Will we need to process text, speech, or will a simpler point-and-click interface be sufficient? Finally, we must decide how to best *answer* the user's questions, whether it be by fetching pre-existing documents, dynamically generating structured database reports, or producing natural language sentences. These five issues do not present us with a series of independent choices that are merely stylistic or cosmetic. The stance we take regarding each of these issues strongly influences design decisions, ease of installation/configuration, and the end-user experience.

Here we solve this problem in the context of ac-

*This research was supported in part by a discovery grant from the Natural Sciences and Engineering Research Council of Canada. The authors would also like to thank the referees for their insights and suggestions.

cessing information from a structured database – a natural language interface to a database (NLIDB) (Kapetanios et al., 2010). However, instead of treating it as a natural language analysis problem, we will consider it as a task involving natural language generation (NLG) where users build natural language questions by making choices that add words and phrases. Using our method, users construct queries in a menu driven manner (Tennant et al., 1983; Evans and Power, 2003) to ask questions that are always unambiguous and easy for anyone to understand, getting answers in the form of interactive database reports (not textual reports) that are both immediate and consistent.

This approach retains the main advantage of traditional NLIDBs that allow input of a question in a free form text – the ability for the user to communicate with the information system in English. There is no need for the user to master a computer query langauge such as SQL or MDX. Many disadvantges of traditional free input NLIDBs are removed (Tennant et al., 1983). Traditional NLIDBs fail to analyze some questions and indicate so to the user, greatly decreasing the user's confidence in the system. The problem is even worse when the NLIDB analyzes the question incorrectly and produces a wrong or unpexpected result. In contrast, our system is able to answer every question correctly. In traditional free input NLIDBs, the user can make grammatical or spelling mistakes that may lead to other errors. Using a menu-based technique, the user is forced to input only valid and wellformed queries. The complexity of the system is greatly reduced as the language that the system has to process is simple and unambiguous. Portability to other domains is improved because there is no need for vocabulary that fully covers the domain.

2 Our approach

We begin with an overview of our approach to this question answering problem involving NLG. We describe how we address each of the afore-mentioned issues and give our rationale for each of those choices. Following a brief discussion of our use of online analytical processing (OLAP) (Janus and Fouche, 2009) in section 2.2, we then decribe how we use the OLAP model as the basis for interactive natural query generation, and describe the database used in our evaluation, along with the grammar used for NLG.

2.1 Overview

Our approach to the question answering problem is based on the following decisions and assumptions:

Linguistic knowledge We use a semantic grammar to support user-controlled NLG rather than language analysis. By guiding the construction process, we avoid difficult analysis tasks, such as resolving ambiguities and clarifying vague language. We also eliminate the possibility of out-of-domain queries.

Domain-specific knowledge We model domain knowledge using an OLAP cube, a widely-used approach to model domain-specific data. OLAP cubes provide a standard semantic representation that is well-suited to historical business data and allows us to automatically generate both the lexicon and the semantic grammar for our system.

Users The prototypical user of our system is familiar with business issues but does not have a high-degree of technical expertise. We provide a simple and intuitive interface suitable for such users but still powerful enough for users of any level of technical proficiency.

Input A web-based, point-and-click interface will guide users in the creation of a natural language query string. Users click on words and phrases to construct a question in plain English.

Answers We will answer questions with an interactive database report. Users can click on parts of the report to get detailed information, making it more of an interactive dashboard rather than a report.

An approach governed by these principles offers many benefits. It simplifies database report creation and lowers the associated costs, allows businesses to leverage existing investments in data warehouse and reporting technology, offers a familiar and comfortable interface, does not require installation on client machines, and is simple to install and configure.

2.2 Role of OLAP

An OLAP cube is produced as a result of processing a datawarehouse into datastructures optimized for query processing. The OLAP query language makes reference to measure groups (that roughly correspond to fact tables), measures (that come from the numerical values in the fact tables) and dimensions (that come from dimension tables). For example, the *order* fact table might include total order price, order quantity, freight cost, and discount amount. These are the essential figures that describe orders, but to know more we need to examine these facts along one or more dimensions. Accordingly, the dimension tables associated with this fact table include time (order date, year, quarter, and month), customer (name, address, city, and zip code), and product (name, category, and price).

2.3 Interactive Natural Language Generation

At the heart of the system is a semantic grammar. Our goal was to create a grammar that is suitable to database querying application, but is simple enough so that it can be automatically adapted to different domains. The semantic model makes use of both entities (unary predicates) and relationships (binary predicates) that are automatically derived from the OLAP model. These entities and relationships can be directly and automatically mapped to the lexical items and phrases that the user sees on the screen during query construction. Once a user has completed the construction of a natural language query, a corresponding first order logic formula is created which can then be translated into a database query in SQL or MDX.

Our assumption was that many database queries can be expressed within the following template

```
Show <Show> and ... and <Show> for
each <GroupBy> and ...  and for
each <GroupBy> limit to <LimitTo>
and ... and  to <LimitTo>
```

where `<Show>`, `<GroupBy>` and `<LimitTo>` are different classes of nominals. `<Show>` may refer to a measure or to a level in a dimension which may take an additional constraint in a form of a prepositional clause. `<GroupBy>` may refer to a level in a dimension which may take a constraint in a form of a prepositional phrase or to a set of members of a dimension. `<LimitTo>` may refer to a set of members of a dimension. A prepositional phrase expressing a constraint has a form

```
with <NounPhrase>
```

```
QuestionElement
    Terminal
        EntityTerminal
            GroupByEntityTerminal
    Nonterminal
        TopLevel
        GroupBy
        LimitTo
        Show
        PrepositionalClause
        Determiner
        NounPhrase
        List
```

Figure 1: Semantic Grammar Element Classes

where the noun phrase consists of a determiner such as "some", "no", "at least N", "exactly N" and a noun referring to a measure.

The semantic grammar makes use of classes in an inheritance hierarchy as shown in Figure 1. Each question element corresponds to a parametrized terminal or nonterminal. That is, it can play a role of one of multiple terminals or nonterminals depending on its initialization parameters. There are altogether 13 classes that comprise the elements of the grammar. The implementations of the different class elements make use of semantic constraints as appropriate. Only minimal human intervention is required when adapting the system to a new OLAP cube. The intervention consists of "cleaning up" the automatically generated terminal symbols of the semantic grammar so that the plural and singular forms that were present in the cube metadata are used consistently and so that the mass vs. countable attribute of each measure is set appropriately.

3 Evaluation

An evaluation of this kind of system requires an examination of three performance metrics: domain coverage, ease of use, and query efficiency. How well the system covers the target domain is crucially important. In order to measure domain coverage, we need to determine how many answerable questions can actually be answered using the system. We can answer this question in part by examining the user interface. Does the interface restrict users' access to domain elements and relationships? A more thorough assessment of domain coverage requires extensive user studies.

Ease of use is often thought of as a qualitative measure of performance, but a systematic, objective evaluation requires us to define a quantitative measure. The primary action used to generate queries in our system is the "click." Users click on items to refine their queries, so the number of clicks required to generate queries seems like a reasonable starting point for evaluating ease of use. The time it takes users to make those clicks is important. A four-click query sounds efficient, but if it takes the user two minutes to figure out which four clicks need to be made, not much is gained. It would be ideal if the number of clicks and the time needed to make those clicks grow proportionally. That is, we do not want to penalize users who need to build longer queries.

Query efficiency is measured by the time between the user submitting a query and the system presenting the answer. How long must a user wait while data is being fetched and the report generated? Unlike ease of use, this is objectively measurable and easy to benchmark.

In our initial evaluation, we applied these metrics to a selection of 12 natural language questions about the data in the Adventure Works (Codeplex Open Source Community, 2008) database that could be answered by our natural language query construction system. These questions were generated by a user with prior exposure to the Adventure Works database but no prior exposure to the query construction software system or its design or algorithms, so the questions are not purposely fine-tuned to yield artificially optimal results. Eight of these questions were directly answerable, while four were indirectly answerable. For each of these questions, we measured the number of clicks required to generate the query string, the time it took to make the required clicks, and the time required to retrieve the needed records and generate a report. The distinction between directly answerable and indirectly answerable questions deserves a short explanation. A question is deemed directly answerable if the answer is the sole result returned in the report or if the answer is included in a group of results returned. A question is deemed indirectly answerable if the report generated based on a related query can be used to calculate the answer or if the information relevant to the answer is a subset of the information returned. So, the question *What are the top 20 products based on internet sales* was directly answerable through the constructed query *Show products with one of 20 highest internet sales amount*, while the question *What is the averagefreight cost for internet orders over $1000* could only be answered *Show internet freight cost for customers with more than 1000 dollars of internet sales amount and for each date.*

We found that a user was able to construct natural language queries using between 2 and 6 clicks which required 10 and 57 seconds of elaspsed time for the construction process. On average 3.3 clicks were required to create a query with an average time of 33 seconds, where the time grew in a linear manner based on the number of clicks. Once a query was constructed, the average time to generate a report was 6.7 seconds with the vast majority of queries producing a report from the database system in 4 seconds or less. The median values for query construction was 2.5 clicks, query construction was 31.5 seconds, and report generation was 4 seconds..

4 Analysis and Conclusions

Our evaluation suggests that the menu driven NLG approach results in the rapid creation of unambiguous queries that can retrieve the relevant database information corresponding to the query. It has been embedded in a system that uses OLAP cubes to produce database reports (and dashboards) that allow user interaction with the retrieved information. The system was automatically adapded to a given OLAP cube (only minimal human intervention was required) and can be equally easily adapted to other OLAP cubes serving other domains.

Our results build on semantic web related work (Paiva et al., 2010) that shows that use of NLG for guided queries construction can be an effective alternative to a natural language interface to an information retrieval system. We deal with a highly constrained natural language (cf. the analysis grammars used by (Nelken and Francez, 2000; Thorne and Calvanese, 2012)) that is effective in generation of database queries and the generation (not analysis) of natural language. Like (Paiva et al., 2010), we rely on a semantic grammar, but instead build on the information that can be automatically extracted from the database model, rather than leveraging knowledge from semantic web resources. Furthermore, we provide a more detailed evaluation as to the effectiveness of the guided query construction technique.

Use of OLAP in NLG has also been explored in the context of content planning (Favero and Robin, 2000), and can play an important role in dealing with domain portability issues not only in the context of NLG but also in other natural language database applications. Our technique for leveraging the data model and OLAP cube avoids human customization techniques like those reported by (Minock, 2010) where an explicit mapping between phrases and database relations and entities needs to be provided, and (Evans and Power, 2003) where explicit domain information needs to be entered.

The NLG query construction approach does have limitations, since users will likely have questions that either cannot be constructed by the semantic grammar, or that cannot be answered from the underlying database. However, issues related to choice or ambiguity that are frequently encountered by NLG systems in particular, and natural language processing systems in general, can be avoided by having a human "in the loop."

Efficiency and effectiveness is derived from how we leverage human knowledge, both in query composition and result interpretation. In traditional, non-intelligent query scenarios, users know what they want to ask but not necessarily how to ask it. By guiding the user through the NLG process, the user can focus on the *what* not the *how*. Database reports are generated quickly, providing unambiguous answers in a clear, flexible format. and in a familiar, comfortable, un-intimidating web-based environment. Aside from usability benefits, this web-based approach has the added benefit of minimizing configuration and maintenance.

Our results are only suggestive, since they involve only 12 questions. They suggest it would be worthwhile to expend the resources for a full study that includes multiple users with different levels of experience, multiple domains and larger sets of questions. A more fine-grained analysis of the difference between the results sets of constructed English queries and the expected answers to original questions should also be performed along with an evaluation of how easy it is for the user to find the answer to the question within the database report.

References

Codeplex Open Source Community. 2008. *Adventureworks SQL Database Product Samples*. CODEPLEX. http://msftdbprodsamples.codeplex.com.

Faraj A. El-Mouadib, Zakaria S. Zubi, Ahmed A. Almagrous, and Irdess S. El-Feghi. 2009. Generic interactive natural language interface to databases (GINLIDB). *Int Journal of Computers*, 3:301–310.

Roger Evans and Richard Power. 2003. WYSIWYM - building user interfaces with natural language feedback. In *Proc. of EACL 2003, 10th Conf. of the European Chapter of the ACL*, pages 203–206, Budapest, Hungary.

Eloi Favero and Jacques Robin. 2000. Using OLAP and data mining for content planning in natural language generation. In *NLDB '00 Proc. 5th International Conference on Applications of Natural Language to Information Systems-Revised Papers*, pages 164–175. Springer-Verlag, London.

Phil Janus and Guy Fouche. 2009. Introduction to olap. In *Pro SQL Server 2008 Analysis Services*, pages 1–14. Springer-Verlag.

Epaminondas Kapetanios, Vijayan Sugumaran, and Myra Spiliopoulou. 2010. Special issue: 13th international conference on natural language and information systems (NLDB 2008) five selected and extended papers. *Data and Knowledge Engineering*, 69.

Boris Katz. 1988. Using english for indexing and retrieving. In *Proceedings of the First RIAO Conference on User-Oriented Content-Based Text and Image Handling (RIAO '88)*. CID.

Michael Minock. 2010. C-PHRASE: a system for building robust natural language interfaces to databases. *Data and Knowledge Engineering*, 69:290–302.

Rani Nelken and Nissim Francez. 2000. Querying temporal databases using controlled natural language. In *Proc 18th International Conference on Computational Linguistics (COLING 2000)*, pages 1076–1080, Saarbrücken, Germany, August.

Sara Paiva, Manuel Ramos-Cabrer, and Alberto Gil-Solla. 2010. Automatic query generation in guided systems: natural language generation from graphically built query. In *Proc 11th ACIS Intl Conf on Software Engineering, Artificial Intelligence, Networking and Parallel/Distributed Computing (SNPD 2010)*, pages 165–170. IEEE Conf Publishing Services.

Harry Tennant, Kenneth Ross, Richard Saenz, Craig Thompson, and James Miller. 1983. Menu-based natural language understanding. In *Proc 21st annual meeting of the Association of Computational Linguistics*, pages 151–158. ACL.

Camilo Thorne and Diego Calvanese. 2012. Tractability and intractability of controlled languages for data access. *Studia Logica, to appear.*

Blogging birds: Generating narratives about reintroduced species to promote public engagement

Advaith Siddharthan, Matthew Green, Kees van Deemter, Chris Mellish & René van der Wal
{advaith, mjgreen, k.vdeemter, c.mellish, r.vanderwal}@abdn.ac.uk
University of Aberdeen

Abstract

This paper proposes the use of NLG to enhance public engagement during the course of species reintroductions. We examine whether ecological insights can be effectively communicated through blogs about satellite-tagged individuals, and whether such blogs can help create a positive perception of the species in readers' minds, a requirement for successful reintroduction. We then discuss the implications for NLG systems that generate blogs from satellite-tag data.

1 Introduction

Conservation of wildlife is an objective to which considerable effort is devoted by governments and NGOs across the world. A variety of web-based approaches can help make the natural world more accessible to the public, which in turn may translate into greater public support for nature conservation initiatives. The present paper explores the role of Natural Language Generation (NLG) in bringing up-to-date information about wild animals in their natural environment to nature enthusiasts.

We focus on the reintroduction of the red kite to the UK. This member of the raptor family was once widespread in the UK, but prolonged and intense persecution led to its near extinction. Since 1989, efforts have been ongoing to reintroduce this species in various locations across the country. We are working together with one of the largest nature conservation charities in Europe to use NLG for public engagement around a small number of satellite-tagged reintroduced red kites.

The public engagement activities surrounding this reintroduction initiative have two subtly different objectives: (i) to communicate ecological insights to increase awareness about the species, and (ii) to create a positive image of the reintroduced species to harness public support for the reintroduction. Currently, data from these satellite tags are being used by the charity to manually create blogs such as:

> ...Ruby (Carrbridge) had an interesting flight down to Loch Duntelchaig via Dochfour on the 6th March before flying back to the Drumsmittal area, spending the 10th March in the Loch Ussie area (possibly also attracted by the feeding potential there!) and then back to Drumsmittal for the 13th...

Such blogs are used by schools which have adopted individual kites, and pupils can read these texts alongside a map plotting the GPS locations of 'their' kite. As can already be seen from the above, there is currently little ecological information about the species in these blogs. Because of the perceived importance of education to the success of reintroductions, there is a clear desire to include more ecological insights. Yet, time and resource limitations have prevented the charity from doing so; they perceive the writing of such blogs already as very time consuming, and indeed, rather mundane.

In this paper, we explore the use of blogs based on satellite tag data for communicating ecological insights and creating a positive image of a species. We consider both aspects, deemed essential for a successful species reintroduction, and focus on how the blogs can be made more informative than those currently being written by the charity.

2 Related work

Data-to-text systems (e.g., Goldberg et al. (1994); Theune et al. (2001); Portet et al. (2009)) have typ-

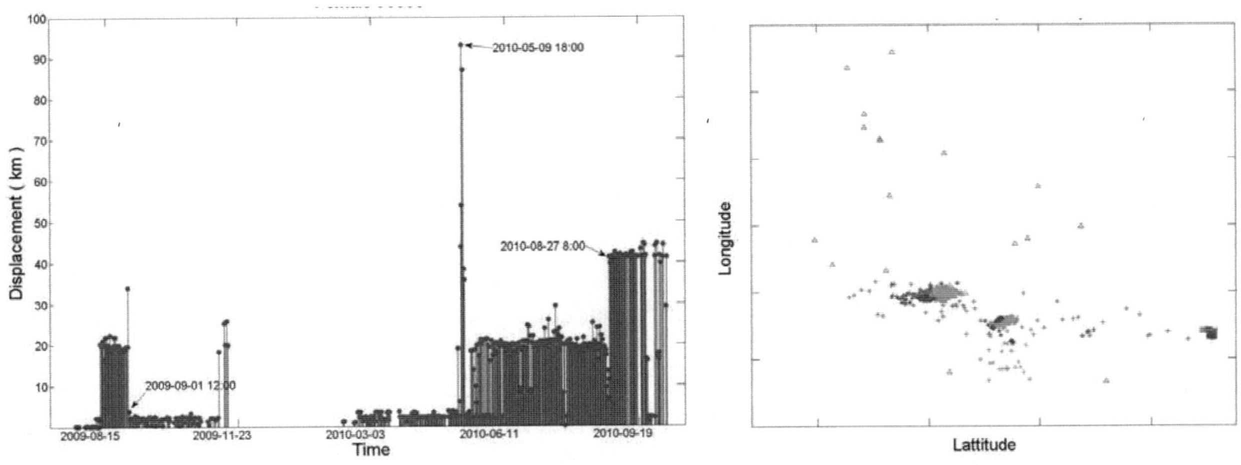

(a) (b)

Figure 1: Plot of (a) distance from nest as a function of time, and (b) clusters of visited locations.

ically been used to generate summaries of technical data for professionals, such as engineers, nurses and oil rig workers. There is some work on the use of data-to-text for lay audiences; e.g., generating narratives from sensor data for automotive (Reddington et al., 2011) and environmental (Molina et al., 2011) applications, generating personal narratives to help children with complex communication needs (Black et al., 2010), and summarising neonatal intensive care data for parents (Mahamood et al., 2008).

Our application differs from the above-mentioned data-to-text applications, in that we aim to generate inspiring as well as informative texts. It bears some resemblance to NLG systems that offer "infotainment", such as Dial Your Disc (Van Deemter and Odijk, 1997) and Ilex (O'Donnell et al., 2001). In fact, Dial Your Disc, which generates spoken monologues about classical music, focused emphatically on generating engaging texts, and achieved linguistic variation through the use of recursive, syntactically structured templates (see also, Theune et al. (2001)). We intend to extend a data-to-text system in similar ways, using ecological insights to make narratives engaging for non-experts.

3 Overall Goals

Our overall aim is to bring satellite tagged animals (in this case study, red kites) "to life" by constructing narratives around their patterns of movement. We require individual locations of a bird to be explained in the context of its wider spatial use, and the ecological interpretations thereof. This paper has the following goals:

1. To illustrate how satellite tag data can be analysed to identify behavioural patterns for use in generating blogs (content selection);
2. To test whether blogs written by an ecologist based on such data analysis can be used to educate as well as create a positive perception of the species;
3. To investigate the challenges for NLG in automating the generation of such blogs.

4 Data analysis for identifying behaviours

From an NLG perspective, our interest in automating the generation of blogs from satellite tag data is in making these narratives more interesting, by using the data to illustrate key aspects of red kite behaviour. To illustrate how we can relate the data to behaviours, we provide two graphical views of GPS fixes from a tagged red kite. Fig. 1(a) shows how far a focal kite is located from its nest over the course of a year. We propose to use such data to construct narratives around ecological insights regarding the exploratory behaviours of red kites during their first year after fledgling. Fig. 1(b) shows the same GPS data, but now spatially, thereby plotting latitude against longitude of all fixes without regard to time. This portrayal highlights the kite's favoured locations (indicated in different colours based on a MATLAB cluster analysis which automatically estimates the parameters of a Gaussian mixture model, even when clusters overlap substantially), as well as its broad range.

These plots illustrate two key aspects of kite behaviour: *exploration* and *site-fidelity* (the presence of favoured locations that the kite tends to return to). In addition, we are interested in communicating various *feeding behaviours* as well as that, unlike many other birds of prey, red kites are *social* birds, often found in groups. Feeding and social behaviours cannot be directly identified from the data. However, they can often be inferred; for instance, a red kite spending its time by the side of a main road is likely to be looking to scavenge on road kill.

5 Study on engaging readers using blogs

We now report a study that explores whether such ecological insights can be effectively communicated through blogs constructed around an individual of the species, and whether such blogs can help create a positive perception of the species in a reader's mind.

This study was based on a text manually constructed by an ecologist based on five weeks of data such as in Fig 1 from a red kite named "Red Baroness". For this study, the data was mapped onto a simplified world with seven features: a lake, a shoreline, fields, a road, a moor, a forest and a river. A sample of the text is shown in Figure 2 for illustration.

> **Week 2:** How different the pattern of movements of Red Baroness was this week! On Monday, she shot off past Bleak Moor, on her longest journey so far north-east of the lake. She appeared not to find much of interest there, and on the next day she was observed combing the edges of Green Park, possibly in search of a group of birds resting in the top half of the trees. The bird was clearly restless however, as on Thursday she was observed following River Rapid, downstream for further than she had been last month, finally stopping when she reached Blue Lake again.

Figure 2: Sample material showing week 2 from the five week blog

5.1 Experimental Design

80 participants were shown the material: a five week blog on the movements of the focal red kite, named Red Baroness, alongside a picture of a red kite and a schematic map marking the seven features of interest. Participants were students at the University of Aberdeen. The experiment was conducted in a lab in a supervised setting. After reading and returning the blog, each participant was asked to (a) summarise the blog they had just read in 5 lines, (b) state what they found most interesting, and (c) state what they did not like about the blog. These textual responses were manually coded for whether the four behaviour types (site fidelity, exploration, feeding and social) were identified by each participant.

To gauge the participants' perceptions of the kite, we used two methods. First, we asked the participant to answer four questions that tested various aspects of their willingness to engage with red kite conservation:

- Q1 Would you be willing to contribute money to a charity that tries to protect kites?
- Q2 The use of rat poison also leads to the death of kites that feed on the bodies of these rats. Would you be willing to sign a campaign against rat poison?
- Q3 Should governments allocate more money than they do currently to protect kites from extinction?
- Q4 Write your email if you wish to be sent more blogs.

Further to this, participants were asked to assess the red kite's personality. We follow (Gosling et al., 2003), who use the 44 question Big Five Inventory (BFI) (John et al., 1991; John et al., 2008) to assess the personality of dogs. We are interested in whether readers did assign personalities to the red kite in the blog and, if so, what these personality profiles looked like.

5.2 Results

We now analyse the extent to which our participants were informed about red kite ecology as well as how willing they were to engage with conservation efforts and how they perceived the species.

5.2.1 Informativeness

More than half the participants identified feeding behaviour (61%) and social (54%) behaviour. The other two ecological concepts were not mentioned explicitly in the blog that participants read, but needed to be inferred. Around a quarter of participants managed to infer the notion of site fidelity

(23%), the most difficult of the concepts, and 41% inferred exploratory behaviour.

5.2.2 Engagement

39% provided their email address to receive further blogs (the only real commitment), and an equal number expressed willingness to contribute money for red kite conservation efforts. 85% expressed willingness to sign a campaign against rat poisoning, and 61% wanted increased government spending for red kite conservation.

We detected a correlation between recall/inference of behaviours and willingness to engage (plotting total number of behaviours recalled/inferred by each participant against the total number of engagement questions answered affirmatively, $r_{pearson} = 0.31$; $p < 0.005$; $n = 80$). One interpretation of this result is that greater insights into the life of this bird has positively influenced the reader's perceptions of it. Further qualitative studies are needed to substantiate this, but we view this result as evidence in favour of incorporating ecological insights into the blogs.

5.2.3 Perception

Table 1 shows the big five personality traits assigned to Red Baroness by participants. The BFI is constructed such that being non-committal about the 44 trait questions would result in scores of 3. The ability of readers to assign human personality traits (significantly different from 3.0) to the red kite indicates a willingness to anthromorphise the bird. The last column shows the average personality of 21 year old humans (from Srivastava et al. (2003)), which is the same age group as our participants. The values for extroversion, agreeableness and conscientiousness are very similar, and the kite has lower neuroticism and openness.

Trait	Red Kite	Conf. Int.	21 yo
Extroversion	3.28	3.07–3.48	3.25
Agreeableness	3.64	3.47–3.80	3.64
Conscientiousness	3.48	3.26–3.69	3.45
Neuroticism	2.60	2.41–2.80	3.32
Openness	3.29	3.11–3.47	3.92

Table 1: Big five personality traits of Red Baroness with 99.9% confidence intervals, compared to average 21 year olds (6076 people) (Srivastava et al., 2003)

6 Implications for NLG

The above study indicates that it is possible to use narratives based on satellite tag data to communicate ecological insights as well as create a positive perception of the species in the readers' minds. To generate texts that are fluent and engaging enough that readers will be both informed and entertained by them poses challenges that are sharply different from the ones facing most data-to-text systems, whose primary purpose is to offer decision support. Our goals are more similar to those of Dial Your Disc (Van Deemter and Odijk, 1997), with the added requirement that texts should be easy to read. For instance, ecological concepts (such as site fidelity) could be communicated by explicitly defining them. However, we would prefer these to be inferred from more engaging narratives.

The blogs currently created by the charity (cf. Section 1) are, stripped down to their essence, a sequence of locations. We propose to interlay these sequences of locations with descriptions of red kite behaviours, broadly categorised as fidelity, exploration, feeding or social. Algorithm 1 outlines the planning process. We have developed an initial prototype that implements this for our simplified world. Using template based generation, we can automatically generate blogs such as the following for arbitrary sequences of locations in our simplified world:

> This week Red Baroness continued to feel like stretching her wings. On Monday she was seen in the fields by the lake, calling out to other kites. On Tuesday and Wednesday she stayed along the road, looking for roadkill on the country lanes. On Thursday she returned to the fields by the lake – clearly there was plenty to eat there.

To scale this up to the real world, work is in progress to augment our data analysis component by using a variety of GIS data to map geo-coordinates to habitat, terrain and demographic features from which we can identify relevant kite behaviours.

Our remaining challenges are to (a) compile a large list of red kite behaviours, (b) use paraphrasing approaches to create variety in descriptions of behaviour and (c) develop means to interweave more

1. Identify place names of interest to the user among the many GIS locations frequented by the red kite
2. For each place of interest (ordered by time):
   (a) describe place in terms of relevant geographical features
   (b) describe one or two behaviours (feeding or social) associated with any of these features
   (c) make a reference to any exploratory behaviour or site fidelity if identified from previous sequence.

Algorithm 1: Generate a blog about a red kite

complex behaviours, such as mating, into the narratives. There is ongoing interdisciplinary work into each of the above. Variation is likely to be critical to the endeavour as these blogs are aimed at engaging the reader, not just at presenting information. This can be achieved both by expanding the range of behaviours we describe, and the range of ways we can realise these through language.

7 Conclusions

This paper reports a study that informs the application of NLG technologies to conservation efforts centred around public engagement. We report on findings which indicate that it is possible to use narratives loosely based on satellite tag data to communicate ecological insights as well as to create a positive perception of the species in readers' minds. This informs an approach to automating the creation of blogs from satellite-tagged red kites by interleaving sequences of locations with descriptions of behaviour. A proof of concept system has been developed for a simplified world, and is in the process of being scaled up to the real world, using GIS data.

Acknowledgments

This research is supported by an award made by the RCUK Digital Economy programme to the dot.rural Digital Economy Hub; award reference: EP/G066051/1.

References

R. Black, J. Reddington, E. Reiter, N. Tintarev, and A. Waller. 2010. Using nlg and sensors to support personal narrative for children with complex communication needs. In *Proceedings of the NAACL HLT 2010 Workshop on Speech and Language Processing for Assistive Technologies*, pages 1–9. Association for Computational Linguistics.

E. Goldberg, N. Driedger, and R.I. Kittredge. 1994. Using natural-language processing to produce weather forecasts. *IEEE Expert*, 9(2):45–53.

S.D. Gosling, V.S.Y. Kwan, and O.P. John. 2003. A dog's got personality: a cross-species comparative approach to personality judgments in dogs and humans. *Journal of Personality and Social Psychology*, 85(6):1161.

O.P. John, E.M. Donahue, and R.L. Kentle. 1991. The big five inventoryversions 4a and 54. *Berkeley: University of California, Berkeley, Institute of Personality and Social Research.*

O.P. John, L.P. Naumann, and C.J. Soto. 2008. Paradigm shift to the integrative big five trait taxonomy. *Handbook of personality: Theory and research*, pages 114–158.

S. Mahamood, E. Reiter, and C. Mellish. 2008. Neonatal intensive care information for parents an affective approach. In *Computer-Based Medical Systems, 2008. CBMS'08. 21st IEEE International Symposium on*, pages 461–463. IEEE.

M. Molina, A. Stent, and E. Parodi. 2011. Generating automated news to explain the meaning of sensor data. *Advances in Intelligent Data Analysis X*, pages 282–293.

M. O'Donnell, C. Mellish, J. Oberlander, and A. Knott. 2001. Ilex: an architecture for a dynamic hypertext generation system. *Natural Language Engineering*, 7(3):225–250.

F. Portet, E. Reiter, A. Gatt, J. Hunter, S. Sripada, Y. Freer, and C. Sykes. 2009. Automatic generation of textual summaries from neonatal intensive care data. *Artificial Intelligence*, 173(7-8):789–816.

J. Reddington, E. Reiter, N. Tintarev, R. Black, and A. Waller. 2011. "Hands Busy, Eyes Busy": Generating Stories from Sensor Data for Automotive applications. In *Proceedings of IUI Workshop on Multimodal Interfaces for Automotive Applications*.

S. Srivastava, O.P. John, S.D. Gosling, and J. Potter. 2003. Development of personality in early and middle adulthood: Set like plaster or persistent change?. *Journal of Personality and Social Psychology*, 84(5):1041.

M. Theune, E. Klabbers, J.R. de Pijper, E. Krahmer, and J. Odijk. 2001. From data to speech: a general approach. *Natural Language Engineering*, 7(01):47–86.

K. Van Deemter and J. Odijk. 1997. Context modeling and the generation of spoken discourse. *Speech Communication*, 21(1-2):101–121.

Natural Language Generation for a Smart Biology Textbook

Eva Banik[1], Eric Kow[1], Vinay Chaudhri[2], Nikhil Dinesh[2], and Umangi Oza[3]

[1]{ebanik,kowey}@comp-ling.co.uk, Computational Linguistics Ltd, London, UK
[2] {chaudhri,dinesh}@ai.sri.com, SRI International, Menlo Park, CA
[3]umangi.oza@evalueserve.com, Evaluserve, New Delhi, India

1 Application Context

In this demo paper we describe the natural language generation component of an electronic textbook application, called Inquire[1]. Inquire interacts with a knowledge base which encodes information from a biology textbook. The application includes a question-understanding module which allows students to ask questions about the contents of the book, and a question-answering module which retrieves the corresponding answer from the knowledge base. The task of the natural language generation module is to present specific parts of the answer in English. Our current generation pipeline handles inputs that describe the biological functions of entities, the steps of biological processes, and the spatial relations between parts of entities. Our ultimate goal is to generate paragraph-length texts from arbitrary paths in the knowledge base. We describe here the natural language generation pipeline and demonstrate the inputs and generated texts. In the demo presentation we will show the textbook application and the knowledge base authoring environment, and provide an opportunity to interact with the system.

2 The Knowledge Base

The knowledge base contains information from a college-level biology textbook[2], encoded by biologists as part of project HALO at SRI[3]. The core of the knowledge base is the CLIB ontology[4], which is extended with biology-specific information. The knowledge base encodes entity-to-event relations (similar to thematic roles in linguistics), event-to-event relations (discourse relations), various property values and relations between properties, spatial relations, cardinality constraints, and roles that participants play in events. The input to the generation pipeline is a set of triples extracted from the biology knowledge base. Currently our content selection includes either an event and the entities that participate in the event, or a set of entities and spatial relations between them.

3 Generation Grammar and Lexicon

Our generation grammar consists of a set of Tree Adjoining Grammar (TAG) elementary trees. Each tree is associated with either a single relation, or a set of relations in the knowledge base. As an example, Fig 1 illustrates the mapping between elementary trees and event participant relations in the KB for the above input. We currently associate up to three different elementary trees with each event and the connected set of participant relations: an active sentential tree, a passive sentential tree and a complex noun phrase.

The knowledge base provides concept-to-word

[1]The work described in this paper and presented in the demo is funded by Vulcan Inc.

[2] **Reece et al. 2010.** Campbell biology. Pearson Publishing.

[3] **Gunning Et al, 2010.** Project halo update progress toward digital aristotle. AI Magazine Fall:33-58. See also http://www.projecthalo.com/

[4]http://www.cs.utexas.edu/users/mfkb/RKF/clib.html

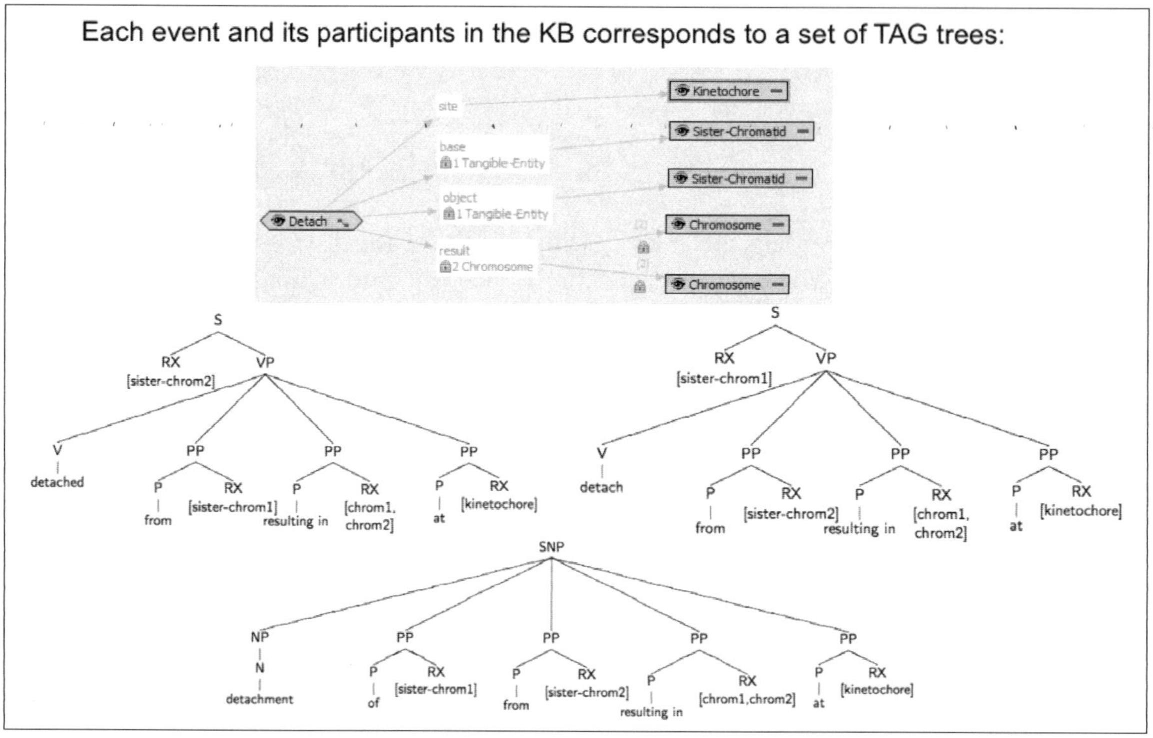

Figure 1: The grammar of the surface realizer

mappings (a list of synonyms) for every concept, and the words are used in the generation lexicon to anchor elementary TAG trees. Our generation grammar consists of a set of TAG tree templates, which are defined as combinations of tree fragments and are compiled using the XMG metgrammar toolkit[5].

These underspecified elementary trees are further specified in the generation lexicon, which maps concepts onto elementary tree templates, and associates a word (an anchor) with the tree, along with other idiosynchratic information (e.g., preposition choice). We create a generation lexicon dynamically at run-time, by mapping tree templates onto concepts based on the number and types of participants, and the lexical information associated with the event (e.g., the preposition requirements of the verb).

Concept names for entities are included in the elementary trees as features on the corresponding NP nodes. These features form part of the input to the referring expression generation module, which looks up the concept name in the concept-to-word mapping to obtain a list of possible noun phrases.

[5]https://sourcesup.renater.fr/xmg/

4 Realization

Our natural language generation pipeline is centered around the GenI surface realizer[6,7]. The set of triples yielded by content selection are first aggregated and converted to GenI's input format, a set of flat semantic literals. We then feed this input to GenI to produce an underspecified surface form in which referring expressions are still underspecified:

NP is detach from NP resulting in NP at NP
NP detach from NP resulting in NP at NP
Detachment of NP from NP resulting in NP at NP

A post-processing module carries out referring expression generation and morphological realization to produce the fully specified output.

[6] **Kow, Eric. 2007.** Surface realisation: ambiguity and determinism. Doctoral Dissertation, Universite de Henri Poincare - Nancy 1.

[7] **Banik, Eva 2010.** A minimalist approach to generating coherent texts. Phd thesis, Department of Computing, The Open University

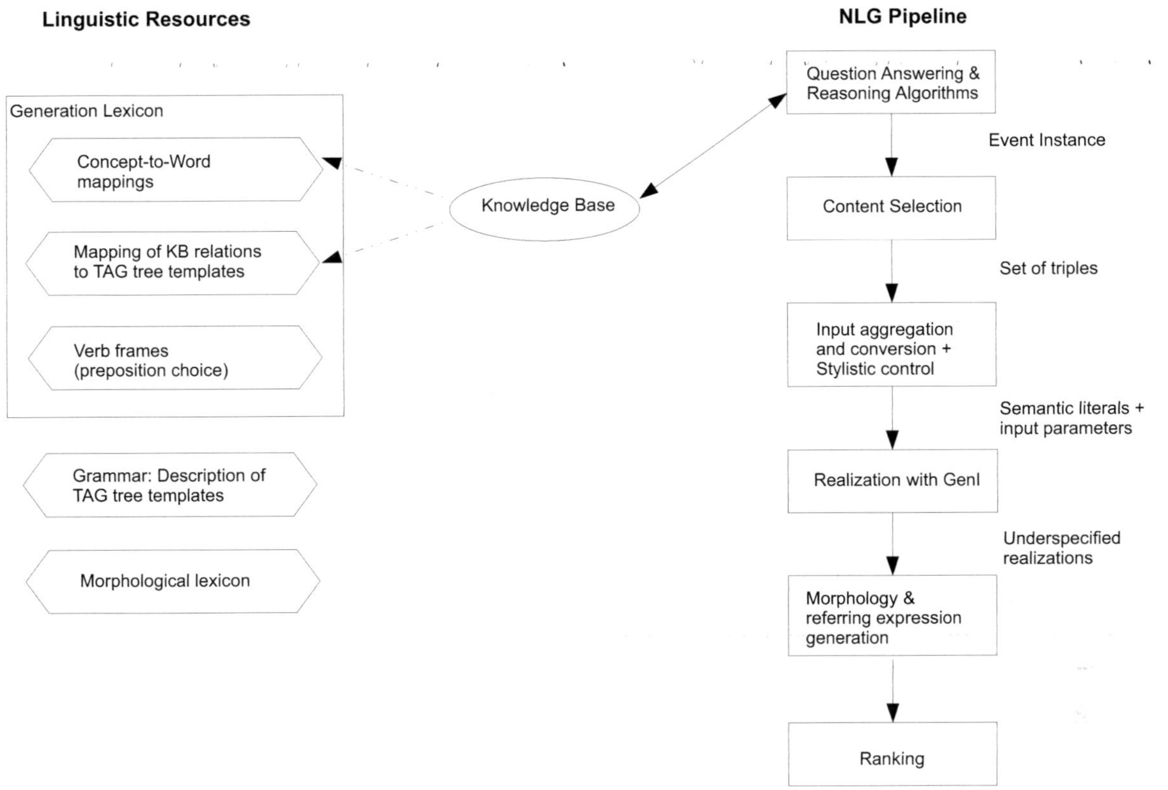

Figure 2: Linguistic resources and the generation pipeline

Our referring expression realization algorithm performs further semantic aggregation where necessary to produce cardinals ("two chromosomes"), and decides on a suitable determiner based on previous mentions of instance names and subclasses in the discourse context (definite/indefinite determiner, "another" or "the same"). For the input shown in Fig 1, our system will produce the following three realizations:

1. A sister chromatid detaches from another sister chromatid resulting in two chromosomes at a kinetochore.
2. A sister chromatid is detached from another sister chromatid resulting in two chromosomes at a kinetochore.
3. Detachment of a sister chromatid from another sister chromatid resulting in two chromosomes at a kinetochore

We rank the generated outputs based on their linguistic properties using optimality theoretic constraints (e.g., active sentences are ranked above passive sentences), where each constraint corresponds to a (set of) tree fragments that contributed to building the tree that appears in the output. Our system also allows for extra input parameters to be sent to GenI to restrict the set of generated outputs to fit a specific context (e.g., syntactic type or focused discourse entity). Our full natural language generation pipeline is illustrated in Fig 2.

5 Future Work

We are currently working on extending the system to handle more relations and other data types in the knowledge base. This involves extending the grammar to new sentence types and other linguistic constructions, and extending the content selection module to return more triples from the knowledge base. Our ultimate goal is to be able to generate arbitrary – but in some sense well-formed – paths from the knowledge base as coherent paragraphs of text.

Generating Natural Language Summaries for Multimedia

Duo Ding, Florian Metze, Shourabh Rawat, Peter F. Schulam, Susanne Burger
School of Computer Science, Carnegie Mellon University
Pittsburgh, PA, USA 15213
{dding, fmetze, srawat, pschulam, sburger}@cs.cmu.edu

Abstract

In this paper we introduce an automatic system that generates textual summaries of Internet-style video clips by first identifying suitable high-level descriptive features that have been detected in the video (e.g. visual concepts, recognized speech, actions, objects, persons, etc.). Then a natural language generator is constructed using SimpleNLG to compile the high-level features into a textual form. The generated summary contains information from both visual and acoustic sources, intending to give a general review and summary of the video. To reduce the complexity of the task, we restrict ourselves to work with videos that show a limited number of "events". In this demo paper, we describe the design of the system and present example outputs generated by the video summarization system.

1 Introduction

The Internet allows us to browse millions of videos. For some of them, the content is well organized with human-generated tags and labels (e.g. wedding ceremony, birthday party, etc.), but the rate at which content is uploaded daily makes it unrealistic to expect that user-provided labels will be sufficient for organizing this information in the future. We believe that automatically generating a brief summary (or "abstract") of videos is both an attractive solution to this problem and an exciting challenge for the natural language generation community. Converting audio and video output into natural language to create a human readable summary that facilitates effective browsing, supports classification decisions, or helps differentiating videos from one another without having to watch them in their entirety has both academic and practical value.

In this paper, we introduce an automatic video summary generation system that uses a natural language realization engine (Gatt and Reiter, 2009) to create sentences based on state-of-the-art video classification features. These features are computed on a large corpus from the TrecVID evaluation (Bao, et al. 2011). In a recent user study (Ding, et al. 2012), we compared automatically generated and manually generated summaries with respect to several tasks. The study shows, for example, that more specific information (e.g. "food" instead of "some object") and temporal information (something happened first and then...) is helpful in improving the quality of machine-generated summaries. This is a first step to implement an automatic system which is not only able to describe videos using natural language, but accomplishes more sophisticated tasks such as differentiating videos, finding supporting evidence for video classification and other tasks.

2 Related Work

Significant work has been done in the field of video summarization. A large part of it is based on the idea that the summarization should be a graphical representation such as visually rich storyboards. These storyboards intended to help users to efficiently browse the videos, e.g. in the Open-Video Archive (Marchionini, Song et al. 2009). Christel, et al. (2006) are mainly focusing on the research in user interface designs for video browsing and summarization. Li, et al. (2010) introduced a maximal marginal relevance algorithm working across video genres to improve the quality of the informative summary for a video, which exploits both audio and video information. Truong et al. (2007) worked on techniques targeting video data from various domains that were developed to summarize and organize the information and present surrogates to the users. Tan et al. (2011) recently have worked on using recognition techniques to obtain audio-visual concept classifiers to generate textual descriptions of videos. They manually defined a template for each concept and built a rule-based language generation system to create textual descriptions. But the template approach, which is directly related to specific events, cannot be adapted to new events. In our work, we use SimpleNLG to generate video-specific summaries, which can be applied to any new event.

3 System Description

3.1 Architecture

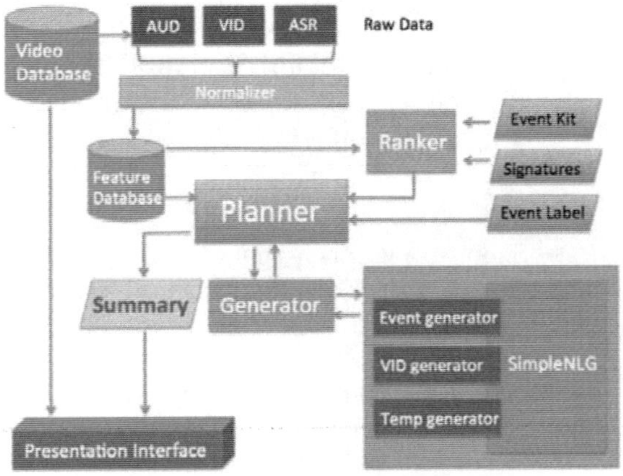

Figure 1. System Architecture.

Figure 1 shows the overall system architecture. The raw data of the videos is extracted and normalized to a format that can be read by the feature database, which stores all the features from the videos. The ranker contains a set of algorithms that rank the features from a video and conduct content determination. For example, when there is a long list of visual conceptual features, the ranker will sort all the features based on their relevance to the specific event's signature and return a ranked list to the planner. The planner is the "commander" of the system; it receives the ranked features and passes them to the language generator. For each set of the features, the language generator uses SimpleNLG to compile a sentence stating the scenario of the video. Eventually, the planner combines all the sentences into a summarization passage presenting the information detected from the video.

3.2 Feature Extraction

High-level features are extracted from the video using the techniques described in (Bao, et al. 2011). Visual conceptual features are detected with SVM classifiers trained on the SIN task in TRECVID 2011 using MOSIFT and CSIFT features to describe keyframes. Other features are also extracted, including event labels, event signatures and the event kit, etc. Event signatures are relevant features describing a certain event, similar to a fingerprint, and the event kit is a textual description of important objects and actions that make up the event. For features that make use of temporal information, we use a GMM based segmenter to cut the audio of each video into small clips (1-3 seconds) and give a label to each clip.

3.3 Language Generation

Taking a series of features, each of the sentence generators composes these features into a human readable sentence using the SimpleNLG generation tool. We use SimpleNLG at the lexical level (i.e. orthography, morphology and simple grammar) and at the phrase and sentence level (i.e. phrase element coordination, clause subordinates). For each set of features, the system generates a sentence specifically mentioning these features.

The VID generator deals with visual concepts, i.e. the probabilities of the occurrence of 346 visual concepts extracted from the video. A list of visual features (e.g. food, people, room) will be processed as follows:

SPhraseSpec p = nlgFactory.createClause();
p.setSubject("the system");
p.setVerb("observe");
p.setObject("food, people, room");
p.setFeature(Feature.TENSE, Tense.PAST);
p.addComplement("in the video")

to generate a sentence like:

The system observed food, people and room in the video.

Another sentence generator is the "temporal information generator", which takes the temporal information and produces a sentence describing what is happening in the video. We first segment the audio into small clips lasting three seconds each, and assign an audio semantic label to each clip (e.g. music, crowd, cheer, speech). Using temporal information, we generate a sentence like:

From the video, the system heard the sound of music at first, then cheer, and then speech.

When the system generates several sentences, we compose them into a summary paragraph of the video. For example, we combine the subordinate clauses using the conjunction "*because*":

The video summarization system thinks this video is about Birthday Party because it found 3 Or More People Meeting in Room.

In this sentence, "Birthday Party" is the event label for the given video, and "3 Or More People", "Meeting", "Room" are the visual concepts extracted from the video.

4 Demo System Interface

We demonstrate the video summarization system in a dynamic web page. A screen shot of the demo page can be seen in Figure 2. The top gallery shows several videos for selection. The user can choose a video by clicking on it, and the selected video will play in the main area of the page. Once a video is selected and playing, a summary paragraph will be automatically generated and displayed underneath the video, presenting the video's information in natural language.

Figure 2. A screen shot of the user interface.

The demo and the interface are currently being tested internally, in order to stabilize and improve all components, and to prepare for task-based and free-form evaluations on platforms such as Amazon Mechanical Turk, which will serve to further develop the NLG system. While the NLG is currently mostly hard-coded, the availability of an evaluation framework will allow us to learn parameters from data, and increase the amount of automation successively. In future work we will also explore and extend the feature sets by extracting additional visual, acoustic, textual features from the video. We also plan to employ more sophisticated NLG techniques (e.g. microplanning and document structuring) to generate more complex and authentic natural language sentences.

Acknowledgments

This work is partly supported by the Intelligence Advanced Research Projects Activity (IARPA) via Department of Interior National Business Center contract number D11PC20068. The U.S. Government is authorized to reproduce and distribute reprints for Governmental purposes notwithstanding any copyright annotation thereon. Disclaimer: The views and conclusions contained herein are those of the authors and should not be interpreted as necessarily representing the official policies or endorsements, either expressed or implied, of IARPA, DoI/NBC, or the U.S. Government.

References

Lei Bao, Shoou-I Yu, Zhen-zhong Lan, Arnold Overwijk, Qin Jin, Brian Langner, Michael Garbus, Susanne Burger, Florian Metze, Alexander Hauptmann. Informedia @TRECVID2011. *TRECVID2011, NIST.*

Michael G. Christel. 2006. Evaluation and User Studies with Respect to Video Summarization and Browsing. In *Proc. "Multimedia Content Analysis, Management, and Retrieval", part of the IS&T/SPIE Symposium on Electronic Imaging.*

Duo Ding, Florian Metze, Shourabh Rawat, Peter Franz Schulam, Susanne Burger, Ehsan Younessian, Lei Bao, Michael G. Christel, Alexander Hauptmann. 2012. Beyond Audio and Video Retrieval: Towards Multimedia Summarization. In *Proc. 2012 International Conference on Multimedia Retrieval.*

Albert Gatt and Ehud Reiter. 2009. SimpleNLG: A realisation engine for practical applications. In *Proc. 12th European Workshop on Natural Language Gneratoin-2009,* pages 90-93.

Yingbo Li, Bernardo Merialdo. 2010.Multi-video Summarization Based on AV-MMR. In *Proc. 2010 Int'l Workshop on Content-Based Multimedia Indexing.*

Gary Marchionini, Yaxiao Song, and Robert Ferrell. 2009. Multimedia Surrogates for Video Gisting: Toward Combining Spoken Words and Imagery. *Information Processing & Management* 45(6), 615-630.

Ba Tu Truong and Svetha Venkatesh. 2007. Video Abstraction: A Systematic Review and Classification. *ACM Trans. (TOMCCAP)* 3(1), 1-37.

Chun Chet Tan, Yu-Gang Jiang, Chong-Wah Ngo. 2011. Towards Textually Describing Complex Video Contents with Audio-Visual Concepts Classifiers. In *Proc. ACM Multimedia-2011.*

Midge: Generating Descriptions of Images*

Margaret Mitchell
University of Aberdeen
m.mitchell@abdn.ac.uk

Xufeng Han
Stony Brook University
xufhan@cs.stonybrook.edu

Jeff Hayes
SignWorks of Oregon
jeff@signworksoforegon.com

Abstract

We demonstrate a novel, robust vision-to-language generation system called Midge. Midge is a prototype system that connects computer vision to syntactic structures with semantic constraints, allowing for the automatic generation of detailed image descriptions. We explain how to connect vision detections to trees in Penn Treebank syntax, which provides the scaffolding necessary to further refine data-driven statistical generation approaches for a variety of end goals.

1 Introduction

There has been a growing interest in tackling the problem of how to describe an image using computer vision detections. This problem is difficult in part because computer vision detections are often wrong: State-of-the-art vision technology predicts things that are not there, and misses things that are obvious to a human observer. This problem is also difficult because it is not clear what kind of language should be generated – the language that makes up a "description" can take many forms.

At the bare minimum, an automatic vision-to-language system, given an image with a single detection of, for example, a dog, should be able to generate *a dog*, and a longer phrase if requested. To be useful in real-world applications, it should be able to create basic descriptions that are as true as possible to the image, as well as descriptions that guess probable information based on language analysis alone. To our knowledge, no current system provides this functionality. Midge is built based on these goals.

Our approach converts object detections to descriptive sentences using a tree-generating derivation process that fleshes out lexicalized syntactic structure around object nouns. Likely subtrees are learned from a cleaned version of the Flickr dataset (Ordonez et al., 2011) parsed using the Berkeley parser. The final structures generated by the system are present-tense declarative sentences in Penn Treebank syntax.

With this in place, the system can generate *a dog*, *a black dog sleeping*, *a furry black dog sleeping by a cat*, etc., while also suggesting further detectors for the vision system to run. Approaching the problem in this way, Midge provides a starting point for generation to meet different goals: from automatically creating stories or summaries based on visual data, to suggesting phrases that a speech-impaired AAC user can select to assist in conversation. There is still much work to be done, but we believe that the basic architecture used by this system is a solid starting point for generating a wide variety of descriptive content, and makes clear some of the issues a vision-to-language system must handle in order to generate natural-sounding descriptions.

2 Background

Previous work on generating image descriptions can be characterized as prioritizing among several goals:

- Creating language that is poetic or metaphorical (Li et al., 2011)
- Creating automatic captions with syntactic variation based on semantic visual information (Farhadi et al., 2010)
- Creating language describing the scene in a basic template-driven way, utilizing attribute detections (Kulkarni et al., 2011) or likely verbs from a language model (Yang et al., 2011)

To meet one goal, other goals are often compromised. Yang et al. (2011) fill in likely verbs to form complete sentences, but limit the generated structures to a simple template, without capturing natural variation in sentence length or surface structure.

* Thanks to the CLSP 2011 summer workshop at Johns Hopkins for making this system possible. Midge is available to try online at http://recognition.cs.stonybrook.edu:8080/~mitchema/midge/ and http://mcvl.cewit.stonybrook.edu//~mitchema/midge/ and screenshots at http://www.abdn.ac.uk/~r07mm9/midge/

Li et al. (2011) aim at more metaphorical and varied language, but the generated structures are often syntactically and semantically ill-formed. Farhadi et al. (2010) generate natural, varied, descriptive language, but this is created by copying captions directly from similar images, resulting in captions that are often not true to the actual query image content.

Midge builds on ideas from these systems, additionally mapping the structures underlying vision detections to syntactic structures and data-driven distributional information underlying natural language descriptions. With this in place, the door is opened for language and vision to communicate at a deep syntactic-semantic level. The language components of the system can filter and expand on given visual information, and can also call back to the visual system itself, specifying further detectors to run (or train) based on semantically related or expected information. We hope that this system not only advances work in generating visual descriptions, but work in training visual detectors as well.

3 Vision to Language Issues

The process of developing Midge brought to light several key issues that any vision-to-language system aiming to generate descriptive, varied, human-like language must handle:

Descriptiveness: Should the system include information about everything there is evidence for, limit that information, or add to it?

World knowledge: What sorts of things in an image are remarkable, and should be mentioned, and which may go without saying?

Object grouping: Which objects should be mentioned together? How do people divide objects among sentences when they describe an image? Which detections should not be mentioned?

Noun ordering: In what order should the objects be named?

Reference plurals and sets: How should sets of objects be described as a whole? Should the exact number be included (*four chairs*), a vague term (*a few chairs*) or a general plural form (*chairs*)?

Modifier ordering: How should the different modifiers common to descriptions be ordered to make the utterances sound fluent?

Determiner selection: When should objects be treated as given (*the sky*), new (*a boy*), mass (*grass*), or count (*a blade*)?

Verb selection: Given that action/pose detection in computer vision does not function reliably, should verbs be hallucinated from a language model alone? Should they be left out?

Preposition selection: How should spatial relations between objects be analyzed, and how does this translate to language describing the scene layout?

Surface realization: What final lexicalization decisions need to be made to realize the generated strings within the output language?

Final string selection: Given a set of possible outputs, how is the final output string decided?

Nonsense detections: How should the system handle computer vision detections that are often wrong?

Many of these issues are well-suited to statistical NLP techniques, and some (modifier ordering, final string selection) have already been addressed in the NLP community. Where appropriate, Midge incorporates this technology alongside novel solutions to issues that have not yet been heavily researched (determiner selection, nominal ordering). We hope to further refine Midge's solutions as technology in these areas advances.

Separating Midge's architecture into components that handle each of these issues separately means that the system is flexible to change the kind of language it generates depending on the goals of the end user. The system offers general solutions to the issues listed above, and can have many of its goals changed if specified at run-time, resulting in different kinds of generated utterances. Midge can successfully create natural, varied descriptions that add descriptive content based on language modeling alone; it can also generate descriptions that are more limited, but as true as possible to the image.

4 Natural Language Generation in Midge

- id: 1, type: 1, label: bus, score: 0.73, bbox: [65.0, 65.0, 415.0, 191.0], attrs: {'blue': 0.01, 'furry':.02, ..., 'shiny': 0.69}
- id: 2, type: 1, label: road, score: 0.95, bbox: [1.0, 95.0, 440.0, 235.0], attrs: {'blue': 0.01, ...}
- preps {1,2}: 'by'

Figure 1: Computer Vision Out / Midge In (Excerpt)

The input to Midge is the output of vision detections, with detectors run for objects and attributes within each object's bounding box. In this demonstration, we incorporate the Kulkarni et al. (2011) vision detections. This provides objects/stuff and associated attributes, bounding boxes, and spatial relations between object pairs derived from the bounding boxes. Object detections are based on Felzenszwalb's multi-scale deformable parts models, and stuff detections are based on linear SVMs for low level region features.

Language generation in Midge is driven by a lexicalized derivation process that uses likely syntactic and distributional information for object nouns to create present-tense declarative sentences. Object detections form the basis of the computer vision detections, and these in turn are linked to nouns that form the basis of the generated output string.

The syntactic trees used to collect and generate likely subtrees for object nouns is outlined in Figure 2. Each anchor noun selects for a set of likely adjectives **a**, determiners **d**, prepositions **p** and present tense verbs **v**.

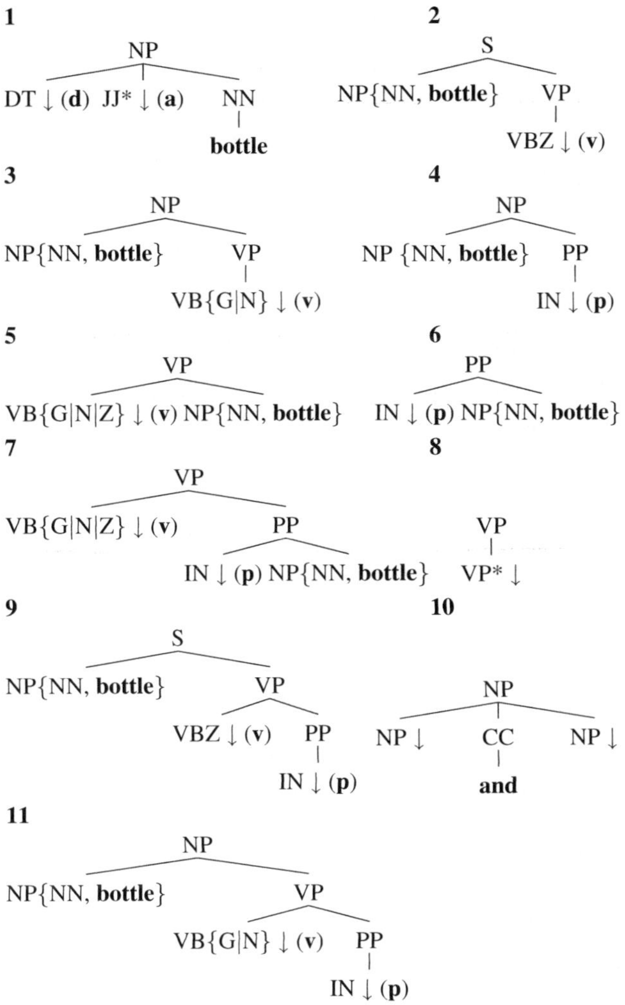

Figure 2: Trees for generation. Each {NN, **noun**} selects for its local subtrees. ↓ marks a substitution site, * marks ≥ 0 sister nodes of this type permitted. **Input:** set of ordered nouns, **Output:** trees preserving nominal ordering.

5 Architecture

Midge can be explained at a high level as a pipelined system incorporating the following steps:

Step 1: Run detectors for objects, stuff, action/pose and attributes; pass as <detection, score> pairs to Midge. Vision output/NLG input is displayed in Figure 1 and in the system demo.

Step 2: Group objects together that will be mentioned together.

Step 3: Order objects within each group – this automatically sets the subject and objects of the sentence. Midge currently order nouns based on WordNet hypernyms.

Step 4: Create all tree structures that can be generated from the object noun node. (See Figure 2). Noun anchors select for adjectives (JJ), determiners (DT), prepositions (IN) and if specified, verbs (VBG, VBN, or VBZ).

Step 5: Limit adjectives (JJ) to the set that are not *mutually exclusive* – different values for the same attribute class. REG comes into play at this step.

Step 6: Create all trees that combine following the given trees until all object nouns in a group are under one node (either NP or S).

Step 7: Order selected adjectives. We use the top-scoring ngram model from (Mitchell et al., 2011).

Step 8: Choose final tree from set of generated trees. Users can select a longest-string or cross entropy calculation.

References

A. Farhadi, M. Hejrati, P. Young Sadeghi, C. Rashtchian, J. Hockenmaier, and D. A. Forsyth. 2010. Every picture tells a story: generating sentences for images. *Proc. ECCV 2010.*

G. Kulkarni, V. Premraj, and S. Dhar, et al. 2011. Baby talk: Understanding and generating image descriptions. *Proc. CVPR 2011.*

S. Li, G. Kulkarni, T. L. Berg, A. C. Berg, and Y. Choi. 2011. Composing simple image descriptions using web-scale n-grams. *Proc. CoNLL 2011.*

M. Mitchell, A. Dunlop, and B. Roark. 2011. Semi-supervised modeling for prenominal modifier ordering. *Proc. ACL 2011.*

V. Ordonez, G. Kulkarni, and T. L. Berg. 2011. Im2text: Describing images using 1 million captioned photographs. *Proc. NIPS 2011.*

Y. Yang, C. L. Teo, H. Daumé III, and Y. Aloimonos. 2011. Corpus-guided sentence generation of natural images. *Proc. EMNLP 2011.*

Preface

Generation Challenges 2012 (GenChal'12) was the sixth of the annual Generation Challenges umbrella events for shared-task evaluation activities in natural language generation. It followed five previous events: the Pilot Attribute Selection for Generating Referring Expressions (ASGRE) Challenge hosted by UCNLG+MT in Copenhagen, Denmark in 2007; Referring Expression Generation (REG) Challenges at INLG'08 in Ohio, US; Generation Challenges 2009 at ENLG'09 in Athens, Greece; Generation Challenges 2010 at INLG'10 in Trim, Ireland, and, most recently, Generation Challenges 2011 at ENLG'11 in Nancy, France. More information about all these events can be found via the links on the Generation Challenges homepage (http://www.nltg.brighton.ac.uk/research/genchal12).

Like its predecessor events, GenChal'12 had a Future Task Proposals Track where researchers were invited to submit papers describing ideas for shared tasks to be run in the future. The responses to this call are the last three papers in the GenChal'12 part of the present volume. White's paper on a Syntactic Paraphrase Reranking task is explicitly proposed as a further development on the outcomes of the Surface Realisation task, with the emphasis on methods to rank realisation alternatives. Banik et al.'s KBGen task proposal focuses on generation of text from structured knowledge sources, while Bouayad-Agha et al.'s proposal focuses on methods for content determination in NLG from semantic web data.

GenChal'12 also included a progress report on the Surface Realisation shared task, currently organised by Anja Belz, Bernd Bohnet, Simon Mille, Leo Wanner and Michael White. The report, which can be found at the beginning of the GenChal'12 part of this volume, describes current work on the SR Task's common-ground input representations and plans for the next edition of the task, SR'13.

The GenChal'12 session at INLG'12 included two further presentations, one an update report on the Question Generation Challenge organised by Vasile Rus, Arthur Graesser and Paul Piwek, which did not run this year. The other was a summary report on the second edition of the Helping Our Own task (HOO'12) organised by Robert Dale, whose full results session was this year hosted at BEA'12. HOO'12 was based on a much more focused task definition than its 2011 predecessor. While HOO'11 addressed the automatic correction of a very broad range of errors in scientific articles in English by non-native authors, this year's edition was centred on errors related to the use of determiners and prepositions. This focus was partly motivated by the results of HOO'11. HOO'12 attracted 14 participating teams.

Preparations are already underway for a seventh NLG shared-task evaluation event next year, Generation Challenges 2013, which may be organised as part of ENLG'13. Hopefully, this will include new tasks from among those proposed in the Future Task Proposals Track of GenChal'11 and GenChal'12. Many of the new proposals share an emphasis on fostering collaboration with members of other research communities, and will, it is to be hoped, serve to broaden the interest in tasks related to the generation of natural language.

Many people contribute to making Generation Challenges happen each year. This year, we would like to thank in particular the INLG'12 organisers, Barbara di Eugenio and Susan McRoy for hosting GenChal'12, and the shared task organising teams for all their hard work.

June 2012 *Anja Belz and Albert Gatt*

Generation Challenges Steering Committee:

Anja Belz, University of Brighton, UK
Robert Dale, Macquarie University, Australia
Albert Gatt, University of Malta and Unversity of Aberdeen, UK
Kevin Knight, ISI, University of Southern California, USA
Alexander Koller, Saarland University, Germany
Chris Mellish, Aberdeen University, UK
Johanna Moore, Edinburgh University, UK
Amanda Stent, Stony Brook University, USA
Kristina Striegnitz, Union College, USA

The Surface Realisation Task: Recent Developments and Future Plans

Anja Belz
Computing, Engineering and Maths
University of Brighton
Brighton BN1 4GJ, UK
a.s.belz@brighton.ac.uk

Bernd Bohnet
Institute for Natural Language Processing
University of Stuttgart
70174 Stuttgart
bohnet@ims.uni-stuttgart.de

Simon Mille, Leo Wanner
Information and Communication Technologies
Pompeu Fabra University
08018 Barcelona
<firstname>.<lastname>@upf.edu

Michael White
Department of Linguistics
Ohio State University
Columbus, OH, 43210, US
mwhite@ling.osu.edu

Abstract

The Surface Realisation Shared Task was first run in 2011. Two common-ground input representations were developed and for the first time several independently developed surface realisers produced realisations from the same shared inputs. However, the input representations had several shortcomings which we have been aiming to address in the time since. This paper reports on our work to date on improving the input representations and on our plans for the next edition of the SR Task. We also briefly summarise other related developments in NLG shared tasks and outline how the different ideas may be usefully brought together in the future.

1 Introduction

The Surface Realisation (SR) Task was introduced as a new shared task at Generation Challenges 2011 (Belz et al., 2011). Our aim in developing the SR Task was to make it possible, for the first time, to directly compare different, independently developed surface realisers by developing a 'common-ground' representation that could be used by all participating systems as input. In fact, we created two different input representations, one shallow, one deep, in order to enable more teams to participate. Correspondingly, there were two tracks in SR'11: In the Shallow Track, the task was to map from shallow syntax-level input representations to realisations; in the Deep Track, the task was to map from deep semantics-level input representations to realisations.

By the time teams submitted their system outputs, it had become clear that the inputs required by some types of surface realisers were more easily derived from the common-ground representation than the inputs required by other types. There were other respects in which the representations were not ideal, e.g. the deep representations retained too many syntactic elements as stopgaps where no deeper information had been available. It was clear that the input representations had to be improved for the next edition of the SR Task. In this paper, we report on our work in this direction so far and relate it to some new shared task proposals which have been developed in part as a response to the above difficulties. We discuss how these developments might usefully be integrated, and outline plans for SR'13, the next edition of the SR Task.

2 SR'11

The SR'11 input representations were created by post-processing the CoNLL 2008 Shared Task data (Surdeanu et al., 2008), for the preparation of which selected sections of the WSJ Treebank were converted to syntactic dependencies with the Pennconverter (Johansson and Nugues, 2007). The resulting dependency bank was then merged with Nombank (Meyers et al., 2004) and Propbank (Palmer et al., 2005). Named entity information from the BBN Entity Type corpus was also incorporated. The SR'11 shallow representation was based on the Pennconverter dependencies, while the deep representation was derived from the merged Nombank, Propbank and syntactic dependencies in a process similar to the graph completion algorithm outlined by Bohnet (2010).

Five teams submitted a total of six systems to SR'11 which we evaluated automatically using a range of intrinsic metrics. In addition, systems were assessed by human judges in terms of Clarity, Readability and Meaning Similarity.

The four top-performing systems were all statistical dependency realisers that do not make use of an explicit, pre-existing grammar. By design, statistical dependency realisers are robust and relatively easy to adapt to new kinds of dependency inputs which made them well suited to the SR'11 Task. In contrast, there were only two systems that employed a grammar, either hand-crafted or treebank-derived, and these did not produce competitive results. Both teams reported substantial difficulties in converting the common ground inputs into the 'native' inputs required by their systems.

The SR'11 results report pointed towards two kinds of possible improvements: (i) introducing (additional) tasks where performance would not depend to the same extent on the relation between common-ground and native inputs, e.g. a text-to-text shared task on sentential paraphrasing; and (ii) improving the representations themselves. In the remainder of this paper we report on developments in both these directions.

3 Towards SR'13

As outlined above, the first SR Shared Task turned up some interesting representational issues that required some in-depth investigation. In the end, it was this fact that led to the decision to postpone the 2nd SR Shared Task until 2013 in order to allow enough time to address these issues properly. In this section, we describe our plans for SR'13 to the extent to which they have progressed.

3.1 Task definition

As in the first SR task, the participating teams will be provided with annotated corpora consisting of common-ground input representations and their corresponding outputs. Two kinds of input will be offered: deep representations and surface representations. The deep input representations will be semantic graphs; the surface representations syntactic trees. Both will be derived from the Penn Treebank. The task will consist in the generation of a text starting from either of the input representations.

3.2 Changes to the input representations

During the working group discussions which followed SR'11, it became apparent that the CoNLL syntactic dependency trees overlaid with Propbank/Nombank relations had turned out to be inadequate in various respects for the purpose of deriving a suitable semantic representation. For instance:

- **Governed prepositions** are not distinguished from semantically loaded prepositions in the CoNLL annotation. In SR'11, only strongly governed prepositions such as *give something TO someone* were removed, but in many cases the meaning of a preposition which introduces an argument (of a verb, a noun, an adjective or an adverb) clearly depends on the predicate: *believe IN something*, *account FOR something*, etc. In those cases, too, the preposition should be removed from the semantic annotation, since the relisers have to be able to introduce non-semantic features un-aided. On the contrary, semantically loaded governed prepositions such as *live IN a flat/ON a roof/NEXT TO the main street* etc. should be retained in the annotation. These prepositions all receive argumental arcs in PropBank/NomBank, so it is not easy to distinguish between them. One possibility would be to target a restricted list of prepositions which are void of meaning most of the time, and remove those prepositions when they introduce arguments.

- The annotation of **relative pronouns** did not survive the conversion of the original Penn Treebank to the CoNLL format unscathed: the antecedent of the relative pronoun is sometimes lost or the relative pronoun is not annotated, predominantly because the predicate which the relative pronoun is an argument of was not considered to be a predicate by annotators, as in *the degree TO WHICH companies are irritated*. However, in the original constituency annotation, the traces allow for retrieving antecedents and semantic governors, hence using this original annotation could be useful in order to get a clean annotation of such phenomena.

Agreement has been reached on a range of other issues, although the feasibility of implementing the corresponding changes might have to be further evaluated:

- **Coordinations** should be annotated in the semantic representation with the conjunction as the head of all the conjuncts. This treatment would allow e.g. an adequate representation of sharing of dependents among the conjuncts.
- The inversion of 'modifier' arcs and the introduction of **meta-semantemes** would avoid anticipating syntactic decisions such as the direction of non-argumental syntactic edges, and allow for connecting unconnected parts of the semantic structures.
- In order to keep the **scope** of various phenomena intact after inverting non-argumental edges, we should explicitly mark the scope of e.g. negations, quantifiers, quotation marks etc. as attribute values on the nodes.
- **Control arcs** should be removed from the semantic representation since they do not provide information relevant at that level.
- **Named entities** will be further specified adding a reduced set of named entity types from the BBN annotations.

Finally, we will perform automatic and manual quality checks in order to ensure that the proposed changes are adequately introduced in the annotation.

3.3 Evaluation

We will once again follow the main data set divisions of the CoNLL'08 data (training set = WSJ Sections 02–21; development set = Section 24; test set = Section 23), with the proviso that we have removed 300 randomly selected sentences from the development set for use in human evaluations. Of these, we used 100 sentences in SR'11 and will use a different 100 in SR'13.

Evaluation criteria identified as important for evaluation of surface realisation output in previous work include Adequacy (preservation of meaning), Fluency (grammaticality/idiomaticity), Clarity, Humanlikeness and Task Effectiveness. We will aim to evaluate system outputs submitted by SR'13 participants in terms of most of these criteria, using both automatic and human-assessed methods.

As in SR'11, the automatic evaluation metrics (assessing Humanlikeness) will be BLEU, NIST, TER and possibly METEOR. We will apply text normalisation to system outputs before scoring them with the automatic metrics. For n-best ranked system outputs, we will again compute a single score for all outputs by computing their weighted sum of their individual scores, where a weight is assigned to a system output in inverse proportion to its rank. For a subset of the test data we may obtain additional alternative realisations via Mechanical Turk for use in the automatic evaluations.

We are planning to expand the range of human-assessed evaluation experiments (assessing Adequacy, Fluency and Clarity) to the following methods:

1. Preference Judgement Experiment (C2, C3): Collect preference judgements using an existing evaluation interface (Kow and Belz, 2012) and directly recruited evaluators. We will present sentences in the context of a chunk of 5 consecutive sentences to the evaluators, and ask for separate judgements for Clarity, Fluency and Meaning Similarity.
2. HTER (Snover et al., 2006): In this evaluation method, human evaluators are asked to post-edit the output of a system, and the edits are then categorised and counted. Crucial to this evaluation method is the construction of clear instructions for evaluators and the categorisation of edits. We will categorise edits as relating to Meaning Similarity, Fluency and/or Clarity; we will also consider further subcategorisations.

We will once again provide evaluation scripts to participants so they can perform automatic evaluations on the development data. These scores serve two purposes. Firstly, development data scores must be included in participants' reports. Secondly, participants may wish to use the evaluation scripts in developing and tuning their systems.

We will report per-system results separately for the automatic metrics (4 sets of results), and for the human-assessed measures (2 sets of results). For each set of results, we will report single-best and n-best results. For single-best results, we may furthermore report results both with and without missing outputs. We will rank systems, and report significance of pairwise differences using bootstrap resampling where necessary (Koehn, 2004; Zhang and Vogel, 2010). We will separately report correlation between human and automatic metrics, and between different automatic metrics.

3.4 Assessing different aspects of realisation separately

In addition, we will consider measuring different aspects of the realisation performance of participating systems (syntax, word order, morphology) since a system can perform well on one and badly on another. For instance, a system might perform well on morphological realisation while it has poor results on linearisation. We would like to capture this fact. This may involve asking participating teams to submit intermediate representations or identifiers to identify the reference words. This more fine-grained approach should help us to obtain a more precise picture of the state of affairs in the field and could help to reveal the respective strengths of different surface realisers more clearly.

4 Related Developments

4.1 Syntactic Paraphrase Ranking

The new shared task on syntactic paraphrase ranking described elsewhere in this volume (White, 2012) is intended to run as a follow-on to the main surface realisation shared task. Taking advantage of the human judgements collected to evaluate the surface realisations produced by competing systems, the task is to automatically rank the realisations that differ from the reference sentence in a way that agrees with the human judgements as often as possible. The task is designed to appeal to developers of surface realisation systems as well as machine translation evaluation metrics. For surface realisation systems, the task sidesteps the thorny issue of converting inputs to a common representation. Developers of realisation systems that can generate and optionally rank multiple outputs for a given input will be encouraged to participate in the task, which will test the system's ability to produce acceptable paraphrases and/or to rank competing realisations. For MT evaluation metrics, the task provides a challenging framework for advancing automatic evaluation, as many of the paraphrases are expected to be of high quality, differing only in subtle syntactic choices.

4.2 Content Selection Challenge

The new shared task on content selection has been put forward (Bouayad-Agha et al., 2012) to initiate work on content selection from a common, standardised semantic-web format input, and thus provide the context for an objective assessment of different content selection strategies. The task consists in selecting the contents communicated in reference biographies of celebrities from a large volume of RDF-triples. The selected triples will be evaluated against a gold triple selection set using standard quality assessment metrics.

The task can be considered complementary to the surface realisation shared task in that it contributes to the medium-term goal of setting up a task that covers all stages of the generation pipeline. In future challenges, it can be explored to what extent and how the output content plans can be mapped onto semantic representations that serve as input to the surface realisers.

5 Plans

We are currently working on the new improved common-ground input representation scheme and converting the data to the new scheme.

The provisional schedule for SR'13 looks as follows:

Announcement and call for expressions of interest:	6 July 2012
Preliminary registration and release of description of new representations:	27 July 2012
Release of data and documentation:	2 Nov 2012
System Submission Deadline:	10 May 2013
Evaluation Period:	10 May– 10 Jul 2013
Provisional dates for results session:	8–9 Aug 2013

6 Conclusion

For a large number of NLP applications (among them, e.g., text generation proper, summarisation, question answering, and dialogue), surface realisation (SR) is a key technology. Unfortunately, so far in nearly all of these applications, idiosyncratic, custom-made SR implementations prevail. However, a look over the fence at the language analysis side shows that the broad use of standard dependency treebanks and semantically annotated resources such as PropBank and NomBank that were created especially with parsing in mind led to standardised high-quality off-the-shelf parser implementations. It seems clear that in order to advance the field of surface realisation, the generation community also needs adequate resources on which large-scale experiments can be run in search of the surface realiser with the best performance, a surface realiser which is commonly accepted, follows general transparent principles and is thus usable as plug-in in the majority of applications.

The SR Shared Task aims to contribute to this goal. On the one hand, it will lead to the creation of NLG-suitable resources in that it will convert the PropBank into a more semantic and more completely annotated resource. On the other hand, it will offer a forum for the presentation and evaluation of various approaches to SR and thus help us to search for the best solution to the SR task with the greatest potential to become a widely accepted off-the-shelf tool.

Acknowledgments

We gratefully acknowledge the contributions to discussions and development of ideas made by the other members of the SR working group: Miguel Ballesteros, Johan Bos, Aoife Cahill, Josef van Genabith, Pablo Gervás, Deirdre Hogan and Amanda Stent.

References

Anja Belz, Michael White, Dominic Espinosa, Deidre Hogan, Eric Kow, and Amanda Stent. 2011. The first surface realisation shared task: Overview and evaluation results. In *Proceedings of the 13th European Workshop on Natural Language Generation (ENLG'11)*, pages 217–226. Association for Computational Linguistics.

Bernd Bohnet, Leo Wanner, Simon Mille, and Alicia Burga. 2010. Broad coverage multilingual deep sentence generation with a stochastic multi-level realizer. In *Proceedings of the 23rd International Conference on Computational Linguistics*, Beijing, China.

Nadjet Bouayad-Agha, Gerard Casamayor, Leo Wanner, and Chris Mellish. 2012. Content selection from semantic web data. In *Proceedings of the 7th International Natural Language Generation Conference (INLG'12)*.

Richard Johansson and Pierre Nugues. 2007. Extended constituent-to-dependency conversion for English. In Joakim Nivre, Heiki-Jaan Kaalep, Kadri Muischnek, and Mare Koit, editors, *Proceedings of NODALIDA 2007*, pages 105–112, Tartu, Estonia.

Philipp Koehn. 2004. Statistical significance tests for machine translation evaluation. In Dekang Lin and Dekai Wu, editors, *Proceedings of EMNLP 2004*, pages 388–395, Barcelona, Spain, July. Association for Computational Linguistics.

Eric Kow and Anja Belz. 2012. LG-Eval: A toolkit for creating online language evaluation experiments. In *Proceedings of the 8th International Conference on Language Resources and Evaluation (LREC'12)*.

Adam Meyers, Ruth Reeves, Catherine Macleod, Rachel Szekely, Veronika Zielinska, Brian Young, and Ralph Grishman. 2004. The NomBank project: An interim report. In *NAACL/HLT Workshop Frontiers in Corpus Annotation*.

Martha Palmer, Daniel Gildea, and Paul Kingsbury. 2005. The Proposition Bank: A corpus annotated with semantic roles. In *Computational Linguistics Journal*, pages 71–105.

Matthew Snover, Bonnie Dorr, Richard Schwartz, Linnea Micciulla, and John Makhoul. 2006. A study of translation edit rate with targeted human annotation. In *In Proceedings of Association for Machine Translation in the Americas*, pages 223–231.

Mihai Surdeanu, Richard Johansson, Adam Meyers, Lluís Màrquez, and Joakim Nivre. 2008. The CoNLL 2008 shared task on joint parsing of syntactic and semantic dependencies. In *Proceedings of the Twelfth Conference on Computational Natural Language Learning (CoNLL'08)*, Manchester, UK.

Michael White. 2012. Shared task proposal: Syntactic paraphrase ranking. In *Proceedings of the 7th International Natural Language Generation Conference (INLG'12)*.

Ying Zhang and Stephan Vogel. 2010. Significance tests of automatic machine translation evaluation metrics. *Machine Translation*, 24:51–65.

KBGen – Text Generation from Knowledge Bases as a New Shared Task

Eva Banik[1], Claire Gardent[2], Donia Scott[3], Nikhil Dinesh[4], and Fennie Liang[5]

[1]`ebanik@comp-ling.co.uk`, Computational Linguistics Ltd, London, UK
[2]`claire.gardent@loria.fr`, CNRS, LORIA, Nancy, France
[3]`D.R.Scott@sussex.ac.uk`, School of Informatics, University of Sussex, Brighton, UK
[4]`dinesh@ai.sri.com`, SRI International, Menlo Park, CA
[5]`fennie.liang@cs.man.ac.uk`, School of Computer Science, University of Manchester, UK

1 Introduction

In this paper we propose a new shared task, KBGen, where the aim is to produce coherent descriptions of concepts and relationships in a frame-based knowledge base (KB). We propose to use the AURA knowledge base for the shared task which contains information about biological entities and processes. We describe how the AURA KB provides an application context for NLG and illustrate how this application context generalizes to other biology KBs. We argue that the easy availability of input data and a research community – both domain experts and knowledge representation experts – which actively uses these knowledge bases, along with regular evaluation experiments, creates an ideal scenario for a shared task.

2 Application Context and Motivation

One of the research challenges in the knowledge representation community is to model complex knowledge in order to be able to answer complex questions from a knowledge base (see e.g. the Deep Knowledge Representation Challenge Workshop at KCAP 2011[1]). There are several applications of such knowledge bases, perhaps most recently and most prominently in the bioinformatics and educational informatics domain, where there are available knowledge bases and reasoners that help scientists answer questions, explain connections between concepts, visualize complex processes, and help students learn about biology. These uses of a knowledge base are however difficult to implement without presenting the resulting answers and explanations to the user in a clear, concise and coherent way, which often requires using natural language.

2.1 The AURA Knowledge Base

The AURA biology knowledge base developed by SRI International (Gunning et al., 2010) encodes information from a biology textbook (Reece et al., 2010)[2]. The purpose of this knowledge base is to help students understand biological concepts by allowing them to ask questions about the material while reading the textbook. The KB is built on top of a generic library of concepts (CLIB, Barker et al., 2001), which are specialized and/or combined to encode biology-specific information, and it is organized into a set of concept maps, where each concept map corresponds to a biological entity or process. The KB is being encoded by biologists and currently encodes over 5,000 concept maps.

The AURA KB and its question answering system is integrated with an electronic textbook application[3]. The applicaton allows the students to ask complex questions about relationships between concepts, which are answered by finding a possible path between the two concepts. The results are presented to the students as graphs, for example the answer produced by the system in response to the question "what is the relationship between glycolysis and glucose?" is illustrated in Fig 1.

These graphs are simplified representations of

[1]http://sites.google.com/site/dkrckcap2011/home

[2]The development of the AURA knowledge base and related tools and applications was funded by Vulcan Inc.

[3]A demo of the application will be presented in the demo session at INLG 2012

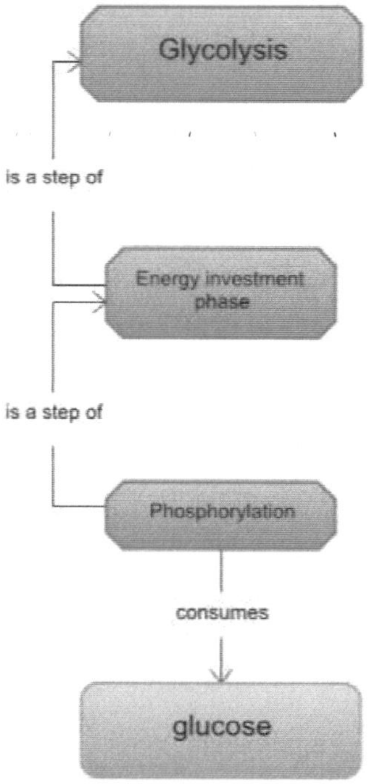

Figure 1: Relationship between glycolysis and glucose

a path in the knowledge base that connects two concepts, because presenting the full concept map where the path was found would make it difficult for the students to clearly see the relationship. However, this simplification often obscures the connection by not showing relevant information.

Given the inclusion of a few more relations from the concept map of glycolysis (Fig 2), the answer to the question could be generated as a complex sentence or a paragraph of text, for example: "Phosphorylation of glucose is the first step of the energy investment phase of glycolysis" or "In the first step of the energy investment phase of glycolysis, called phosphorylation, hexokinase catalyses the synthesis of glucose-6-phosphate from glucose and a phosphate ion."

2.2 BioCyc

Another situation in which graph-based representations are presented to the user is metabolic pathway and genome databases, such as the BioCyc knowledge base. BioCyc describes the genome, metabolic pathways, and other important aspects of organisms such as molecular components and their interactions and currently contains information from 1,763 pathway/genome databases[4].

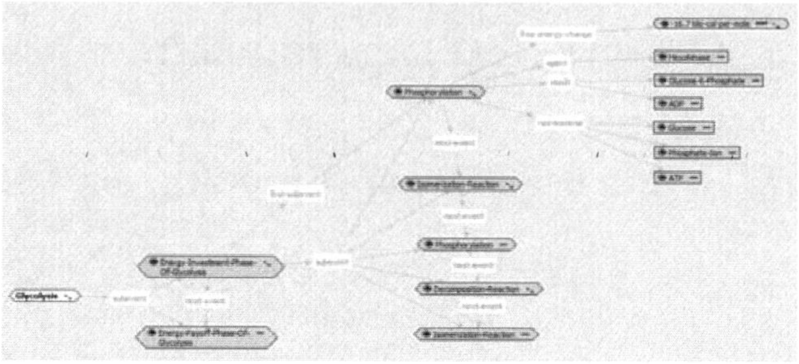

Figure 2: Concept map of glycolysis

When users query parts of the BioCyc knowledge base, the system automatically produces a graph to visualize complex biological processes. For example, Fig 3 illustrates an automatically generated graph from the knowledge base which shows the process of glycolysis in an E. coli cell. Hovering the mouse over the ⊕ and ⊖ signs on the graph brings up popups with additional information about gene expressions , detailed chemical reactions in the process, enzymes activated by certain chemicals, etc..

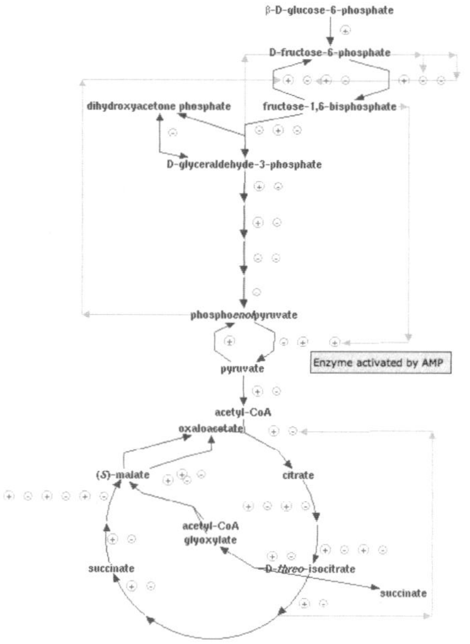

Figure 3: The process of glycolysis in E.coli

3 Input Data for Generation

Although there is a clear benefit from visualizing complex processes in a graph form, one also has to

[4]http://www.biocyc.org

be well-versed in the notation and details of biological processes in order to make sense of these representations. Students of biology and non-experts would certainly benefit from a more detailed explanation of the process, presented as a few paraphraphs of text along with graphs to emphasize the most salient features of processes.

The paths and relations returned by reasoning algorithms also present a good opportunity to provide inputs for natural language generation. These chunks of data typically contain the right amount of data because they consist of the information needed to answer a question or describe a concept. Additionally, many knowledge bases (including both BioCyc and AURA) are encoded in a frame-based representation, which has the advantage that frames naturally correspond to linguistic units.

Frame-based systems (Minsky, 1981) are based around the notion of frames or classes which represent collections of concepts. Each frame has an associated set of slots or attributes which can be filled either by specific values or by other frames. Intuitively, frames correspond to situations, and each terminal in the frame corresponds to answers to questions that could be asked about the situation, including the participants in the situation, causes and consequences, preceding and following situations, purpose, etc. Frame-based representations may either contain frames of generic concepts or instance frames which represent information about particular instances. Frames also have a kind-of slot, which allows the assertion of a frame taxonomy, and the inheritance of slots.

In the knowledge representation community, frame-based representations are popular because they make the encoding process more intuitive. From a natural language generation perspective, each frame (or a set of slots) corresponds to a linguistic unit (sentence, noun phrase, clause, verb phrase, etc), depending on the type of the frame and the slots it contains. This organization of concepts and relations in the knowledge base makes it easier to select chunks of data from which coherent texts can be generated.

Slots in these frame-based representations also naturally correspond to the kind of flat semantic representations and dependency structures that have served as input to surface realization (Koller and Striegnitz, 2002; Carroll and Oepen, 2005; White, 2006; Gardent and Kow, 2007; Nakatsu and White, 2010).

4 The shared task

We propose two tracks for the KBGen shared task: a "complex surface realization" track, where the task is to generate complex sentences from shorter inputs, and a "discourse generation" track, where the task is to generate longer texts made up from several paragraphs. In the following, we describe the data set from which the input to generation will be selected; the methology we plan to use to extract text size input for the generation challenge; and the two tracks making up the KBGen challenge.

4.1 The AURA knowledge base as Input Dataset

We propose to use the AURA knowledge base as input data for the shared task for several reasons. AURA contains a number of relations and therefore provides varied input for generation[5]. The AURA knowledge base contains linguistic resources that can be used for generation (a morphological lexicon and a list of synonyms for each concept) and the electronic textbook provides an application context to evaluate the generated texts. There are regular evaluation efforts to assess the educational benefits of using the textbook application, and the next round of these experiments will involve over 400 students and biology teachers who will use the application over an extended period of time. The evaluation of the outputs generated for the shared task could form part of these experiments.

4.2 Selecting Text Size Content for the Shared Task

We propose to select data from the knowledge base manually or semi-automatically, by selecting a set of concepts to be described and including relevant relations associated with the concepts. We would first select a set of concept maps that are encoded in most detail and have been reviewed by the encoders for quality assurance. The input data for each concept will then be a manually selected set of frames

[5]If there is interest, the systems developed to generate from AURA could also be applied to the BioCyc data, which has a more restricted set of relations.

from the concept map. The selected relations will be reviewed one more time for quality and consistency to filter out any errors in the data.

If there is interest in the community, we can also envision a content selection challenge which could provide input to the generation task. Although frames in the knowledge base correspond well to chunks of data for generation of descriptions, content selection for other communicative goals is far from a trivial problem. One such challenge could be for example comparing two concepts, or explaining the relation between a process and its sub-type (another process that is taxonomically related, but different in certain parts).

4.3 Complex Surface Realization Track

For the complex surface realization track, a small number of frames would be selected from the knowledge base along with a small number of other relevant relations (e.g., important parts or properties of certain event participants, or certain relations between them, depending on the context). The output texts to be generated would be complex sentences describing the central entity/event in the data, or the relationship between two concepts, such as the glycolysis example in section 2.1. This task would involve aggregation and generating intrasentential pronouns governed by syntax where necessary, but it would not require the generation of any discourse anaphora or referring expressions.

This track will differ from the deep generation track of the Surface Realization Shared Task both in form and in content. The form of the KBGen input is a concept map extracted from an ontology rather than a deep semantics extracted by conversion from dependency parse trees. Similarly, its content is that of a biology knowledge base rather than that of the Penn Treebank textual corpus.

4.4 Discourse Generation Track

Inputs for the discourse generation task would include most frames from the concept map of an entity or process. The output would be longer paragraphs or 2-3 paragraphs of text, typically a description of the subevents, results, etc, of a biological process, or the description of the structure and function of an entity. This task would involve text structuring and the generation of pronouns.

4.5 Lexical Resources and potential multilingual tracks

The knowledge base provides a mapping from concepts to lexical items and a list of synonyms. It also provides information about how specific slots in event frames are mapped onto prepositions.

If there is interest in the community, the lexical resources corresponding to the selected content could be translated to different languages semi-automatically: the translation could be attempted first automatically, with the help of available biology/medical lexicons, and then the output would be hand-corrected. Candidate languages for a multilingual challenge would be French and Spanish. To run the multilingual tracks we would need to create multilingual development and test data and would need to have access to French/Spanish speaking biologists.

5 Evaluation

Evaluation of the generated texts could be done both with automatic evaluation metrics and using human judgements. Automatic evaluation metrics could include BLUE (Papineni et al., 2002) or measuring Levenshtein distance (Levenshtein, 1966) from human written texts. To obtain human judgements, biologists will be asked to compose texts conveying the same content as the input for the generated texts. The human-written texts will be presented to subjects along with the generated outputs to obtain fluency judgements, but the subjects will not be told which kind of text they are judging. The evaluation campaign could be coordinated with the evaluation of the knowledge base and the electronic textbook application, and/or publicized on social networking sites or mechanical turk.

6 Next Steps

We invite feedback on this proposal with the aim of refining our plan and discussing a suitable input representation for the shared task in the next few months. If there is sufficient interest in the shared task, we would make the input data available in the agreed format in late 2012, with the first evaluation taking place in 2013. We would like to hear any comments/suggestions/critisisms about the plan and we are actively looking for people who would be interested in getting involved in planning and running the challenge.

References

Barker, K., B. Porter, and P. Clark. 2001. A library of generic concepts for composing knowledgebases. In *Proceedings of the 1st Int Conf on Knowledge Capture (K-Cap'01)*, 14–21.

Carroll, J., and S. Oepen. 2005. High efficiency realization for a wide-coverage unification grammar. *2nd IJCNLP* .

Gardent, C., and E. Kow. 2007. A symbolic approach to near-deterministic surface realisation using tree adjoining grammar. In *In 45th Annual Meeting of the ACL.*

Gunning, D., V. K. Chaudhri, P. Clark, K. Barker, Shaw-Yi Chaw, M. Greaves, B. Grosof, A. Leung, D. McDonald, S. Mishra, J. Pacheco, B. Porter, A. Spaulding, D. Tecuci, and J. Tien. 2010. Project halo update - progress toward digital aristotle. *AI Magazine* Fall:33–58.

Koller, Alexander, and Kristina Striegnitz. 2002. Generation as dependency parsing. In *Proceedings of ACL.*

Levenshtein, Vladimir I. 1966. Binary codes capable of correcting deletions, insertions, and reversals. *Soviet Physics Doklady* 10:707–710.

Minsky, Marvin. 1981. *Mind design*, chapter A Framework for Representing Knowledge, 95–128. MIT Press.

Nakatsu, Crystal, and Michael White. 2010. Generating with discourse combinatory categorial grammar. *submitted to Linguistic Issues in Language Technology* .

Papineni, Kishore, Salim Roukos, Todd Ward, and Wei jing Zhu. 2002. Bleu: a method for automatic evaluation of machine translation. 311–318.

Reece, Jane B., Lisa A. Urry, Michael L. Cain, Steven A. Wasserman, Peter V. Minorsky, and Robert B. Jackson. 2010. *Campbell biology*. Pearson Publishing.

White, Michael. 2006. Ccg chart realization from disjunctive inputs. In *Proceedings of the Fourth International Natural Language Generation Conference*, 12–19. Sydney, Australia: Association for Computational Linguistics.

Content Selection From Semantic Web Data

Nadjet Bouayad-Agha[1]
Gerard Casamayor[1]
Leo Wanner[1,2]
[1]DTIC, University Pompeu Fabra
[2]Institució Catalana de Recerca i Estudis Avançats
Barcelona, Spain
`firstname.lastname@upf.edu`

Chris Mellish
Computing Science
University of Aberdeen
Aberdeen AB24 3UE, UK
`c.mellish@abdn.ac.uk`

Abstract

So far, there has been little success in Natural Language Generation in coming up with general models of the content selection process. Nonetheless, there has been some work on content selection that employ Machine learning or heuristic search. On the other side, there is a clear tendency in NLG towards the use of resources encoded in standard Semantic Web representation formats. For these reasons, we believe that time has come to propose an initial challenge on content selection from Semantic Web data. In this paper, we briefly outline the idea and plan for the execution of this task.

1 Motivation

So far, there has been little success in Natural Language Generation in coming up with general models of the content selection process. Most of the researchers in the field agree that this lack of success is because the knowledge and context (communicative goals, user profile, discourse history, query, etc) needed for this task depend on the application domain. This often led in the past to template- or graph-based combined content selection and discourse structuring approaches operating on idiosyncratically encoded small sets of input data. Furthermore, in many NLG-applications, target texts and sometimes even empirical data are not available, which makes it difficult to employ empirical approaches to knowledge elicitation. Nonetheless, during the last decade, there has been a steady flow of new work on content selection that employed Machine learning (Barzilay and Lapata, 2005; Duboue and McKeown, 2003; Jordan and Walker, 2005; Kelly et al., 2009), heuristic search (O'Donnell et al., 2001; Demir et al., 2010; Mellish and Pan, 2008), or a combination thereof (Bouayad-Agha et al., 2011). All of these strategies can deal with large volumes of data.

On the other side, there is a clear tendency in NLG towards the use of resources encoded in terms of standard Semantic Web representation formats such as OWL and RDF, e.g., (Wilcock and Jokinen, 2003; Bontcheva and Wilks, 2004; Mellish and Pan, 2008; Power and Third, 2010; Bouayad-Agha et al., 2011; Dannells et al., 2012), to name but a few. However, although most of these works make a good attempt at realisation, the problem of content determination from Semantic Web data is relatively untouched.

For these reasons, we believe that the time has come to bring together researchers working on (or interested in working on) content selection to participate in a challenge for this task using standard freely available web data as input. The availability of open modular multi-domain multi-billion triple data and of open ontological resources (Bizer et al., 2009) presented in a standard knowledge representation formalism make semantic web data a natural choice for such a challenge.

As will be presented below, this initial challenge presents a relatively simple content selection task with no user model and a straightforward communicative goal so that people are encouraged to take part and motivated to stay on for later challenges, in which the task will be successively enhanced from gained experience.

A content determination challenge would be a chance to (i) directly compare the performance of different types of content selection strategies; (ii) contribute towards developing a standard "off-the-shelf" content selection module; and (iii) contribute towards a standard interface between text planning and linguistic generation.

To get the widest reception possible, the challenge will be open to any approach, be it template-, rule- or heuristic-based, or empirical. Furthermore, it will be advertised in the Semantic Web Community to get contributors from other horizons, see, e.g., (Dai et al., 2010).

In what follows, we briefly outline the idea and plan for the execution of the challenge. In Section 2, we outline a description of the task. In Section 3, the data and domain that will be used are presented. Section 4 describes how this data is to be prepared for the task, and Section 5 how it will be released to the participants. In Section 6, we sketch the evaluation including the preparation of the evaluation dataset. Section 7 gives a proposed schedule for each of the tasks involved in organizing the challenge. Finally, in Section 8, we provide short biographies of the members of the organization team, focusing on their experience in the proposed task.

2 Task Description

The core of the task to be addressed can be formulated as follows:

> Build a system which, given a set of RDF triples containing facts about a celebrity and a target text (for instance, a wikipedia-style article about that person), selects those triples that are reflected in the target text.

The participants are also free to consider the semantics defined by the data sources in their approach, rely on additional resources like ontologies from other sources, or disregard the semantics completely.

The implemented system should output its results in a predefined standard format that can be used for automatic evaluation.

It could be that the RDF data does not contain everything that would ideally be included in such an article, but that is ignored here. The task consists in selecting content that is communicated in the target text.

3 The data

The domain will be constituted by short biographies of famous people. This is an interesting domain for the challenge because Semantic Web data and corresponding texts for this domain are available in large quantities (e.g., DBPedia or Freebase for the data and many other sources for biography texts, among them Wikipedia).

The data will consist, for each famous person, of a pair of RDF-triple set and associated text(s). For each pair, the RDF data will include both information communicated and excluded from the text. The text may convey information not present in the RDF-triples, but this will be kept to a minimum, always subject to using naturally-occurring texts. All pairs should contain enough RDF-triples and text to make the pair interesting for the content selection task.

When choosing data for the challenge, we will prefer semantic contents classified under consistent ontologies over plain Linked Data with no explicit semantics. The semantics of the RDF data (vocabularies, ontologies) will be provided, preferably encoded in Semantic Web standards (e.g., in RDFS or OWL).

4 Data Preparation

The task of data preparation consists in 1) data gathering and preparation, which is to be carried out by the organizers, and 2) working dataset selection and annotation, which is to be carried out by both the organizers and participants.

4.1 Data gathering and preparation

This preparatory stage consists in choosing the repository sources, downloading the relevant ontologies (to the extent those will be provided), and downloading and pairing the data and associated texts (= the paired corpus).

4.2 Working Dataset selection and annotation

The participants will be asked to participate in a preliminary task consisting in marking which triples are included in the text given a subset of the paired corpus (the size of the subset still has to be decided). This task could be supported by some automatic anchoring techniques such as used in (Duboue and McKeown, 2003; Barzilay and Lapata, 2005). The objectives of the task are threefold: (1) to provide all participants with a common set of "correct answers" to be exploited in their approach, (2) to familiarize the participants with the nature of the contents, their semantics and the texts, and (3) to provide the task with a ceiling for the evaluation, i.e. inter-annotator agreement.

Annotation guidelines will be needed to ensure that all participants follow the same procedure when annotating texts. For this purpose, an early document will be produced detailing the procedure together with examples and descriptions of relevant problems such as ambiguities in the annotation. The guidelines will be improved in multiple stages of annotation and revision with the goal of maximizing inter-annotator agreement.

5 Data release

The participants in the challenge will be given access to the set of all correct answers and a large portion of the non-marked paired corpus, as well as their semantics (i.e., ontologies and the like). The remaining unseen, non-marked set will be kept for evaluation.

6 Evaluation

The evaluation consists of 1) a preparatory stage for selecting and annotating the evaluation dataset, and 2) an evaluation stage.

6.1 Evaluation dataset selection and annotation

Once all participants have submitted their executable to solve the task, the evaluation set will be processed. If timing is tight, however, this could be done whilst the participants are still working on the task or extra effort (for instance, from the organizers) could be brought in. A subset of the data is randomly selected and annotated with the selected triples by the participants. This two-stage approach to triple selection annotation is proposed in order to avoid any bias on the evaluation data.

6.2 Evaluation

Each executable is run against the test corpus and the selected triples evaluated against the gold triple selection set. Since this is formally a relatively simple task of selecting a subset of a given set, we will use for evaluation standard precision, recall and F measures. In addition, other appropriate metrics will be explored—for instance, certain metrics for extractive summarisation (which is to some extent a similar task).

The organizers will explore whether it will be feasible to select and annotate some test examples from a different corpus and have the systems evaluated on these as a separate task.

7 Schedule

Table 1 presents the different tasks, protagonists and the schedule involved in the organization of the challenge. The challenge proper will take place between November 2012 and May/June 2013.

8 Organizers

Nadjet Bouayad-Agha has been a lecturer and researcher at DTIC, UPF, since 2002. She obtained her PhD on Text Planning in 2001 from the University of Brighton and has been working ever since her postgraduate studies at the University of Paris VII in NLG, more specifically on Text Planning. In recent years her focus has been on how to exploit semantic web representations and technologies for Text Planning in general and content selection in particular.

Gerard Casamayor is a PhD student at DTIC, UPF, working on text planning from general-purpose semantic data. His main interests are machine learning and interactive, collaborative text planning. As part of his thesis, he is developing a text planning approach that can be trained directly by domain experts, minimizing the need of encoding or annotating prior knowledge about how to solve the task.

Chris Mellish has been a professor at the University of Aberdeen since 2003, when he moved from a similar position at the University of Edinburgh. He has been doing research in NLG since 1984 and organised the second European NLG workshop. His work on content selection includes the opportunistic planning approach used by the ILEX system and a rule-based approach to content selection from semantic web data presented in ENLG 2011.

Leo Wanner has been ICREA Research Professor at DTIC, UPF, since 2005. Before, he was

What?	Who?	When?
Data gathering and preparation	Organizers	Summer 2012
Working dataset selection and annotation	Organizers and Participants	Sept/Oct 2012
Data Release	Organizers	November 2012
Evaluation dataset selection and annotation	Organizers and Participants	May 2013
Evaluation	Organizers	June 2013
Publication@INLG	Organizers	August 2013

Table 1: Content Selection Challenge Organization Schedule

affiliated as Assistant Professor with the University of Stuttgart. Wanner is involved in research on multilingual text generation since the late 80ies. Among his research foci are user-oriented content selection and the interface between language-independent ontology-based and linguistic representations in text generation.

References

Regina Barzilay and Mirella Lapata. 2005. Collective Content Selection for Concept-to-Text Generation. *Proceedings of the Joint Human Language Technology and Empirical Methods in Natural Language Processing Conferences (HLT/EMNLP-2005)* Vancouver, Canada.

Christian Bizer, Tom Heath and Tim Berners-Lee 2009. Linked Data - The Story So Far. *International Journal on Semantic Web and Information Systems* 5(3) 1–22

Kalina Bontcheva and Yorick Wilks 2004. Automatic Report Generation from Ontologies: the MIAKT approach *Nineth International Conference on Applications of Natural Language to Information Systems (NLDB'2004)* 324–335.

Nadjet Bouayad-Agha, Gerard Casamayor and Leo Wanner. 2011. Content selection from an ontology-based knowledge base for the generation of football summaries *Proceedings of the 13th European Workshop on Natural Language Generation (ENLG'2011)* 72–81 Nancy, France.

Yintang Dai, Shiyong Zhang, Jidong Chen, Tianyuan Chen and Wei Zhang. 2010 Semantic Network Language Generation based on a Semantic Networks Serialization Grammar *World Wide Web* 13:307341

Dana Dannélls, Mariana Damova, Ramona Enache and Milen Chechev. 2012 Multilingual Online Generation from Semantic Web Ontologies *Proceedings of the 21st International Conference on World Wide Web (WWW'12)* 239–242

Seniz Demir, Sandra Carberry and Kathleen F. McCoy. 2010. A Discourse-Aware Graph-Based Content-Selection Framework. *Proceedings of the International Language Generation Conference*. Sweden.

Pablo A. Duboue and Kathleen R. McKeown. 2003. Statistical Acquisition of Content Selection Rules for Natural Language Generation. *Proceedings of the 2003 conference on Empirical Methods in Natural Language Processing (EMNLP).* Sapporo, Japan.

Dimitrios Galanis and Ion Androutsopoulos. 2007. Generating Multilingual Personalized Descriptions from OWL Ontologies on the Semantic Web: the NaturalOWL System. *Proceedings of the Eleventh European Workshop on Natural Language Generation (ENLG07)*

Pamela W. Jordan and Marilyn A. Walker 2005 *Learning content selection rules for generating object descriptions in dialogue* Journal of Artificial Intelligence Research 24, 157–194.

Colin Kelly, Ann Copestake, and Nikiforos Karamanis. 2009 Investigating content selection for language generation using machine learning. *Proceedings of the 12th European Workshop on Natural Language Generation.*. 130–137.

Chris Mellish and Jeff Z. Pan. 2008 Language Directed Inference from Ontologies. *Artificial Intelligence.* 172(10):1285-1315.

Mick ODonnell, Chris Mellish, Jon Oberlander, and Alistair Knott. 2001. ILEX: an architecture for a dynamic hypertext generation system. *Natural Language Engineering.* 7(3):225–250.

Richard Power and Allan Third 2010 Expressing OWL axioms by English sentences: dubious in theory, feasible in practice *Proceedings of the 23rd International Conference on Computational Linguistics (CICLING'01).* 1006–1013.

Graham Wilcok and Kristiina Jokinen 2003 Generating Responses and Explanations from RDF/XML and DAML+OIL. *IJCAI03 Workshop on Knowledge and Reasoning in Practical Dialogue Systems.* 58–63.

Shared Task Proposal: Syntactic Paraphrase Ranking

Michael White
Department of Linguistics
The Ohio State University
Columbus, OH 43210 USA
mwhite@ling.ohio-state.edu

Abstract

We describe a new shared task on syntactic paraphrase ranking that is intended to run in conjunction with the main surface realization shared task. Taking advantage of the human judgments collected to evaluate the surface realizations produced by competing systems, the task is to automatically rank these realizations—viewed as syntactic paraphrases—in a way that agrees with the human judgments as often as possible. The task is designed to appeal to developers of surface realization systems as well as machine translation evaluation metrics: for surface realization systems, the task sidesteps the thorny issue of converting inputs to a common representation; for MT evaluation metrics, the task provides a challenging framework for advancing automatic evaluation, as many of the paraphrases are expected to be of high quality, differing only in subtle syntactic choices.

1 Introduction

For the first surface realization shared task, the organizers considered running a follow-on task for evaluating automatic evaluation metrics—along the lines of similar meta-evaluations carried out for machine translation in recent years—though it was deferred for lack of time. For the second surface realization shared task, we propose to generalize this metrics meta-evaluation task to also usefully encompass realization ranking, where the various realizations generated for a given input in the main task are viewed as syntactic paraphrases of the original corpus sentence. The syntactic paraphrasing shared task comprises three tracks, described in the next section; in each case, the task is to automatically reproduce the relative preference judgments gathered during the human evaluation of the surface realization main task. As explained further below, developers of realization systems that can generate and optionally rank multiple outputs for a given input will be encouraged to participate in the task, which will test the system's ability to produce acceptable paraphrases and/or to rank competing realizations.

The objectives of the shared task are as follows:

broaden participation We expect developers of automatic quality metrics in the MT community to be interested in the proposed task, which is anticipated to be both more focused (with lexical choice largely excluded) and more challenging than in the MT case, given the generally high level of quality in realization results: as realization quality increases, the metrics' task becomes more difficult, since the paraphrases of a given sentence often involve subtle differences between acceptable and unacceptable variation. In an earlier study of the utility of automatic metrics with Penn Treebank (PTB) surface realization data (Espinosa et al., 2010), we observed moderate correlations between the most popular metrics and human judgments, though lower than the levels seen with MT data.

promote reuse of human judgments The task is intended to test the effectiveness of realization ranking models in a way that reuses human judgments, making it possible to carry out re-

Track	Reference Sentence	PTB Gold	PTB Auto
Realization Ranking	N	Y	N
Hybrid	Y	Y	N
Metrics Meta-Eval	Y	N	Y

Table 1: Additional inputs for the three realization tracks

producible system comparisons.

mitigate input conversion issues Realizer evaluations have typically focused on single-best outputs, where the depth and specificity of system inputs has a large impact on quality, making comparative evaluation difficult. While the surface realization shared task seeks to address this issue by developing common ground input representations, to date it has proved to be difficult to adapt existing systems to work with these inputs. By focusing on ranking paraphrases that are distinct from the reference sentence, the proposed task may provide a way to mitigate these issues, as discussed below.

2 Three Tracks: From Realization Ranking to Metrics Meta-Evaluation

We propose three tracks for the task, going from pure realization ranking to metrics meta-evaluation, with a hybrid case in the middle. For all three tracks, the input is a set of pairs of syntactic paraphrases (distinct from the reference sentence), and the output is the preferred member of each pair, where the goal is to match the human judgments of relative preference. The tracks differ in the additional inputs that systems may use in determining which member of each pair is preferred (see Table 1). In the realization ranking track, the task is to rank order the paraphrases for a given sentence, *without* having access to the reference sentence, using a realization ranking model. To do so, each system is allowed to use its own "native" inputs derived from the Penn Treebank and PTB-based resources. To the extent that a system's statistical ranking model can be used to assign a score to any possible realization, the ranking task can be accomplished by simply ranking the realizations by model score. As such, following this strategy, the task is one of **analysis by synthesis**.

For non-statistical realizers, or ones that cannot assign a score to any possible realization, there is an alternative strategy available, namely to **automatically approximate HTER**. Snover et al. (2006) demonstrate that the human-targeted translation edit rate (HTER) represents a reliable and easily interpretable method of evaluating MT output. With this method, a human annotator produces a targeted reference sentence which is as close as possible to the MT hypothesis while being fully acceptable; from the targeted reference, the TER score then represents a normalized post-edit score, which has been shown to correlate with human ratings at least as well as more complex competing metrics. As Madnani (2010) points out, generated paraphrases of the reference sentence can be used to approximate HTER scoring, as the closest acceptable paraphrase of a reference sentence should correspond to the version of the MT hypothesis with minimal changes to make it acceptable. Indeed, in the limit, it should be possible to use a system that can enumerate all and only the acceptable paraphrases of a reference sentence to fully implement HTER scoring.

Naturally, it is possible to combine the analysis-by-synthesis and approximating HTER strategies. One particularly simple way to do so is to (1) use an n-best list of realizations with normalized scores, (2) find the realization with the minimum TER score for each paraphrase to rank, then (3) combine the realizer's model score with the TER score, e.g. just by subtraction (weights for the combination could also be optimized using machine learning).

Regarding the issue of whether fair comparisons can be made when each system is allowed to use its own PTB-derived "native" input, note that it is unclear whether using shallow, specific inputs is necessarily advantageous for ranking a range of possible realizations, all distinct from the reference sentence: in the limit, a realizer input that completely specifies the reference sentence (and no other variants) is of no help at all, as in this case the approximating HTER strategy reduces to just doing TER scoring against the reference sentence.

Turning now to the metrics meta-evaluation track, here the the task is to rank order a set of realizations for a given sentence, starting with the reference sentence and *nothing else*. In principle, it should be possible to use any MT metric for this task off-the-shelf. It should also be possible for realization systems to participate in this track, if they can be paired with a parser that produces inputs for the realizer, or a parser whose outputs can be converted to realizer inputs. To do so, strategies employed in the realization ranking track can be combined with ones that make use of the reference sentence.

Finally, between these two tracks is a hybrid track, where one is allowed to substitute automatic parses with gold parses. This track can be viewed as providing a way to estimate an upper bound on approaches that pay attention to how well a sentence expresses an intended meaning, while also arguably representing the most sensible way to automatically evaluate outputs in a data-to-text setting, where intended meanings can be reliably represented.

3 Pilot Experiments

In this section, we present two pilot experiments intended to demonstrate the feasibility of the task. The experiments use the human judgments collected in Espinosa et al.'s (2010) study, which consist of adequacy and fluency ratings from two judges for a variety of realizations for PTB Section 00. The realizations in the corpus were generated using several OpenCCG realization ranking models (White and Rajkumar, 2009) and using the XLE symbolic realizer with subsequent n-gram ranking (paraphrases involving WordNet substitutions were excluded). For comparison purposes, three well-known metrics (BLEU, METEOR and TER) were tested, along with three OpenCCG ranking models: (I) a generative baseline model, incorporating three n-gram models as well as Hockenmaier's (2003) generative model; (II) a model additionally incorporating a slew of discriminative features, extending White & Rajkumar's model with dependency ordering features; and (III) a model adding one additional feature for minimizing dependency length. Note that Models II and III are very similar, usually yielding the same single-best output, though occasionally differing in important ways; by contrast, both models represent a substantial refinement of Model I.

The two experiments investigate different strategies for approaching the hybrid task. The first experiment investigates the approximating-HTER strategy (with an analysis-by-synthesis component) using a 20-best list. For simplicity, edit rate (edit distance normalized by the number of words in the reference sentence) was used to find the realization in the 20-best list that was closest to the paraphrase to be ranked. The score for the paraphrase was then calculated by normalizing the realizer model score for the closest realization (linearly interpolating using the min and max scores across all 20-best lists), subtracting the edit rate, and adding in the metric score, for each of BLEU, METEOR and TER.[1] Since edit rate is less reliable than TER, as it overly penalizes phrasal shifts, the metric score was used alone in cases where the edit rate exceeded 0.5.

The results of the first experiment appear in Table 2. Human judgments were combined by averaging the summed adequacy and fluency ratings from each judge. Excluding exact match realizations, 2838 pairs of realizations with distinct combined scores (from approximately 250 sentences) were used to judge ranking accuracy. Here, BLEU substantially outperforms METEOR and TER, and combining Models I-III with BLEU does not yield significant differences in ranking accuracy. Note, however, that using TER scores rather than edit rate, and optimizing the way the model scores are combined with the TER score and BLEU score, could perhaps yield significant improvements. With METEOR and TER, combining the model score, edit rate and metric score in the simplest way does yield highly significant improvements. With the METEOR combination, Model II achieves a highly significant improvement over Model I, though in other cases, only trends are observed across models.

The second experiment investigates the analysis-by-synthesis strategy more directly. Here, the realizer's search was guided to reproduce each paraphrase where possible, with model scores then calculated where an exact match could be achieved. The results appear in Table 3 for 474 pairs with differing combined human judgments. The first column shows the ranking accuracy using the model scores by themselves; the subsequent columns compare the accuracy using BLEU, METEOR and TER against using the model score added to the metric score. Here we see from the first column that Model II substantially outperforms Model I, showing the

[1] TER scores were inverted for consistency.

	BLEU	Model+BLEU	METEOR	Model+METEOR	TER	Model+TER
Model I	71.2	70.2	58.6	65.4 (***)	59.7	68.7 (***)
Model II	-	70.8	-	66.7 (***† † †)	-	69.4 (***†)
Model III	-	**71.3** (†)	-	**67.1** (***)	-	**69.9** (***)

Table 2: Pairwise accuracy percentage on reproducing human judgments of relative adequacy plus fluency of syntactic paraphrases, using **n-best realizations** from three OpenCCG ranking models and minimum edit rate in combination with MT metrics (significance: * for $p < 0.1$, ** for $p < 0.05$, *** for $p < 0.01$ in comparison to MT metric, using McNemar's test; similarly for number of daggers in comparison to model in previous row)

	Model	BLEU	Model+BLEU	METEOR	Model+METEOR	TER	Model+TER
Model I	62.2	67.7	**73.0** (***)	49.2	65.4 (***)	50.6	73.8 (***)
Model II	**67.1** († † †)	-	72.2 (***)	-	68.6 (***††)	-	74.9 (***)
Model III	66.2	-	72.6 (***)	-	**68.8** (***)	-	**75.1** (***)

Table 3: Pairwise accuracy percentage on reproducing human judgments of relative adequacy plus fluency of syntactic paraphrases, using **exact targeted realizations** from three OpenCCG ranking models and minimum edit rate in combination with MT metrics (significance: * for $p < 0.1$, ** for $p < 0.05$, *** for $p < 0.01$ in comparison to MT metric, using McNemar's test; similarly for number of daggers in comparison to model in previous row)

ability of the ranking task to discriminate among models of varying sophistication, though the model differences are largely washed out when the model scores are combined with metric scores. In the subsequent columns, we see that METEOR and TER are only performing at chance (50%) on these particular ranking cases, while adding the model scores and metric scores does much better, with Model III plus TER performing the best overall, as might have been expected. Even with BLEU, which performs decently on its own, adding in the model scores achieves substantial (and highly significant) gains.

4 Task Organization

The proposed syntactic paraphrase ranking task is intended to be run as a straightforward extension of the main surface realization shared task. For development and training purposes, the human judgments collected for the first surface realization shared task will be made available; the data from Espinosa et al.'s study is already publicly available as well. For test data, the human judgments collected for evaluation during the second surface realization shared task will be used. Ideally enough systems will enter the main task to enable many pairwise comparisons per sentence, and enough judges can be employed to allow majority preferences to be used as the gold standard. As baselines for the metrics meta-eval and hybrid tracks, the BLEU, NIST, METEOR and TER metrics will be run by the organizers. Time permitting, a baseline system that works with n-best realization scores will also be made available, so that any developer of a realization system that can produce n-best outputs can easily participate.

Acknowledgments

This work was supported in part by NSF grant no. IIS-1143635. Thanks go to the anonymous reviewers for helpful comments and discussion.

References

Dominic Espinosa, Rajakrishnan Rajkumar, Michael White, and Shoshana Berleant. 2010. Further meta-evaluation of broad-coverage surface realization. In *Proc. of EMNLP-10*, pages 564–574.

Julia Hockenmaier. 2003. *Data and models for statistical parsing with Combinatory Categorial Grammar*. Ph.D. thesis, University of Edinburgh.

Nitin Madnani. 2010. *The Circle of Meaning: From Translation to Paraphrasing and Back*. Ph.D. thesis, University of Maryland.

Matthew Snover, Bonnie Dorr, Richard Schwartz, Linnea Micciulla, and John Makhoul. 2006. A study of translation edit rate with targeted human annotation. In *Proc. of AMTA-06*, pages 223–231.

Michael White and Rajakrishnan Rajkumar. 2009. Perceptron reranking for CCG realization. In *Proc. of EMNLP-09*, pages 410–419.

Author Index

Albacete, Patricia, 95
Allman, Tod, 59

Banik, Eva, 125, 141
Beale, Stephen, 59
Belz, Anja, 136
Bohnet, Bernd, 22, 136
Bouayad-Agha, Nadjet, 146
Brockmann, Carsten, 40
Burger, Susanne, 128
Buschmeier, Hendrik, 12

Casamayor, Gerard, 146
Challenge, Generation, 134
Chaudri, Vinay, 125

Dannélls, Dana, 76
Denton, Richard, 59
Dethlefs, Nina, 49
Dinesh, Nikhil, 125, 141
Ding, Duo, 128
Duboue, Pablo, 85

El Kholy, Ahmed, 90
Emiel, Krahmer, 3

Ford, Michael, 95

Gardent, Claire, 31, 141
Gill, Alastair, 40
Green, Matthew, 120

Habash, Nizar, 90
Han, Xufeng, 131
Hastie, Helen, 49
Hayes, Jeff, 131

Jordan, Pamela, 95

Katz, Sandra, 95
Kopp, Stefan, 12
Kow, Eric, 125
Kruszewski, German, 31

Lemon, Oliver, 49
Lester, James, 2
Liang, Fennie, 141
Lindberg, David, 115

Mahamood, Saad, 100
Mariët, Theune, 3
Mazzei, Alessandro, 105
McCoy, Kathleen, 1
Melero, Yolanda, 17
Mellish, Chris, 17, 120, 146
Metze, Florian, 128
Mille, Simon, 22, 136
Mitchell, Margaret, 131
Mosny, Milan, 115

Nguyen, Tu Anh T., 110

Oberlander, Jon, 40
Oza, Umangi, 125

Piwek, Paul, 110
Popowich, Fred, 115
Power, Richard, 110

Rawat, Shourabh, 128
Reiter, Ehud, 100
Rieser, Verena, 49
Ruud, Koolen, 3

Schulam, Peter, 128
Scott, Donia, 141
Siddharthan, Advaith, 120
Sripada, Somayajulu, 17
Striegnitz, Kristina, 12

Tait, Elizabeth, 17

Third, Allan, 67
Tintarev, Nava, 17

van Deemter, Kees, 120
Van Der Wal, Rene, 17
van der Wal, Rene, 120

Wanner, Leo, 22, 136, 146
White, Michael, 136, 150
Williams, Sandra, 110
Wilson, Christine, 95